CONTEMPLATIVE PSYCHOTHERAPY ESSENTIALS

CONTEMPLATIVE PSYCHOTHERAPY ESSENTIALS

Enriching Your Practice With Buddhist Psychology

KAREN KISSEL WEGELA

W. W. Norton & Company
New York • London

For information about permission to reproduce selections from this book,
write to Permissions, W. W. Norton & Company, Inc.,
500 Fifth Avenue, New York, NY 10110

For information about special discounts for bulk purchases,
please contact W. W. Norton Special Sales at
specialsales@wwnorton.com or 800-233-4830

Manufacturing by Quad Graphics Fairfield
Production manager: Leeann Graham

Library of Congress Cataloging-in-Publication Data

Wegela, Karen Kissel.
   Contemplative psychotherapy essentials : enriching your practice
with Buddhist psychology / Karen Kissel Wegela. — First edition.
      pages   cm
   "A Norton Professional Book."
   Includes bibliographical references and index.
   ISBN 978-0-393-70867-7 (hardcover)
   1. Existential psychotherapy.   2. Psychotherapist and patient.
3. Psychotherapy—Religious aspects.   I. Title.
   RC489.E93W44 2014
   616.89'14—dc23   2014021359

ISBN: 978-0-393-70867-7

W. W. Norton & Company, Inc., 500 Fifth Avenue, New York, N.Y. 10110
www.wwnorton.com
W. W. Norton & Company Ltd., Castle House,
75/76 Wells Street, London W1T 3QT

1 2 3 4 5 6 7 8 9 0

For two compassionate psychotherapists:

My niece, Debbie
and
My wise colleague, Bill

CONTENTS

ACKNOWLEDGMENTS

When I work with clients in individual psychotherapy, there appear to be only two of us in the room. In truth, however, we are both a unique and ever-changing coming together of many disparate causes, conditions, and influences. So many people contribute to who any of us are. I have become aware, once again, that without the generosity of many people, both living and dead, I could not be in a position to have written this book on the integration of psychotherapy and Buddhist psychology.

When I remember the many teachers I have had, I feel overwhelmed with gratitude. An early teacher who fanned the sparks of my brilliant sanity, though she had never heard the term, was Mrs. Amelia Coffey, my high school French teacher. It is her kindness and precision that I still attempt to emulate as a teacher myself. My graduate advisor, Dr. Robert S. Sproat, spent extra time with me when I was ready to give up on my first master's degree program. His willingness to meet me as one human being to another in the midst of a large, impersonal university reminds me how little it can take to encourage a student, a client, or a friend.

It has been my great good fortune to have had the opportunity to meet personally with and receive direct teachings from a host of Tibetan Buddhist teachers including Chagdud Tulku, Khenpo Kartar Rinpoche, Dzigar Kongtrül Rinpoche, H. H. Dilgo Khyentse Rinpoche, Mingyur Rinpoche, Anam Thubten Rinpoche, Khenchen Thrangu Rinpoche, Tulku Ugyen Rinpoche, and His Holiness, the 14th Dalai Lama. My dharma sisters, Pema Chödrön, Dale Asrael, Judy Lief, and Judith Simmer-Brown, have been valued teachers, as well. Most importantly, I was fortunate to have received transmissions and teachings from my root guru, the Vidyadhara, the Venerable

Chögyam Trungpa Rinpoche from the early 1970s until his passing in 1987. His son and dharma heir, Sakyong Mipham Rinpoche, is an important teacher in my life now.

In addition, the Vietnamese Zen teacher Thich Nhat Hanh has had a strong influence on me. I am grateful, too, to other Buddhist teachers in the Zen and Insight traditions: Roshi Bernie Tetsugen Glassman, Roshi Joan Halifax, Jack Kornfield, and Sharon Salzberg. Reb Zalman Schachter-Shalomi's kindness and vast mind have been a blessing, as well.

Without the creative and dedicated Contemplative Psychotherapy colleagues with whom I have gotten to work since I came to Naropa University in 1980, I might still be struggling on my own to figure out how to combine the meditative part of my life with the psychotherapy part. Along with the late Edward M. Podvoll and the late Virginia Hilliker, I have been privileged to work with Paul Bialek, Lauren Casalino, Paul Cashman, Sharon Conlin, Jeff Fortuna, MacAndrew Jack, Ugur Kocataskin, Bonnie Rabin, Robert Unger, Robert Walker, and Antonio Wood.

In addition, other colleagues whose generosity and guidance I wish to acknowledge include Stephen Batchelor, Mark Epstein, Rick Hanson, Joe Loizzo, Jeremy Lowry, Elaine Miller-Karas, William Staudenmaier, and Gay Watson. Colleagues have a way of becoming friends, and in addition to those already named, I want to thank the following for their humor and support: Kathy Emery, Marilyn Chodosh Kruegel, and the Not-Yet-Over-the-Hill bridge group: Terry, Sharon, and Russ.

My students over the past 34 years of teaching at Naropa have been a constant source of inspiration and learning. I thank them, as ever, for not letting me get away with anything. A special thank you goes to Elizabeth Driscoll, who drew the first written mandala of a client's brilliant sanity.

My appreciation goes also to the many clients with whom I have had the privilege and honor to work over the years. Their willingness to let me into their lives has taught me so much about how to do therapy and about myself, as well. I particularly wish to thank the client who appears in this book as "Whitney" for her openness and fearlessness.

My family, both alive and no longer alive, is a group of eccentric people who value humor, intelligence, and compassion. There is no way to repay their generosity.

Finally, my life partner Fred Wegela, who is also the novelist Freddie Owens, has continued to support me with his writer's wisdom, quirky humor, and good companionship.

INTRODUCTION

When I first began practicing Buddhist meditation, I mentioned it to my mother. Her reaction was perhaps a bit extreme, but not really so unusual. "Will you have to shave your head? Will you wear robes? Are you joining a cult?" Her idea of Buddhism was of something exotic and a bit threatening. Would I become unavailable and strange? Would I still be normal? Sometimes when people hear of Contemplative Psychotherapy and find out that it draws on Buddhist psychological principles, they wonder, as my mother did, just how alien it might be. As you may see below, when I began to look further into Buddhist psychology, I discovered that it wasn't alien at all.

My intention in writing this book is to show how the Contemplative Psychotherapy approach, originated and developed at Naropa University since the mid-1970s may enrich the work of therapists with different theoretical orientations. I hope to share something of my own journey with the Buddhist principles that underlie the contemplative approach and to present how they may be applied in the work of all kinds of therapists and helpers. People often wonder if they need to be Buddhists to be contemplative psychotherapists—definitely not.

I didn't set out to be a therapist. I had studied English in college and had a master's degree in English language and literature. I was happy teaching high school English in a rural junior-senior high school in upstate Connecticut in the late 1960s and early 1970s. I enjoyed working with the teenagers in my classes and sharing with them my love of reading and writing. I especially liked meeting one-on-one with students who came in to talk about their personal concerns. One year, following my former husband to Denver, Colorado, for his one-year clinical psychology internship, I went back to school to get the 30 extra credits that would pay me more as a teacher. I nearly began a program in French. At the last minute, due to scheduling conflicts perhaps, I signed up for a counseling class.

To my surprise and delight, I realized that I could have a professional career doing what already felt natural to me and what I loved: helping my students, family, and friends deal with their personal concerns. During that year in Denver, I completed an MA in guidance and counseling. Upon returning to Connecticut, I taught for another year and a half before leaving to pursue a doctoral degree in psychology.

In those years, it was not uncommon for friends and even acquaintances who were having bad recreational drug experiences to show up on my doorstep. I had no idea what would help them. More often than not, I simply invited them in and said, "Would you like a cup of tea?" Then I would just sit with them. As we sat together, many times the person who had been frightened or intensely confused would begin to settle down. Looking back, I see that this had much to do with my willingness simply to be present with them. Once I had begun my doctoral training, it was clear that I still had much more to learn about being genuinely helpful. In the years since then I have added to my original training, which was in the client-centered approach of Carl Rogers. Early on, I also completed a course in Gestalt therapy, and more recently received training in Eye Movement Desensitization and Reprocessing therapy (EMDR) and in the Trauma Resiliency Model (TRM).[1]

I didn't plan on becoming a Buddhist practitioner, either. Just after I completed my doctoral training in 1977, my best friend from high school died of leukemia. We had fallen out of touch for about a year, and the news of her death came as a shock. I began having the symptoms I could now recognize as anxiety and panic. Knowing that didn't help much. My usual comforts and distractions were of no help either, and I grew even more frightened that these horrible feelings would never stop. I remember talking on the phone to my mother, who was just as anxious and distressed as I was. "Oh no," I thought. "Just getting older isn't going to help." Looking back, it would have made sense to seek out a therapist. For whatever reason, I did not. Perhaps I hesitated because the therapists I knew were friends or colleagues. Then another friend, who was a meditation instructor, suggested that I try sitting meditation. I will always remember his kind words: "Karen, why don't you sit?" Though I had read about meditation, and had tried it once or twice, I had never done it for more than a few minutes at a time.

So, I sat down on a cushion on the floor—sweaty palms, dry mouth, shaky limbs, speedy mind, and all—and tried to find my breath. Again and again, as I had been instructed by my friend, I brought my attention back to the sensation of my breathing, in and out. Especially out. When I noticed that I was lost in thoughts, I did my best to gently return to my breathing. I didn't feel less awful, but there began to be a shift in my relationship toward my suffering. Instead of trying to escape it, I discovered that I could just be with it. This, in itself, brought some relief.

I began to practice meditation regularly, and I joined a small local group. We listened to recorded lectures by Chögyam Trungpa, a Tibetan Buddhist meditation master, and I began to study Buddhist teachings. I found that they were about how to work with psychological issues such as painful emotions, the sense of self, the source of psychological pain and its relief, and how to be genuinely helpful to others. They were not about worshiping a guy with a big belly like the statues I'd seen in Chinese restaurants. It wasn't about worship at all. It was about how to cultivate compassion and insight in relation to oneself and others A few years later, I received the training to become a meditation instructor myself.

By this time, I was working with therapy clients. So far, these two parts of my life had not come together. I had the sense that they were somehow part of the same endeavor, but how they connected was unclear. What did the interpersonal relationship essential to talk therapy have to do with the solitary practice of sitting silently with oneself? Was it appropriate to teach meditation to clients? Wasn't that mixing together two different roles, meditation instructor and therapist? Should I tell my clients to meditate? I had more questions than answers. I knew therapists and I knew meditators. I didn't know anyone else in my small Connecticut town who was both, so I had no one to bounce my questions off.

My questions led me, in 1979, to Boulder, Colorado, to a Naropa Institute summer program on Buddhism and psychotherapy. At last I found colleagues who were exploring the same issues I was. A year later, I moved to Boulder, and I have been a faculty member at Naropa (now University) for more than 30 years.

In the past several years, mindfulness, a key teaching in Buddhist psychology, has become an increasingly common term in the field of psychotherapy. In this book, my intention is to go further and to present what my colleagues and I have learned about how to apply not only mindfulness but also some of the other rich teachings of Buddhist psychology to our therapeutic work. Throughout the book I share how we approach our work with clients, along with suggestions for the practical application of Buddhist principles to the therapeutic journey. Clinical case examples, strategies, exercises, and guided meditation instructions are offered throughout the book.

In Chapter 1, I explore the Buddhist teachings that form the foundation of Contemplative Psychotherapy. In the following chapters, I focus more on how to apply those teachings in preparing to work with others and in the therapeutic journey itself.

Throughout the book, any clients used as clinical examples are presented with identifiable details changed or are composites of several different clients. Any errors in presenting the Buddhist teachings are my own.

CONTEMPLATIVE PSYCHOTHERAPY ESSENTIALS

Chapter 1

FOUNDATIONS OF
CONTEMPLATIVE
PSYCHOTHERAPY

In Contemplative Psychotherapy we use the term "Buddhist psychology" rather than "Buddhist religion" because, unlike most religions, Buddhism takes no position about the existence of a supreme being. It is neither theistic nor atheistic. Instead, Buddhism is more like what we think of as psychology, providing us with a method and set of teachings for exploring the nature of the mind and the problem of how to relieve suffering. In this chapter, we look at the basic Buddhist ideas that are important in Contemplative Psychotherapy.

The man who is now known as the Buddha never did psychotherapy, so Contemplative Psychotherapy is not exactly Buddhist psychotherapy. I like to think of Contemplative Psychotherapy as the child of two different parents: the Western psychological traditions of talk therapy and the ancient Eastern teachings of the sixth-century BCE teacher known to us as the Buddha or "the awakened one." Just like all offspring, this Contemplative Psychotherapy child has much in common with both its parents, but it has grown up to become something different from either one. Though my focus in this book is primarily on the Buddhist parent, the psychotherapy parent is always playing a role as well. On the one hand, I do not go into great detail about contemporary psychotherapy, which I trust my readers can find elsewhere. And, on the other hand, this book is not an attempt at a scholarly presentation of the Buddhist teachings. Instead I focus on the basic teachings of Buddhism as they may be applied to our work with therapy clients. Those readers who would like to explore the Buddhist teachings more deeply will find suggested readings in the notes.

HOW TO APPROACH THIS CHAPTER

Buddhist teachings emphasize the importance of exploring one's own personal experience. So, from the beginning, I would suggest that you read this chapter about Buddhist ideas with an open, curious, and slightly skeptical mind. Test everything against your own experience. At Naropa we encourage our students and ourselves to live with the questions we have and not to close our minds down by reaching premature conclusions. Sometimes we even say "the question is the answer" as a way of expressing how valuable having an open and inquiring mind can be (Asrael, 2012). If you are doubtful about the truth of anything you find in this chapter or the rest of the book, see if you can simply be with the direct experience of doubt and not conclude that something is true or not true until you feel some clarity about your own personal sense of it. If it feels true and makes sense to you, then, and only then, apply it in your own life or work. If you decide something does not meet that test, then discard it. The Buddha was himself a person who explored and questioned things, and we can follow his example in testing out for ourselves what to accept and what to reject. The teachings, the Buddha said, should be tested and hammered like gold (Trungpa, 1987).

WHO WAS THE BUDDHA?

The Buddha was born in what is now Nepal, the son of a ruler of a small domain. Like many fathers, the Buddha's did not want his son, known as Siddhartha, to go too far afield of his own kingly concerns. He was dismayed when a sage made a prophecy at Siddhartha's birth predicting that this special child could become either a universal ruler or a great spiritual teacher (Narada, 1992). The king wanted to make sure that his son would become a ruler.

An important event happened when Siddhartha was a child. He accompanied his father to a plowing festival. While sitting under a rose-apple tree, he had a moment of complete clarity. Some legends say that the sun stood still, but the idea is that he was fully alert and present, perhaps even joyful (J. Simmer-Brown, personal communication, 1983).

Since the king wanted young Siddhartha to grow up to join the family business, taking over the kingdom after his own reign, he made the prince's life as appealing and pleasurable as possible. Behind the palace's high walls, Siddhartha was entertained by dancing girls, musicians, fabulous food, and rich furnishings. He was taught all the skills of a nobleman's son: "art, science, metaphysics, medicine, and even sports such as wrestling" (Karthar, 1992, p. 35). All unhappy things and the evidence of suffering were hidden away from him.

Nonetheless, as the prince grew up, his life of pleasure became less satisfying, and he yearned to go beyond the palace walls to see the world for himself. As the story goes, he was allowed to go into the city with his chariot driver. Imagine if you had never seen anyone in pain, had never seen an old person or a sick one. As his driver drove them along the busy road, Siddhartha saw—in the traditional formula—the signs of birth, old age, sickness, and death. He asked his driver what was wrong with these people, and his driver explained that if we live long enough, we all become sick and old. Everyone, he told Siddhartha, dies. This was quite shocking to the prince, who had been shielded from all of life's sorrows. He was touched to the core of his being.

On that trip, Siddhartha saw one more noteworthy thing: he saw a spiritual seeker, "a dignified hermit" (Narada, 1992, p. 15). When I imagine this encounter, I think of the great teachers I have been fortunate to meet. From whatever tradition they have come, they shared the qualities of gentleness, peacefulness, and liveliness. Perhaps this man was like that, too. In any case, he made a deep impression on the young man, who had never seen anyone like that before.

Soon afterward, with the collusion of his chariot driver, the prince left the palace. Exchanging clothes with the driver, he made his way into the world to seek out spiritual teachings. He met a number of different spiritual teachers with whom he studied and practiced, including those who practiced extreme asceticism. He was a gifted student and mastered everything he was taught. "What else?" he

3

would say. "What else can you teach me?" Based on his own inner sense, he knew there was more.

Finally, he decided to go off on his own. He remembered the experience he had had under the rose-apple tree. The clarity he had experienced then had not required self-denial or special practices. Instead of continuing his asceticism, he accepted the offering of a sort of yogurt-based drink from a young woman, created a seat of soft kusha grass, and simply sat down with himself, vowing to stay there until he experienced what he could recognize himself as the truth of things. As the story goes, he sat down in Bodhgaya under a bodhi tree, and he attained Buddhahood, full awakening and realization of the nature of reality and of his own mind. This is why he is known as the Buddha, the awakened one.

For the rest of his long life, he taught others what he had learned: sit down and see for yourself what is true and what is not. He gave many talks that have come down to the present day, teaching that all of us are able to realize our own natural wisdom and compassion. These talks, along with the experiences of those who practiced what he taught, form the teachings of the Buddhist lineages.

As in many spiritual traditions, not unlike Christianity, Judaism, or Islam, many different branches have evolved. The dharma, or the living tradition of the Buddhist teachings, has been expounded in a number of different styles as the teachings have made their way around the world. Japanese Zen, South Asian Theravada, Tibetan, Burmese, and now American Buddhism all reflect the cultures in which they are practiced. In true American fashion, all of the different Asian traditions are represented in the United States. My own training was primarily in the Vajrayana tradition of Tibetan Buddhism, and that is reflected in how I present the Buddhist teachings. Again, any mistakes here are my own.

The rest of this chapter presents some of the basic concepts of Contemplative Psychotherapy drawn from Buddhist teachings.

BRILLIANT SANITY

"Buddhist psychology is based on the notion that human beings are fundamentally good. Their most basic qualities are positive ones: openness, intelligence, and warmth" (Trungpa, 2005, p. 8).

The root teaching in Contemplative Psychotherapy is the idea of brilliant sanity.[1] Closely related to the Buddhist idea of Buddha nature, brilliant sanity suggests that all beings have a nature that is fundamentally good: wise, compassionate, and open. Our overarching goal in Contemplative Psychotherapy is to help our clients connect, or reconnect, with their own worthiness, their brilliant sanity. Being able to recognize the signs of brilliant sanity in our clients is an important part of our work and is explored in Chapter 5.

Let us look at this notion of brilliant sanity more closely, as it forms the basis of everything else in the contemplative psychotherapeutic approach. First, brilliant sanity is not something that can be fully captured in words. This, of course, makes it difficult to present it in a book. We tend to experience it in small glimpses. Still, it is not foreign to us, so perhaps I can evoke it or remind you of your own sense of it through some descriptions and examples.

You might think of a time in your life—it could be just a moment or longer—when you felt fully alive and present. It could be a time of great bliss, pleasure, or delight. Or, equally, it could be a time of shock, pain, or sorrow. Such moments are often free of self-consciousness, and whatever thinking occurs tends to be about the needs of the present moment. Sometimes these moments occur when the expected does not happen, and we are suddenly without our usual reference points. Maybe we are the recipient of a surprise party. Or maybe the car breaks down. Or perhaps something catastrophic happens. We may find ourselves very present and clear minded. We may feel vulnerable or even sweetly touched. Some people feel that sense of being fully present when they meet someone with whom they fall in love. There is an absence of planning, a welcoming of the novel, a feeling of one's heart opening. Then we may try to deliberately recapture such moments and are disappointed to find that it does not work. Our experiences of brilliant sanity are often temporary and fleeting. Still, they may be times when we feel most alive.

I remember a time when an old boyfriend—actually, my first serious one—told me that he thought we should stop seeing each other.[2] I felt like the ground had fallen away beneath me. I remember precisely the look on his face—the furrowing of his brow, the sapphire blue of his eyes, the slightly rumpled look of his dark hair. I felt a pain in my solar plexus as though I had been hit there. I felt sadly tender, and tears began to run down my face. I looked down and noticed the muted white and green vertical stripes of my Oxford shirt. For the first few moments there were no particular thoughts. There was great simplicity; I was just there with a sore heart.

It did not take long, though, before I began churning out thoughts about the past, present, and future. "Why is this happening? What have I done wrong? Was it the comment I made yesterday? Am I just unlovable? Will I be alone for the rest of my life?" I lost the sense of simplicity. The sense of tender heart vanished from my awareness, and I became less present as I rocketed into fearful fantasies of what this might mean about me and my life.

Before I fell into that cauldron of whirling thoughts, the experience may have been a glimpse of brilliant sanity characterized by a sense of presence, clarity, and tenderheartedness. The instances you thought of may have some of the same traits as well.

Openness

Openness, clarity, and compassion are the three main qualities of brilliant sanity or natural wisdom. While I look at each separately, they are also inseparable from each other.

Before we go any further, what is meant by "mind" in this context? In Buddhism there are many different terms for the mind. Some refer to "that which perceives an other" and is thus a dualistic sense of what mind is (Trungpa, 2005, p. 64). Others refer, as brilliant sanity does, to the unconditioned nature of human experience: that is, the underlying nature of who and what we are regardless of the specifics of what we are experiencing. Even the word "experience" is a bit tricky, though, since it may imply an experiencer separate from an experience. Instead, mind here is understood to be nondual: there is no separation between a putative experiencer of whatever experience we may be having and the experience itself. It is like the question posed in the Yeats poem, "Among School Children" (Yeats, 1990, p. 242), "How can we know the dancer from the dance?"

Brilliant sanity, then, is a description of the nondual, unconditioned mind that all of us have or are. Its first quality is openness. Openness points to the spacious aspect of mind that is accommodating to all phenomena (Trungpa, 2005). This use of "openness" differs from some other common uses of the word. For example, we might say we feel open if we are undefended or vulnerable. We might also say we are open when we can take in new ideas. Or we might say that an event is open when there are no restrictions on who may attend it. These meanings are related but not as vast in scope as the meaning of openness with respect to brilliant sanity.

Openness here refers to what is sometimes called our "sky-like" nature (Sogyal, 1992, p. 57). The suggestion is that our minds, like the sky, can be vast and open, able to include or accommodate any experience at all. All kinds of things may appear in the sky, but the sky itself is unchanged: airplanes, birds, bees, clouds, tornadoes, hot air balloons, rockets, missiles, explosions. None of these actually changes the sky, the background of space in which they appear. The sky passes no judgment on them. In the same way, we can feel all of our feelings, think all of our thoughts, perceive all of our perceptions, and none of these experiences affects or changes the underlying space of the mind.

Sometimes this quality is called "emptiness," and we will look further at that below. For now, the point to note about emptiness is that it is not the same as a void or nothingness, a point sometimes misunderstood about Buddhist psychology (Fremantle, 2001). Our minds are open, vast, and fundamentally unobstructed.

Clarity

The second quality of brilliant sanity is clarity or awareness. Not only are our minds vast and spacious, they are also precise and clear. Clarity refers to our ability to directly experience our sense perceptions and to recognize the contents of our thoughts and mental imagery without distortion. We can see, hear, smell, taste, and touch things in our environment, and in our own bodies, just as they are. What this means is that we can experience our own experience without filtering it through any expectations or judgments. So, for example, when I am watching a movie on TV, and I cannot actually make out the words the actor is saying, I hear what I hear—indistinct and fuzzy. Clarity does not mean that I can hear the specific words he may have actually said, just that I can hear what I can hear. In the same way, when I look at the actor who is speaking, I see him how I see him, not the way I would see him if my vision were corrected to 20/20 with glasses. His shirt may look rosy to me. Of course, if I am wearing my glasses, I see whatever it is more accurately and his shirt reveals itself to be a white and red plaid, but that experience is not more clear from the point of view of brilliant sanity. My perception of the rosy shirt and the plaid one while wearing my glasses could both be examples of clarity.

The Buddhists add one more sense to the usual five: the ability to recognize the activity of the mind itself (Trungpa, 1995). In the same way we see sights or hear sounds, we can mind the mind. We can notice our thoughts and the images that appear in our minds. Once again, it is the quality of clarity being manifested when we can simply notice what occurs in the mind without trying to hang on to it or push it away.

The quality of clarity is sometimes called mindfulness. Our ability to note our experiences directly, without adding layers of thought, judgment, or expectation, is mindfulness, and it is regarded as part of our fundamental nature of brilliant sanity.

Compassion

The third quality of brilliant sanity is compassion. The suggestion here is that it is our very nature to be compassionate, caring beings who wish to alleviate the suffering we find in others and in ourselves. Personally, I find this the most interesting one. What I find so interesting is the idea that we do not have to learn compassion or somehow inject it into our clients. Instead, it can be uncovered because it is already there, though we may not be in touch with it.

When I visited Kathmandu in the early 1990s, I saw many mothers with small children begging on the streets. I remember one woman, in particular, who still lives in my memory. She was about my own height, and she held an infant cradled in her left arm. She was dirty and thin, and the baby looked apathetic. I had two opposite reactions. I felt drawn toward her. I wanted to give her some money or food or help of some kind. I also felt like pulling away and not looking. It was too painful to look and to know I could not change the situation. Both of my reactions—wanting to go toward her and wanting to turn away—were based in the compassionate quality of brilliant sanity. Both were a response to feeling deeply touched by her suffering. Of course, my impulse to turn away was not acting on that compassionate response, but its root was the same as what underlay the desire to help.

THE FOUR NOBLE TRUTHS: THE BUDDHIST PRESCRIPTION

If we have brilliant sanity, why do we not experience it more? We often do not behave compassionately or with openness and clarity. Our minds are often closed down and confused. We need not look very far to see that there is much suffering in the world. Our clients come to us with anxiety, confusion, depression, addiction, and the aftereffects of abuse and other kinds of trauma. The news is filled with stories of casual and organized killings. There is conflict over water, land, religion, and more. There seems to be no end of evidence that brilliant sanity is not manifesting most of the time. So what is going on?

Among the very earliest teachings of the Buddha are the four noble truths (Karthar, 1992). Following the Indian medical approach of the day, they begin with the disease: suffering.[3] The next three teachings of the four noble truths cover the etiology, the prognosis, and the treatment plan for our "suffering illness."

The First Noble Truth: Suffering

The problem, according to the Buddha, is that we suffer. Suffering includes the experiences of getting what we do not want, not getting what we do want, and even when we get what we want, having it change. Simply being born in a body inevitably leads to pain: birth, old age, sickness, and death. These were the very things that so shocked Siddhartha when he took his chariot ride and inspired him to leave his life of luxury.

Suffering refers to the struggle we engage in to escape the pain of being alive. It is contrasted with the simple direct experience of unpleasantness usually called pain. A common saying is that pain is inevitable, but suffering is optional (Murakami, 2008). The Buddhist path is about just this distinction and how to work with our minds so as not to turn unavoidable pain into unnecessary suffering.

As some people who work with those dealing with chronic pain have told us, learning to recognize the difference between our direct experience of painful sensations and our added thoughts, beliefs, and emotions about our pain can alleviate a good deal of our suffering (Kabat-Zinn, 1990). When one experiences pain mindfully, it can lead to better decisions about what needs to be done or what does not in order to skillfully address it.

The main thing that leads people to seek out a therapist is their experience of pain and suffering. It may manifest in many different ways including anxiety, depression, agitation, addiction, aggression, difficulty in working with emotions, dysfunctional relationships, or negative habitual patterns.

Often, one of the first things that we need to help our clients with is simply acknowledging that they are in pain and that how they work with that situation is their responsibility. Until any of us recognizes our personal experience of pain in the present, little can be done to change the situation. As therapists know, many clients begin by blaming others for their suffering. Of course it is often true that others have caused them pain. Helping our clients to begin to tease apart the direct experience of pain from the extra added struggle of suffering, including blaming, is one of the things we offer to our clients. Sometimes it takes quite a long time for clients to own their pain.

Understanding how that suffering arises and how it can be worked with is exactly what the Buddha's Four Noble Truths are about.

The Second Noble Truth: The Cause of Suffering

What does suffering have to do with brilliant sanity? As noted above, the experience of brilliant sanity is not always pleasant. Sometimes we glimpse it in the midst of difficult and painful situations. Why do we suffer? Why do we not experience our brilliant sanity continuously?

From the Buddhist point of view, the main obstacle to experiencing our true nature of brilliant sanity is our attempt to maintain and defend a mistaken sense of who and what we are. Instead of recognizing that we are open and fluid beings, ever-changing and permeable, we try to construct and hold onto a fixed identity.

Sometimes this fixed sense of self is called ego, though it is not the same ego to which Western psychology refers. The Western idea of ego usually refers to things like the ability to know our own experience, to be able to judge clearly, or to have a sense of self-confidence. These qualities are not problematic from a Buddhist point of view.

The mistaken identity that we try to maintain, in the contemplative view, is somewhat different. The mistake is that we believe that there is something in us that is unchanging, separate, and solid. Sometimes it is more of a gut feeling than a conscious belief, but we generally act as though we believe we are separate from others, that something in us is the same as when we were children, and that each of us is somehow a palpable "me."

People often think that Buddhism teaches us to get rid of our ego or self. That is not so. What Buddhist psychology suggests is that an unchanging, independent self just does not exist. It encourages us to let go of a confused belief in a self that we do not have. We cannot give up something that does not exist. However, we feel as though it does. For further clarification, let me also say again that we do exist, just not in the way that most of us take for granted.

This mistaken conviction, and the projections that result from it, come from our failure to recognize what is known as the egolessness, or insubstantiality, of self. Not only do we inaccurately regard ourselves as solidly existent, we regard others and the phenomenal world in the same way (Thrangu, 2012).

When we invest ourselves in maintaining and protecting a mistaken sense of permanence, separation, and solidity, it leads us to suffer unnecessarily. Basically, we have centered our experience around something that is not true, and it leads us into painful misunderstandings and bad choices. One of the most important aspects of this attempt to perpetuate such a false sense of self and phenomena is that it is fundamentally aggressive. Instead of opening to experiencing ourselves as we actually are, we repeatedly push away anything that challenges our misguided beliefs. Clinically, we often find that this appears in clients as a strong conviction that they themselves are bad, irreparably damaged, or somehow flawed. As therapists, we can help our clients to recognize both their positive and negative solidified views of themselves, which are obstacles to their relaxing into their basic nature of brilliant sanity and goodness.

Generally, we try to maintain our mistaken view by hanging on to experiences that support it, by pushing away those things that challenge or undermine it, and by disregarding those which are irrelevant to it.

Let us look a bit more closely at three qualities that a belief in a solid, separate identity attempts to ignore: impermanence, interconnectedness, and emptiness.

Impermanence

One of the main teachings of Buddhism is impermanence. Very simply, everything—inside of us and outside of us—changes and nothing remains the same. Our bodies, our emotions, our thoughts, our roles, the rising and setting of the sun, the sweep of the seasons, the weather: all are changing, increasing and decreasing. Our bodies are aging, our health is in flux, the abilities we may have had in youth fade away. If we identify ourselves with our bodies, we find that our identities fall apart.

When I was 19, about half of my hair fell out in reaction to a medical treatment. I was quite thoroughly identified with the abundant strawberry-blonde hair I had had since birth. It was quite a shock, and my hair never fully came back. My sense of self suffered an equally upsetting shift.

If we try to establish a sense of self based on our emotions, that too leads to disappointment. Nonetheless, we may try to maintain a particular emotion. If I identify myself as an activist, for example, I will have an investment in maintaining a sense of anger toward whatever it is that I want to see changed. I will make that emotion as solid and unassailable as I can. This will require a good deal of maintenance work since the nature of emotions is impermanent. Even a positive emotion like love will change. It may increase or decrease. It may be replaced in turn by some other emotion like jealousy or pride. Trying to keep an emotion going when it is fading leads to increasingly ignoring what we are actually experiencing.

Our thoughts, roles, and relationships also change. One of the main things that brings clients into therapy is pain and confusion based on the experience of impermanence. They come when relationships begin, end, or undergo some kind of significant change. They come when they or their family members become ill. They come when someone dies. They come because they fear that things will change, and they come when they fear that they will not. They seek therapy when their roles change, and they no longer are sure who they are: people who have lost their jobs, retirees, people with new jobs, new mothers and fathers, empty-nesters. To the extent that any of us, our clients or ourselves, identify with occupational and family roles, we may suffer a sense of groundlessness and confusion when our roles are revealed to be impermanent.

Even cherished beliefs may change. I have seen clients who seek out therapy when they have begun to question their sense of what really matters to them or what they believe, for example, about the nature of death. Such existential crises are also based on impermanence.

Interconnectedness

Another key tenet of Buddhism is that we are not truly separate from one another or from the environment. Thich Nhat Hanh (1987b), a Vietnamese Zen teacher, uses the term interbeing to describe our interconnectedness or interdependence.[4] As he describes it, we do not exist independently, but instead we inter-are. He has used the example of a flower and a compost heap. The flower, he points out, is made up entirely of nonflower elements. These could include the sun, the clouds, the minerals in the soil, the care of the gardener, and all of the things that influence the care the gardener can provide, like what he had for breakfast and whether he had a fight with his wife that morning, the truck that brought the seeds to the market where the gardener bought them, the gas in the truck, and the international agreements that allowed the oil that made the gas to be imported. There is no end to the many elements we could think of that make up the flower.

Moreover, the flower is impermanent. It is on its way to the compost heap. It is changing every day or even every moment. Thich Nhat Hanh points out that the compost is also on its way to becoming a flower. It, too, is made up of noncompost elements. There is no separate compost heap and flower. They inter-are. At the same time, we can still enjoy the flower. To say it is interdependent or empty is not to say that it does not exist at all.

As neuroscience is increasingly showing us, we are deeply and pervasively connected with each other.[5] In the language of Contemplative Psychotherapy, we readily exchange with each other (Olson, Unger, Kaklauskas, & Swann, 2008). We are viscerally touched by others' pain and joy. We reflect within ourselves what we perceive outside of ourselves. The inside and the outside are not nearly as separate as we may have thought.

When I sit with a client who is experiencing hopelessness, for example, I may begin to feel hopeless myself. I may start to think that the therapy is going nowhere and maybe we had better just stop meeting. This is not merely a reaction to what I am hearing. From a Buddhist point of view, I may have directly picked up on the experience of the client. I may then add my own thoughts on top of that experience. How to work with exchange is discussed further in Chapters 4 and 11.

Believing and behaving as though others are completely separate from us and that we are separate from them leads to misunderstandings and suffering on both sides.

Emptiness

The final mistaken idea underlying the attempt to maintain a fixed sense of self is the belief that there is something in us that is not made up of other things. In the Buddhist view, every particle may be further divided into its constituent parts and none of these parts is a self. The classic example is "the cart" (Thrangu, 2012, pp. 34–37). A modern car, similarly, is made up of many parts, none of which is the car in itself. The school of Buddhism known as Madhyamaka explores such questions thoroughly.[6] How many parts would have to be removed, for example, before the object would no longer be a car? Similarly, how many aspects of our seeming self would have to change for us still to be the self we know as our self? Am I myself if I am no longer smart? Am I myself if I can no longer give birth? Am I myself if I lose my memory? Am I myself if I lose my job? These and similar questions also bring our clients to us.

In Buddhist language, these questions point to what is known as emptiness. That is, phenomena do not exist in a substantial way. Instead, they are the result of the coming together and falling apart of causes and conditions. Things do happen, but they are not solid. We do exist, but not in the solid way we usually think that we do. A related idea is "egolessness" or "selflessness." People often mistake the idea of emptiness or egolessness to mean some kind of nothingness. This is not the case.

Emptiness is the same as the openness and spaciousness we

explored a bit above. Our minds are empty in the sense that there is nothing unchanging, separate, and solid in us. And yet experiences keep arising out of that emptiness. Creativity and spontaneity can occur because we are not solid and fixed. Emptiness is pregnant with all kinds of phenomena.

The Third Noble Truth: The Cessation of Suffering

Also known as the truth of the goal, the third noble truth is the prognosis for our disease of suffering. The prognosis is good; our suffering can cease. Instead of being lost in the confusion, and sometimes intense distress, of suffering, we can recognize our true nature. Again, this does not mean that there will be no pain, but we do not need to suffer. In some Buddhist traditions the notion of cessation is not addressed until the first two noble truths have been presented. In the Tibetan tradition, especially in what is known as the dzogchen teachings, the outcome of the cessation of suffering, or the fruition, is taken as the ground of the whole enterprise and presented first.[7] That is why Contemplative Psychotherapy, with its roots in Tibetan Buddhism, begins with brilliant sanity. So we could also say that the third noble truth is the truth of brilliant sanity. We can connect with our direct experience and open to the wisdom and compassion that are already present in us.

When I work with clients, I translate the idea of uncovering brilliant sanity into simpler goals: mindfulness, loving-kindness, and courage. To help clients cultivate the aspect of clarity, I assist them in developing mindfulness and refraining from mindlessness. Helping clients connect with the compassion aspect of natural wisdom usually begins with helping them to recognize and reverse the self-aggression that underlies much of what they bring to therapy. The antidote to self-aggression is known as *maitri* or loving-kindness. Helping clients to cultivate a sense of loving-kindness toward themselves is an important aspect of contemplative work and is the necessary ground for applying mindfulness and awareness to their experiences. And finally, I translate the sense of openness that is part of brilliant sanity into supporting my clients in becoming more fearless. It requires courage to open to all aspects of one's experience. In the chapters that follow, we will explore further how to apply these ideas in therapy.

The Fourth Noble Truth: The Path

The fourth noble truth is the treatment plan. Since our belief in a mistaken sense of self is strong and has been well established for a long time, it is not easy to recognize that it is not actually true. Buddhist psychology suggests that, like the Buddha, we explore our experience for ourselves and see what we find. Is there something in us that corresponds to such a self? Equally, is there such a thing as brilliant sanity? When we look closely at our moment-to-moment experience, what do we discover?

How do we conduct such an exploration? In the Buddhist tradition, this is done through applying mindfulness and meditation to all areas of our lives. The Buddha presented this in the eightfold path.[8] The Tibetan traditions usually reduce it to the three main aspects of the path: *shila* (discipline), *samadhi* (meditation), and *prajna* (wisdom) (Trungpa, 1995). Either way, the idea is to cultivate mindfulness and awareness (discussed below) in all areas of our life. By bringing our own—and our clients'—attention and curiosity to experiences in the present moment, no matter what we are doing, we begin to see through our confusion and start to uncover our innate wisdom and compassion.

A key aspect of the fourth truth is the idea of a gradual journey: a path. As therapists know, it takes time to integrate what one learns about oneself. Similarly, it takes time to undo the habit of mind that clings to a mistaken sense of self and phenomena as well as the habit of trying to escape from unavoidable discomfort. Therefore, bringing compassion and gentleness to oneself throughout the path is essential.

In Chapter 2, we will go through the details of how to practice sitting meditation, But first, let us take a look at mindfulness and awareness, two of the qualities that sitting meditation helps us to cultivate.

MINDFULNESS

As mindfulness has become an increasingly popular term in the field of psychology, it has been used in a number of different ways. Sometimes it refers to our ability to place our mind on an object and keep it there. Sometimes a term popularized by Pema Chödrön, a well-known writer and American-born Buddhist nun, "learning to stay [present]" (2001, p. 23), is used as a description of mindfulness. More generally, mindfulness has come to mean paying attention to the details of one's experience without grasping it, pushing it away, or judging it. Very simply, mindfulness is paying precise attention in the present moment to whatever object we have chosen to observe. Sometimes it is called bare attention: attention without anything extra added to it (Gunaratana, 2002).

Mindfulness is a natural quality of the mind and reflects the clarity aspect of brilliant sanity. In some sense, psychotherapists and counselors have always been interested in helping their clients become more mindful. We all ask our clients to tell us about some aspects of their experiences. Tracking free associations requires mindfulness. Behavioral therapists ask clients to notice the details of their behavior and activities. Cognitive therapists ask them to track their thoughts and emotions. Other therapists may attend to other specific experiences. In that sense, mindfulness is not something new.

As we will see in Chapter 2, mindfulness meditation practice helps us to cultivate unconditional mindfulness: mindfulness of whatever is arising in the present moment. It is this kind of mindfulness that is especially valuable for a counselor or therapist to have. It gives us the opportunity to experience our own minds and all aspects of experience without pushing away what we find. We become more able to feel and to stay present with all states of body and mind, and this, in turn, expands our ability to be present with the many kinds of experiences our clients bring to us. As noted above, because we are interconnected, we pick up on the feelings and experiences of others, including our clients. If we have learned how to be present with our own states of mind, whether pleasant, unpleasant, or neutral, we are more able to stay connected and present with our clients' varying states of mind.

Mindfulness practice is the tool that lets us explore for ourselves whether brilliant sanity is true in our own experiences. It also lets us see whether Buddhist psychology is correct in saying that there is nothing in us that corresponds to a fixed self.

AWARENESS

Beyond mindfulness, there is also awareness. Awareness has a larger perspective than mindfulness. For example, in listening to a piece of music, mindfulness would attend to each moment, each note, as it was played. It could track the precision of the clarinet in my favorite piece of music, the second movement of Mozart's *Clarinet Concerto in A* (K. 622). Awareness would notice not just the notes, but also the themes, the coming together of all the different aspects of the piece, and also the overall sense of the music. It would notice when the clarinet was joined by other instruments, not only in identifying each one, but in noticing, too, the sense of vastness and space that I always find in the piece. Awareness goes beyond the details of each instrument. We might say awareness notices the whole gestalt.

Awareness can go even further: it may include a larger sense altogether. We may have a sense of the space within which our experience arises. For example, if we are mindful of a pain we are experiencing someplace in our body, we could also have a larger sense of the whole body and the environment in which our body rests, without losing our sense of the painful body part. Being able to do this can help us to relax with what is happening and not add to our suffering. Without having a larger sense, we may make things worse by spinning out fearful thoughts about the pain or narrowing our focus so much that all we experience is pain.

We need both mindfulness and awareness, as do our clients. As we will see, Contemplative Psychotherapy emphasizes attending to the details of what occurs in the present moment (mindfulness), but it also pays attention to the larger picture of how the present moment is born from previous moments and what implications are already indicated for the future (awareness). When we limit our attention to just the details of this very moment, we may miss how one thing leads to another and how we cause ourselves to suffer.

PSYCHOTHERAPY ON THE PATH

For many people, engaging in therapy is part of their personal path of uncovering brilliant sanity or a sense of workability in their lives as well as exploring suffering and its relief. From a contemplative point of view, the therapeutic relationship itself is a key part of that path. As I explore more thoroughly in Chapter 4, cultivating a genuine relationship with our clients based on our interconnectedness, and our shared brilliant sanity is at the heart of the contemplative approach.

As I was working on this chapter, I realized that the one time when I am most fully present is when I am meeting with therapy clients. There is often an effortless quality to my presence in sessions. My mind tends to remain quite open and interested in whatever my clients need to explore, and my heart is also warmly receptive. I am able to accommodate all sorts of mind states including boredom, excitement, hopelessness, and pain. Tracking my own experience happens quite naturally and without much self-consciousness. What became obvious—and was surprisingly overlooked all these years— is that I am most in touch with brilliant sanity while I am working as a psychotherapist. I have long known that I am at my best doing this work. It is not only my clients who find therapy as part of their own paths; serving as a psychotherapist forms part of my own personal path as well. That may well be the case for other therapists too.

Chapter 2

BEGINNING WITH ONESELF: PERSONAL MEDITATION PRACTICE

A key principle in Contemplative Psychotherapy is the need to begin with oneself. As we will explore more deeply in Chapter 4, cultivating a genuine relationship with our clients forms the necessary ground of Contemplative Psychotherapy as well as many other therapeutic approaches. A genuine relationship requires us to be present with an open heart. If we are not fully present in a warm-hearted way with our own experience, how can we ask our clients to be open and vulnerable with us? Carl Rogers said something similar when he noted, "One way of putting this which may seem strange to you is that if I can form a helping relationship to myself—if I can be sensitively aware of and acceptant toward my own feelings—then the likelihood is great that I can form a helping relationship toward another" (1961, p. 51).

So we begin by working first with ourselves in order to recognize and let go of our own obstacles to being fully available to our own experience. Of course, working through our own confusion is a gradual process. The more we are able to do so, the more we tap into the qualities of brilliant sanity—openness, clarity, and compassion— and can bring them into our relationships with our clients. The primary method used in Contemplative Psychotherapy for training ourselves to show up in this way is the practice of mindfulness-awareness sitting meditation.

Many clinical training programs address the same idea by requiring their trainees to engage in their own therapy, and certainly that is an excellent idea. The interpersonal discoveries made in therapy can form an invaluable foundation for the practice of being in therapeutic relationships with our clients. It may well be that some readers of this book will not become practitioners of sitting meditation practice. They may choose to take what is valuable for them in this book and leave the rest, and, of course, that is fine. Some may engage in other methods of mindfulness and awareness practice like yoga or tai chi. Others may regard their clinical work as their main practice. Still, in the interest of presenting the contemplative approach faithfully, let me note that for a therapist who chooses to practice Contemplative Psychotherapy, sitting meditation is indispensable both as part of one's training and as an ongoing discipline throughout one's clinical life.

THE UNIQUE OPPORTUNITY OF MINDFULNESS-AWARENESS SITTING MEDITATION

What do we discover through mindfulness-awareness meditation that we might not learn in our own personal psychotherapy or through other mindfulness practices and activities? What does sitting practice offer that is unique? First, while it shares some aspects with other formal mindfulness and awareness practices, such as being done alone or in silence, it is unique in providing an opportunity to experience oneself without adding anything extra. When we practice sitting meditation, we do very little else. As we will see in the instructions that follow about how to do the practice, when we sit, for the most part we just sit. There are no unusual postures or movements, no sounds to make, no images to visualize, and no thoughts to maintain.

In the absence of such things, we have the chance to see what we are like without them. It is actually quite rare to take the time to just be present with ourselves in this way. For most of us, time, especially time devoted to ourselves, is a precious commodity. There is no need, I am sure, to convince anyone that our lives in the 21st century tend to be busy ones.

What can happen when we do take the time to just sit down with ourselves?

Being Present, Touching Our Experience

Through sitting practice, we cultivate our ability to be present with whatever arises in our body, emotions, and mind. This practice cultivates unconditional presence (Welwood, 1992). That is, no matter what arises, we learn to be with it. If we cannot be present with ourselves, how can we expect to be present with our clients? It is easy to say, "Be in the present moment," but it can be quite difficult to actually do it.

Over the years, I have sat with a great many different states of mind and emotions. What had seemed unimaginable—tolerating the pain that arose when I lost first my father and then my mother— became workable. I found that feeling the intensely sad pain in my heart and allowing it to be there was easier than shutting down or distracting myself.

Over the years meditators I have known have discovered that they actually can sit with intense fear, brokenheartedness, anger, confusion, obsessive thinking, self-doubt, jealousy, depression, and even mania.

Sometimes I can stay present with unfolding internal narratives and dramas. Other times I become caught up in them. When I sit on my meditation cushion, I become vividly aware of how easily my mind becomes distracted. Even after more than 30 years of practicing meditation, I see that I can go from a flickering random thought like, "It must be nearly lunchtime," to a fantasy about what I would like to have for lunch today, and then seamlessly segue into what I had yesterday, and how the price of cheese has gone up, particularly the cheese I like that is similar to what we had for lunch when we were traveling in Mexico, and really when are we ever going to get back to San Miguel Allende, and how are my friends Shoshana and David who live there? At some point I will notice that I am long gone and apply the technique of the practice and return to the present moment, sitting on my cushion feeling the mild rumblings of hunger in my belly.

Over the time that I have been meditating, my ability to come back has increased. In any case, my relationship to my distractible mind has changed, which leads us to the second benefit of sitting practice.

Finding Kindness, Opening the Heart

Sharon Salzberg, a well-known meditation teacher, said in a talk I heard her give at a conference in San Diego in 2010 something along the lines that the most important moment in meditation practice is the moment when we realize that we have been distracted or lost in thought. How we deal with that recognition is key.

We may become self-aggressive: "No! Wrong! Get back to the practice!" Or "You idiot, what are you doing thinking about that!" Or "I'm hopeless, I can't do this meditation thing." The actual instruction, when we notice that we have been distracted is to gently return to doing the technique of the practice. The most important word there is "gently." Each time we treat ourselves with gentleness, we cultivate our ability to be kind not only to ourselves but also to others. As we train our ability to be gentle, we uncover the natural compassion that is part of our brilliant sanity.

As noted in Chapter 1, we use the Sanskrit word *maitri* to describe this quality of loving-kindness that we develop first toward ourselves and then extend to others.

Making Friends With Ourselves

Closely related to finding kindness toward ourselves and others is making friends with ourselves (Chödrön, 1998). When we practice mindfulness-awareness meditation, we get to know ourselves really well. There is nothing like sitting with oneself and not doing anything else to reveal us to ourselves. Our habitual patterns of leaving the present moment become quite apparent. We remember times in the past when we behaved poorly, and we may experience shame. We recall times when we achieved something we had worked hard for, and we may feel pride. We spend time wondering and planning for the future. We become lost in all kinds of fantasies: of sexual desires being met, of aggressive scenarios playing out, and of ordinary life just chugging along in a pleasant way.

As we practice, all manner of thoughts, images, sense perceptions, and emotions arise. In sitting practice we do not try to get rid of these experiences. We are not trying to change anything. Instead, the practice provides us with the opportunity to see that we can stay present both with intense states of mind and emotion and also with the times when not much at all is happening. Discomfort and even boredom can be included.

As we sit, there are fewer and fewer hidden corners in our experience. If we are practicing gentleness, our relationship to these scary or unpleasant places shifts from one of avoidance to one of acceptance. Accepting our experience means letting it be what it is; it does not mean that we have to like it or view it in a positive light. It does not even mean that we will not try to change it once we are done sitting. Getting to know ourselves means we can tolerate an increasing range of direct experience without pushing it away. Another way to say the same thing is that we become less self-aggressive.

Courage

Opening again and again to whatever arises in our experience while practicing sitting meditation also gives us the opportunity to develop the courage not to turn away from ourselves. Many of us have learned to disconnect from aspects of our experience. We may even have a habit of becoming dissociated. Perhaps we are afraid to experience anger, or we may have learned it is dangerous to feel vulnerable. As we practice sitting meditation and begin to make friends with all the ways we are, we naturally become more brave. We become less afraid of what might arise next. Unconditional confidence, the confidence that we can touch any aspect of our experience, starts to dawn in us. In turn, this expands what we can stay present with in our clients' experience as well.

Letting Go

Not only may we become more able to touch and stay present with all aspects of our experience, sitting practice also teaches us how to let go. Probably everyone knows what it is like to be so caught up with a thought or a feeling that we feel stuck or haunted. This is a common experience for therapists who find themselves mentally carrying their clients with them long after sessions are over.

The need to be able to let go is not limited to our work with clients. The technique of touch and go allows us to contact our experience fully and also let it dissolve again (Trungpa, 2005). We can apply the basic theme of touching our experience and letting it go both in our meditation practice and in our clinical work. We will explore this technique in detail in Chapter 3 when we look at the five basic competencies of the contemplative psychotherapist.

Seeing for Ourselves

Finally, sitting meditation practice gives us the opportunity to see for ourselves who and what we are. Do we have brilliant sanity? Do we have anything in us that is unchanging, solid, and separate? Are these Buddhist and contemplative ideas true for us or not? As noted in Chapter 1, it is important to be inquisitive and see for ourselves what parts of what is presented here are useful or valuable. In Buddhist traditions, intellectual questioning of ideas is balanced with an experiential investigation. Sitting meditation provides the laboratory for examining our own experience and seeing for ourselves.

INSTRUCTIONS FOR PRACTICING MINDFULNESS-AWARENESS MEDITATION

There are many different traditions and styles of sitting meditation. For example, some are designed to help one relax, while others are devotional in nature. The specific technique presented here is the one we teach our students in the Contemplative Psychotherapy training program at Naropa. We have chosen this particular style of meditation because it cultivates our ability to be unconditionally mindful and aware both with ourselves and with others. It is especially well-suited to preparing us to remain present with our clients. For example, in this practice we keep our eyes open.

Even though the practice itself is quite simple, it takes a great many words to describe all the concerns that might arise for a newcomer to the practice. I suggest that you read through the instructions below in their entirety, and then go back and follow them one step at a time. At the end of this chapter you will find a summary of the practice for easier reference.

It is generally best to receive meditation instruction in person, but you can still begin by working with what is here. At some point, if you feel inspired to continue an ongoing daily practice, it is good to find a meditation instructor with whom you can discuss how your practice is going.[1]

Setting Up the Environment

The first step is to find a place to sit. This may seem obvious, but it is often a challenge to find a good spot. In the same way that we would not choose to do intensive therapy in a noisy room with other people wandering in and out, we try to find a relatively quiet and calm place to engage in our meditation practice. Sometimes we have no choice about where we see clients, and sometimes we do not have much choice about where we can do our meditation practice either. It is just easier if we are able to withdraw from our ordinary life concerns and let our meditation practice be an opportunity to rest the mind (Mingyur, 2007).

Some people are lucky enough to have a room they can devote to their meditation practice. Most of us designate a place, a corner of a room perhaps, where we will practice. Others meditate in community settings. Many towns have meditation groups who hold regular group sitting sessions or simply have an open meditation hall or shrine room where anyone may come and practice throughout the day. Sometimes it is possible to practice in a chapel or church. Since this is a silent practice, our meditation need not disturb anyone else.

Since this practice is done with the eyes open, what we place in front of us can matter. Many people create an altar or shrine as a source of inspiration and as a reminder of why they are practicing meditation. If you wish to create some kind of altar, you might add pictures or objects that are meaningful to you drawn from whatever traditions you feel a connection with. You may want to add candles and incense as reminders of impermanence or as invitations to open your sense perceptions in the practice. Personally, I like to light Japanese incense, which tends to have a lighter scent than Indian or Tibetan varieties. Incense comes in many forms and may be found in shops or online. Fresh flowers are another common addition to an altar.

Part of setting up the environment includes determining how we will know when our meditation session is finished. We can, of course, simply use a clock. Personally, I find that I end up looking at the clock many times during a session if I use that method. Instead, I prefer to use a specially designed clock that emits a soft gonging sound when its timer runs out. There are also quite a number of good applications for smartphones, computer pads, and laptops that are designed to time meditation. Another way to time your practice is by using a stick of incense. Most long sticks burn for about an hour, and short ones burn for about 30 minutes. You can experiment with breaking long ones into different sizes to find the size that meets your needs.

In general, it is best if we decide beforehand how long we will practice and then stick to it. Otherwise, if we have a pleasant session, we are likely to judge it as good and perhaps sit longer, and if we have a challenging session, we are likely to end it early. Since this practice is about developing an unconditional attitude, being with whatever arises, it works better not to determine how long we will practice based on how well it is going. If we just sit for a predetermined time, we can discover that even difficult emotions or thoughts can be included and sometimes may even dissolve on their own without any further effort on our part.

When people are starting out, it is best to do short sessions of about 10 minutes. It may be helpful to sit two or more times a day at the beginning and to keep the sessions quite short. Over time you may choose to reduce the number of sessions and make them longer. Many people like to sit twice a day for about 20 minutes to half an hour. Others prefer to sit once a day for as much as an hour. Most days I sit 45 minutes to an hour in the morning. Generally, it is helpful to practice at the same time each day so that it becomes part of your ordinary routine. Some people choose to practice first thing in the morning as a way to enter their day, while others prefer to sit before dinner, letting their practice mark the transition between the end of their work day and the beginning of their evening. Still others sit as the last thing they do each day. Sometimes our schedules do not allow for that kind of consistency, so we just do whatever we can.

Finding a Good Meditation Seat

Having set up a place to practice, the next concern is to choose a seat. Traditionally, we sit on meditation cushions. These come in a variety of styles, including round Japanese-style zafus, wooden meditation benches, boxy Tibetan gomdens, and crescent-shaped cushions. Some are filled with kapok, others with foam, and still others with buckwheat hulls that let practitioners wriggle around to make them conform to the shape of their bottoms.

It is also fine to fold up a blanket or use another kind of cushion to begin with. If we use a meditation cushion or bench, we want also to have either a larger pad, called a zabuton, underneath or sit on a carpeted floor. Sitting on a cushion placed directly on a hard, bare floor will lead to pain in the feet or ankles pretty quickly. Many people find that they do better sitting in a chair. A chair with a firm and level seat works best. If it is too soft and we sink into it, it will probably become uncomfortable after only a short time.

An important guideline is to have the knees lower than the hips. The back will begin to hurt if the hips are lower than the knees. This is true for both floor and chair sitting. To achieve this, long-legged people may need to add an additional layer below or on top of their cushion, folded blanket, or chair, while short-legged people, like me, will need a cushion that is low enough to keep some weight in the legs and feet as they rest on the floor. When I sit in a chair, I need to put something under my feet so that my feet have weight in them.

It does not matter in the least what we sit on as long as the body is comfortable enough to let us turn our minds to the other aspects of the practice as well. It is best to have a seat that feels firm and stable so that we do not feel like we will tip over. We may need to experiment with different seats until we find one that works for us.

Embodiment

Once we have found an acceptable seat, we begin the practice by sitting down and adjusting our posture. We want to take a posture that lets us feel grounded and embodied. If our posture is too uncomfortable, we are likely either to spend all our time paying attention to our discomfort or to become lost in distractions to escape the pain we feel. The advantage of cushions and benches designed for meditation is that they are likely to be more comfortable. At the same time, many people experience some bodily discomfort with sitting practice. This is especially true for beginners and for people doing long practice sessions.

The posture itself is upright but not rigid. In this practice we take a simple posture. If we sit on a cushion, we cross our legs in front of us with our knees higher than our feet, perhaps the way we did as a child. There is no need to take a challenging posture like the full lotus, in which the feet rest on the opposite thighs. If we use a meditation bench, the knees rest on the ground while the legs go under the bench, pointing behind us. When we meditate sitting in a chair, we try to sit upright without leaning against the back of the chair. Feet are placed squarely on the floor, with or without something under them.

Having taken a good seat, we let the back rise from it. I was once told to imagine that my spine was like a tree and to lean against it. The idea is to let the back take its natural shape: upright and with its natural curve in the lower back. When we are unused to this posture it may feel awkward at first. We can try leaning a bit to the left and right and then to the front and back. This lets us find where our own natural balance is. It may take some getting used to. Sometimes we say, "Strong back, soft front." The front of the body is open so that we can breathe easily. We might notice that we have a habit of rounding our shoulders and letting our front collapse. We can try to gently come upright and let the chest area be open.

Then, we place the hands, facing down, on the thighs or knees. They just rest there; we should not need to use them to hold ourselves up. If we find that we are hanging on to our knees as though for dear life, then we need to readjust our setup, probably so that the hips are a bit higher.

Those who have physical limitations that prevent them from easily sitting upright should do whatever they need to do to feel well supported. For example, if they are using a chair, they may choose to put a cushion or pillow behind their backs and lean against it. Sitting on the floor, they might put a small cushion or rolled-up towel under one or both knees.

The head is upright with the chin tucked in just a little to prevent our looking upward and craning our necks. We face squarely to the front.

Many meditation practices are done with the eyes closed, with the intention to turn away from the outside environment, but in this one we let all of our senses be open: sight, hearing, smelling, tasting, and touching. We are training ourselves to be present with all of our experiences, so we leave the eyes open. The gaze is downward but not uncomfortably tight: around 5 or 6 feet in front and resting on the floor is good. The gaze can be soft or focused, but if we become too caught up with the visual sense, we may find we get a headache. So, generally, it is best to let whatever is front of us just be there. If it is a busily patterned carpet, let it be there. If it is the back of another person, just see that. If it is a peaceful, plain wall, that is fine, too.

Having taken our seat and adjusted our posture, we direct our attention to being present. It is helpful to take a minute or two to notice the environment in which we are sitting. Then we turn our attention to the direct experience of feeling what we feel in our body.

Being embodied is inseparable from being present, so we take a few minutes to feel what we feel. Maybe we notice a tightness in the neck or a numb area in our back. Whatever it is, we just notice it. There is no reason to try to change what we find. On the other hand, we may naturally relax a tight place or feel an area that was outside our awareness. The whole tenor of this practice is to be with ourselves as we are, so we do not get caught up in trying to fix ourselves.

Feeling our bodies is not just a preparation for the practice; it is an ongoing aspect of meditation.

Breath

The next aspect of the practice is working with the breath as a reference point for nowness. If we are with our breathing, we are grounded in the present moment. No special breathing is used in this practice. Whether our breath is shallow or deep, ragged or rhythmic, it does not matter. We just let it be however it is. This is part of becoming friends with all aspects of our experience.

Different meditation techniques relate to the breath in a variety of ways. In this practice, we put more emphasis on the outbreath. As a breath goes out, we lightly place our attention on it. As that breath dissolves into space, the attention we have placed on it dissolves as well. There may be a sense of letting go at the end of the breath. The object of our attention has vanished, and we cannot hang on to it.

Then the inbreath happens naturally. We do not ignore it, and we also do not do anything special with it. We can also come back to a sense of posture and embodiment. Then we go out again with the next outbreath.

Practicing in this way introduces a sense of space and letting go into our practice that we may not find if we follow the breath closely throughout its cycle of going out and coming in.

To repeat, we place our attention only lightly on the breath. The rest of our attention will automatically be on our sense of embodiment and environment. Sometimes this is described as placing 25% of our attention on the breath (Trungpa, 1995). We do not need to try to achieve this percentage; it is, rather, a description of what naturally occurs when we touch the breath gently and leave the rest of our attention to take care of itself.

By doing this, we have the opportunity to discover and make friends with whatever else arises in our experience. Practices that hold the mind more tightly to the breath lead to good concentration and a sense of calmness, but that is a somewhat different intention from that of this practice, which is to cultivate unconditional mindfulness and awareness.

Distraction

Having set up our practice space and seat, taken our posture, and brought our attention to our breathing, the last piece of the technique is to work with distractions. It is important to note that we are not trying to get ourselves to stop thinking or becoming distracted. Minds think. They get lost in images and thoughts, caught up with sense perceptions, and captured by emotions. Our intention is to bring mindfulness and awareness to our experience as we find it. If we forcefully push our distractions away, we will not find out much about who and what we are. Instead, we will learn only about the experience of aggression, the action of rejecting our experience.

At the same time, in order to develop mindfulness, awareness, familiarity with all aspects of our experiences, and letting go, we cannot just indulge in distraction mindlessly. A common guideline for meditation practice is "not too tight and not too loose" (Trungpa, 1987 p. 10). That is, we do not hold our minds to the breath too determinedly, and we also do not just hope for the best and let the mind meander all over the place without any restraint. Working with this balance is an ongoing part of the practice. We all fall into the two extremes of too tight and too loose. When we notice, we simply adjust ourselves.

Labeling "Thinking"

A useful technique is to use the label "thinking" when we notice we have been lost in distraction. We use the same label for all distractions, whether they are mental, physical, or emotional, since the mind is involved in all of them. Using just one label for everything simplifies things.

The label is said silently in the mind as a way of acknowledging what is happening. I like to think of it as a kind of weather report: "Thinking has just occurred in the local region." It is not meant to be a judgment of any kind. It is not, "You should not be thinking," or "You are doing this wrong." We can greet the information that we were distracted with a friendly attitude. It is more along the lines of, "Ah, yes, thinking occurred. No big deal. That's what happens."

Fresh Start

Occasionally we may find that we are completely lost: we may be labeling our breath and following our thoughts. Or we have become so caught up in struggling with a personal problem or so distracted by pain somewhere in our body that we have really stopped applying the technique of returning to the breath. When that happens, we can take a fresh start. We can drop the whole project, adjust our posture, notice the environment, and then gently return to the technique.

If a leg has gone to sleep, it is useful to just rearrange our legs, reversing which one is in front, or rest them by pulling the knees up straight in front of us for a few minutes. If we find ourselves readjusting our posture many times in a session, we may need to change our seat in some way. There is no need at all to put up with strong pain.

Summary of the Meditation Technique

There are three main parts to the practice. First, we work with the body and environment. We establish the environment and take our seat on a cushion or chair. We notice the environment in which we are sitting and then tune in to what we feel in our bodies.

Second, we turn our attention to our breathing. We gently join our attention with the outbreath. As it goes out and dissolves into space, our attention dissolves as well. We may have a sense of letting go at the end of the breath. Then we return to a sense of posture and presence. The inbreath happens naturally and requires no special treatment.

Third, we notice whatever arises in our experience: bodily sensations, emotions, thoughts, and images. When we become caught up or lost in any of those events, we note it gently by labeling it "thinking" silently in our mind. Then we simply return to the present moment and going out with the breath.

WORKING WITH AN ONGOING MEDITATION PRACTICE

In this section we will look at some concerns that may arise both for new and experienced meditators.

Daily and Retreat Practice

It is best if we can develop a daily practice. The point is to be steady if we want to accrue the benefits of the practice. At the same time, we do what we can reasonably do. Even a short session can be helpful in interrupting our habitually speedy lives and minds. Settling down for as little as 5 minutes can create a break in our tendency to mindlessly go from one thing to another. Sometimes just taking three deep breaths in a mindful fashion can help us land back on the ground and bring us into the present moment (Bayda, 2005).

For those of us who feel so inspired, participating in a group retreat for a weekend or for a week or more can be a wonderful chance to slow down and be with ourselves and take a break from the hectic pace of our contemporary lives. I usually participate in a retreat of about 2 weeks most summers. I would also highly recommend individual retreats for those who have practiced for a year or more. There are retreat centers all over the world that provide the facilities and support for both group and individual meditation retreats in different Buddhist and other traditions.

Doing It Right

What does "doing it right" mean when it comes to practicing meditation? Most simply, it means that we take the time to practice. Beyond that, if we are making a reasonable attempt to work with the technique, that is enough. If we just sit on our cushion or chair and daydream, we are not meditating; but if, when we notice our minds wandering, we return our attention to the breath, we are applying the technique. We can remember the slogan, "not too tight, not too loose." No one else can really tell us if we are too tight or too loose; we have to feel our way for ourselves. If we hold our minds too tightly, we will quickly become fed up with meditation. It will be too much of a struggle and will feel like we are just doing time. If we hold our minds too loosely, we will not cultivate our ability to be present and kind. We will not be around enough to make friends with ourselves.

People often make the mistake of thinking that they are having a good practice session if they are not thinking a lot. That is not the case with this practice. The mind may begin to settle down, and it may not. Basically, however we are is fine. Distracted mind, calm mind, it does not matter. We can make friends with however our minds are, and we will see that they change. Sometimes we can be present most of the practice session, and other times we find that we are all over the place. Both are good practice sessions. Over time, we may discover that we can be present and make friends even with a wild, unruly mind.

Another mistake people can make is to think that they should feel a particular way either while they are practicing or afterward. Maybe we think we should become peaceful, calm, and loving. Paradoxically, we may actually become more of those things if we are willing to be however we really are. Being peaceful can be understood as the willingness to be present with our experience no matter what it is. If we are angry, peacefulness is feeling angry. Out of that may very well come the qualities of spacious calm, increased clarity, and kindness, but we will not find those qualities by trying to make them happen on purpose. Trying to be a particular way is the activity of creating a false sense of self, which Buddhist psychology identifies as the problem, not the solution, to our suffering. It is just a more subtle version of self-aggression.

Ongoing Meditation Instruction

For those who are inspired to continue their practice, it can be helpful and supportive to work with a qualified meditation instructor from time to time. Meditation instructors, in many traditions, offer their services as part of their own practice. Sometimes a nominal fee or offering is given to an instructor. In the community in which I serve as a meditation instructor, I do not receive payment, and I usually see people for about half an hour perhaps a few times a year. We pay attention especially to working with the balance of not too tight, and not too loose. In addition, I try to answer any questions about the technique or the theory underlying the practice. At Naropa our students meet with a meditation instructor twice or more during each semester and usually work with the same instructor for the duration of the 3-year program. There is no need to prepare for such an interview or even to have questions ready to ask.

Others may connect with a teacher of a contemplative practice within Christian, Jewish, Hindu, Sufi (Islamic), or another contemplative tradition.

Working With Resistance to Practice

Our final topic is how to deal with resistance to meditation practice. Many people find that they experience times when it is hard to get to the cushion.

Sometimes, we go through periods when we want to jump up at the slightest thought of doing something else. Staying on our meditation seat seems impossible. It can be amazing how important it may seem to check our e-mail or something else that can easily wait until our practice session is over. Feeling antsy in this way is known as hot boredom (Nichtern, 2010). The best thing to do with that is to label it "thinking" and just keep going. If we give in to it, we just reinforce our belief that we cannot sit with this particular state of mind. It usually does not take long to see that it is workable, after all. Other times, we find that not much is happening. Many of us have learned to avoid this experience. We are apt to find it boring and conclude that we ourselves are boring. We call this cool boredom, and it can be useful to reframe it as a sense of spaciousness rather than as a problem (Nichtern, 2010).

It can also happen that we have no idea why we are finding it hard to get to our practice. This might be what is happening when, despite our good intentions to practice, we never seem to get there. There may be things beginning to arise that we are not ready to face alone. The more we practice sitting meditation, the more forgotten or avoided memories may tend to show up. If we find that buried memories of trauma are arising, it may be time to seek out a therapist as a complement to our sitting practice. We may even choose to take a break from practice while we work through past trauma that makes staying embodied too difficult.

For many of us, when we experience resistance to meditation practice, it can be helpful just to do it anyway. My own approach is to imagine placing a friendly arm around my own shoulder and "together" go to my cushion. Once I sit down, I am usually okay. The hardest part of practice for me can be just getting there.

Chapter 3

THE FIVE COMPETENCIES OF THE CONTEMPLATIVE PSYCHOTHERAPIST

The five competencies are expressions of our natural wisdom, our brilliant sanity. They are based on what are known in Tibetan Buddhism as the five Buddha family wisdoms or energies (Trungpa, 1987). Cultivated through our mindfulness-awareness practices, these competencies underlie all that a contemplative therapist does. We develop these competencies over time and are able to tap into them more strongly at some times than at others.

The five contemplative competencies have much in common with the qualities aspired to by therapists who are not contemplatively trained. For example, all therapists are encouraged to receive their clients nonjudgmentally or to appreciate and value differences. Yet many therapists are never actually introduced ways to develop those skills. As we have seen, mindfulness-awareness practice can provide training that develops these and other abilities.

The ability to be present is the first of the five competencies and is the foundation for the other four. While we will look at the five as separate, they overlap with each other and are ultimately inseparable. The five competencies are:

1. Being present and letting be
2. Seeing clearly and not judging

3. Recognizing and appreciating differences
4. Connecting with others and cultivating relationship
5. Acting skillfully and letting go

A series of guided exercises at the end of this chapter is designed to evoke an experiential sense of each of the five.

THE FIRST COMPETENCY: BEING PRESENT AND LETTING BE

In 1985, I attended a large gathering in Phoenix, Arizona, the first Evolution of Psychotherapy Conference. It brought together practitioners and students of every stripe of psychotherapy. Among the presenters were R. D. Laing, Carl Rogers, Carl Whitaker, James Bugental, Thomas Szasz, Virginia Satir, and many others. There were thousands of participants. I was struck by how often the presenters pointed to the same ability as the most important asset that a therapist could have: the ability to be present with clients. Then, just as often, they would go to say something like, "Too bad we can't train that." They seemed to think we had to be born with it. As I sat with a few of my Naropa colleagues, we turned and looked at each other in surprise. We knew that this quality could be trained, and we knew that meditation practice could train it. The following are different aspects of the first competency of being present and letting be.

Being Present With All of Our Experience

The ability to remain present with all aspects of our own experience is probably the most important thing we offer to our clients. If we can be with whatever state of mind or emotion arises for us as we sit with our clients, then we can truly be present for them. If we cannot tolerate particular feelings or states of mind, then we will pull back. We may not even be aware that we are doing so, but we will do something to lower the intensity like changing the subject or asking about a nonthreatening aspect of what the client has brought up. We may even become numb or space out. Clients may not be completely aware of what we have done, but they may begin to notice that not much seems to be happening in therapy. This may even be welcome; it will let them off the hook. It will not, however, help clients to address what they need to.

Resting in Spacious Mind and Practicing Not Knowing

Closely related to being present is resting in the kind of spaciousness that is an aspect of brilliant sanity. The Buddha family wisdom that this skill is related to is called the wisdom of all-encompassing space (Trungpa, 1987). An open or spacious mind is one that can accommodate experiences without having to pull away or draw any conclusions. Another way to say this is that we can allow ourselves not to know what to say or do next.

Like many other therapists, I was well trained from elementary school onward in the belief that knowing is better than not knowing. For a contemplative therapist, though, being able to stay present with not knowing is a valuable skill: it is being open and letting be.

I sometimes found it challenging to stay present with my client Martha, who was having trouble with intimacy. She often indulged in a variety of distractions, including drinking alcohol, as a way to avoid the intimacy of her relationship with her partner. Among other things, we tracked her experience of being present with me. Over time, she was increasingly able to look me in the eye despite a sense of anxiety and uneasiness. I invited her to experiment with turning away from me and then returning back to looking at me in accordance with what seemed possible for her in the moment. I noticed that I often found it difficult to stay present as well. I felt awkward and found myself thinking of things that might make it easier for both of us. Just as in my meditation practice, once I recognized these thoughts, I let them be and returned again and again to just being present and embodied. Like Martha, I was feeling uncomfortable with the open space, the sense of uncertainty.

I was tempted to withdraw from the immediacy of our shared experience by offering explanations or bringing up a safer topic. If I had pulled back from the intimacy we were experiencing in those moments, I would be doing exactly what Martha usually did, and that would not have served her. Meeting as two human beings in the relative safety of the therapeutic relationship could let Martha discover her own obstacles to intimacy. I needed to show up.

My job was to be as available as I could when Martha turned back to me. In meditation, we can learn to tolerate such openness by going out with the outbreath and experiencing a gap at the end of the breath as it dissolves into space. We come back into the present moment by returning to the direct experience of our bodies and our sense perceptions.

Not Trying to Change Clients' Experiences

Along with this ability to be present with uncertainty and whatever else arises, this first competency is also about letting our own and our clients' experiences be what they are. We practice this in meditation every time we simply label "thinking."

Letting be can be difficult for those of us who became therapists in order to not only be helpful but feel helpful. It feels satisfying to know that we have helped someone by changing things for the better. Letting things be as they are may go against the grain. Of course, it feels good to see someone's pain subside. At the same time, if we cannot tolerate staying present with our clients' discomfort, then we really do not know what will be helpful. I see this often with graduate students training to be therapists. "What do I do when . . . ? What do I do if . . . ?" They seek answers as a way to escape the uncomfortable experience of not knowing. And experienced therapists may do the same.

When I was with Martha, letting be also meant staying present with the feelings of helplessness and anger that arose for me as she described her long history of avoiding closeness and its roots in early sexual abuse and negligent parents. Does this mean that we just sit and listen and never do anything else? No, of course not. But first, we need to just be there, and that often requires us to stay open to experiences we might prefer to avoid.

THE SECOND COMPETENCY: SEEING CLEARLY AND NOT JUDGING

The second competency is seeing clearly and not judging. This is one of those things that sounds simple but can be quite difficult in practice. What makes it difficult? From a contemplative point of view, what prevents us from seeing clearly is our allegiance to maintaining a fixed view of ourselves and of the phenomenal world. In other words, we find it challenging to recognize emptiness and interdependence. We might prefer to hold onto a fixed view of ourselves as competent, knowledgeable, and helpful. Feelings of incompetence, not knowing, and helplessness may be extremely uncomfortable.

Instead, we may prefer to have the certainty of a conceptual framework into which we can slot our experience. Getting caught up in intellectual certainties can be an obstacle to recognizing what is going on in our own and our clients' experience. We may privilege our thoughts and projections over the messiness of direct experience. "Truth, uncompromisingly told," said Melville, "will always have its ragged edges" (2010, p. 109).

Misusing Diagnostic Categories

As psychotherapists, we may look at our clients through the lens of diagnostic categories. It is certainly not uncommon to hear a client described by clinicians as a borderline or a schizophrenic. When we do this we are creating an identity, a fixed sense of a person's being. This misuse of labeling to "pinpoint, categorize, and pigeonhole" has been called "psychological materialism" (Trungpa, 2005, p. 138). When we use labels in this way, we narrow down our ability to see clearly, and we miss seeing the whole person.

There are, of course, skillful ways to make use of diagnostic labels. They can help us to communicate with our colleagues. Having a diagnosis can sometimes let clients relax, knowing that what they experience has been experienced by others. Labels can point us toward useful treatment options. We get into trouble, however, when our reliance on them clouds our ability to see our clients clearly.

Going Beyond Countertransference and Judgments

Understanding how we misperceive our clients based on our own preconceptions is familiar ground to many therapists as countertransference. Clarifying what we are projecting onto our clients, based on our own personal histories and expectations, enhances not only our ability to see the client more clearly, it also helps us be present. Instead of becoming limited by our thoughts or projections, we can practice recognizing and letting go of them, just as we do in our sitting practice.

Another brand of thinking that can interfere with our ability to see our clients clearly is forming judgments about them. This can be fairly subtle or quite obvious. We have all had the experience, I suspect, of finding that opinions we had formed about clients were wrong. I remember, for example, making the mistake of thinking that a client of mine, Leon, was not very bright, when it turned out he was merely thoughtful. He was often quiet and noncommittal. What I learned was that Leon took his time before reaching conclusions, but when he reached them, they were often thorough and nuanced.

Working With Sense Perceptions

An important aspect of clarity is working with our sense percep- tions. As both cognitive psychology and Buddhist teachings point out, we filter our experiences through our thoughts, expectations, habit- ual patterns, and prejudices. We tend to perceive what we expect to perceive. Meditation practice, bringing mindfulness and awareness to the ongoing flow of our experience, helps us recognize how we may be distorting simple sense perceptions. As I examine more closely in Chapter 6, working with clients' sense perceptions is often a good way to invite them into their experience of the present moment. First, though, we need to do what we can to be in touch with our own.

Finding Clarity Through Basic Listening Skills

Another part of the second competency is using all of the basic listening skills we may have learned at the beginning of our training. These include paraphrasing, reflecting content and emotions, and summarizing. By employing these skills, we let our clients know that we are hearing them. The wisdom associated with seeing clearly is mirror-like wisdom (Trungpa, 1987), and we practice it by being a clean mirror reflecting back to our clients what we are hearing and seeing without distortion.

Practicing Stupidity

I sometimes suggest to students that they "be more stupid" and not assume they already know what the client means. Like embracing not knowing, being stupid may not come easily to well-trained professionals. It is easy to think we can guess where the client is going with something, but we are often wrong.

In one of our first sessions, Anita told me, "My parents sent me off to boarding school in the seventh grade." I jumped to the conclusion that she felt abandoned or pushed away when she said "sent me off."

"How was that for you?" I asked, expecting my assumptions to be confirmed.

"It was wonderful! I couldn't wait to get out of that house and away from my nagging mother."

Some other simple interventions that let us practice being more stupid might include these:

- "What do you mean when you say 'depressed'?"
- "Tell me more about the argument you had with your partner."
- "As I listen to you, I think you're telling me you are sad. Is that right?"

THE THIRD COMPETENCY: RECOGNIZING AND APPRECIATING DIFFERENCES

Many of the principles in Buddhist psychology highlight what we all have in common: the natural wisdom of brilliant sanity, the obstacle of a fixed sense of identity, the value of mindfulness, and the power of compassion. With the third competency, we shift our focus to the uniqueness of own experience and that of our clients.

Recognizing Differences

Buddhist psychology teachings emphasize how we are interconnected, interdependent, and not separate from each other. This can easily be misunderstood as saying that we are all the same. Sometimes new meditators fear that mindfulness awareness practice will blunt their distinctive qualities. They worry that they will lose their uniqueness and become bland and boring people. I call this fear the mashed potatoes fallacy: the belief that one will become mush, like mashed potatoes without salt or pepper (Wegela, 2009).

There could be a kernel of truth in this fear. To the extent that we are identified with being special because we cling to a particular identity and way of being, meditation can very well reveal the illusory nature of such specialness. On the other hand, however, what I have learned in my studies and in my experience of longtime meditators is that they become more vividly who they are. They become more courageous and lighthearted. Letting go of the straitjacket of a mistaken sense of self lets them become more creative, less afraid of disagreeing with the norms of a peer group, and more alive altogether.

Even more unconventional stories are told of teachers in the "crazy wisdom" lineage of Tibetan Buddhism and of Zen masters who startle their students with their outrageousness (Midal, 2004). One such teacher was Drukpa Künley, the Mad Yogi of Bhutan, who is said to have brought Vajrayana Buddhism to Bhutan in the 15th century and to have used "outrage and laughter" to "shock people out of their lethargic acceptance of the neurotic status quo of their minds, and out of their attachment to conventional forms" (Dowman, 1980, p. 27).

As therapists, if we can be open and clear, we can recognize how each client is unique. As we let go of our expectations and preconceptions, again and again, we meet our clients right where they are in each moment of nowness. On the basis of the first two competencies, we can bring curiosity and interest to the particular qualities of each client we work with.

Maitri

In the context of the third competency, maitri (introduced in Chapter 1) is a way of recognizing and appreciating ourselves as well as our clients. We cultivate it first through making friends with ourselves in our mindfulness-awareness practices. We also can practice and increase maitri in our work with our clients. As we sit with them, all kinds of experiences will arise for us. We can practice maitri on the spot by practicing touch and go: we notice our experience and feel it directly without pushing it away, and then we let it go again. As we do this, we are practicing appreciating ourselves in the same way that we aspire to value and respect all the different aspects of our clients.

Beginning Diversity Awareness With Oneself

Although it was not true when I received my own training many years ago, thankfully diversity awareness training has now become very much a part of clinical training. Like much else in a contemplative approach, recognizing diversity and difference begins with working with oneself.

One aspect of this is recognizing and appreciating our own status as privileged or marginalized. Most of us have privileges and also challenges based on groups of which we may be members. For example, I am privileged in the United States by being white. I can go into most stores and know that I will probably not be followed by suspicious staff members who think I might be there to steal merchandise. When I drive, I do not get stopped by officials who ask to see my license in order to see if I am an undocumented alien. I grew up with the privileges of living in a safe place and having the financial means that allowed me to go to good schools from kindergarten through graduate school. My family could afford good food and health care. I did not do anything personally to receive those privileges.

On the other hand, I was challenged by being a woman. In the mid-1960s I chose to apply to a particular college that accepted many more men than women. As I remember it, their ratio at the time was something like eight men for every one woman. I recall my high school guidance counselor telling me that I would have had a better chance of being accepted if I "came from Missouri and played the bull fiddle." I was penalized, not because I was a poor candidate for the academic demands of the school, but because I was a member of two groups: women and residents of the greater New York area.

Similarly, after interviewing for my first teaching position in a Connecticut high school, the English department chairman told me I had the job. I was ecstatic. When I called a few weeks later to follow up, he told me—with no apparent qualms—that the school had decided that they wanted to hire a man, so they were withdrawing their offer to me.

One thing that meditators often discover is internalized oppression: directing society's prejudices toward oneself (Watson, 2013). For example, as a young woman, I expected that I could not be as smart as a man. Certainly, the acceptance ratios at colleges seemed to support that. I somehow was able to overlook my good grades and college board scores. If I had a question, I was more likely to ask a man than a woman even though I had been exposed to some exceptional female teachers in high school. I had internalized the messages from my culture that women were simply less intelligent than men.

Meditation practice can be extremely helpful in showing us these internalized judgments. If we practice over a long enough period of time, not much remains hidden from us. Sometimes this can be quite challenging. It can be very painful to see that one has treated oneself with the same unkindness, prejudice, and even hatred as the dominant culture in which one has grown up. Cultivating gentleness toward oneself through meditation practice can help heal the wounds of internalized oppression.

Some groups and diversity awareness classes of various kinds can also be invaluable. Being a member of a leaderless women's group in the early 1970s was eye-opening for me. I discovered that there were twice as many smart, creative, and interesting people in the world than I had assumed. In turn, this let me see that I, too, had qualities I either had not recognized or had downplayed (my generation of girls had been taught not to compete with the boys because it might damage their fragile egos).

Being a One-of-a-Kind Therapist

Sometimes I hear from students that they have an expectation that being a contemplative therapist means that they should behave in specific ways or that they will have only certain personal qualities. This mistaken belief is akin to the mashed potatoes fallacy. They expect that they should be gentle and quiet, listening and speaking only in soft and calming tones. Such an image is just another fixed identity: a problem, not a goal.

There are as many ways of being a contemplative therapist as there are people. In fact, each of us may be quite different with different clients and even with the same client on different days. The point is to be genuine and responsive to the situation as it is.

Each of us will pick up on different aspects of what a client brings us. Therapist A might notice a client's tone of voice and the sadness it seems to convey. Therapist B, working with the same client, may notice her posture and how she has collapsed her chest, making it hard to take a full breath. Still another, Therapist C, might notice the repetition of certain words and gestures.

We have different temperaments as well. Therapist A may be quiet and provide a steady presence. Therapist B might be warm and curious, gently asking the client to see what happens when she sits up and takes a breath. Therapist C might be more active and ask a direct question about what the client experiences when she says the word she keeps repeating.

Note that in all of these examples the three therapists were noticing and responding to the client's experience in the present moment. Even with an approach that emphasizes the present moment, we respond in our own ways. When we add the other dimensions of training and orientation, it is easy to see how differently we may approach things. This is part of our richness as therapists. This competency values and celebrates those differences.

Appreciating Differences in Others

The third competency is associated with the wisdom of equanimity (Trungpa, 1987). Equanimity, according to Buddhist teachings, has several meanings. I explore equanimity more thoroughly in Chapter 9, but here we can note that it is the ability to bring a quality of warmth, or even affection, toward all whom we encounter. It has to do with recognizing that all of us wish to be happy and none of us wants to suffer. With equanimity, we recognize that while we are all in some sense the same, we still have utterly different experiences of life.

This recognition is the ground of compassion and empathy. We not only see the ways our clients' experiences differ from our own, we go beyond merely seeing to imagining what it would be like to have their experiences. This lets us genuinely appreciate them.

Of course, we cannot always fully imagine what it is like for someone else. I might never know what it was like for an African American client of mine, Sandra, to grow up in the United States. She may tell me some things, and I might read or hear of things that might be common in the experience of being black in America, but I cannot know her experience unless she can somehow convey it to me.

One of my colleagues, Dr. Robert Unger, emphasizes that every client's experience is "other." If we are quick to point out, even to ourselves, how we and our clients are the same, we may short-circuit our ability to really appreciate differences.

I have noticed, at times, my own eagerness to find points in common with my clients. Sometimes it may be useful to a particular client to hear that I, too, have experienced the groundlessness of divorce and survived, but more often it is not at all helpful. Instead, it may well become a way for me to interfere with clients accessing their own fear, sadness, relief, or anger. Allowing ourselves to feel the aloneness that comes with the recognition of otherness is an essential part of appreciating difference.

In my Gestalt training, denying differences was called confluence and was recognized as a way to avoid genuine contact (Perls, 1969). Sometimes spiritual practitioners dismiss the necessity for exploring our own privileges and prejudices by saying something like, "We are all one." Applying such an approach to diversity is a distortion of spiritual teachings and can even perpetuate harm caused by failing to recognize how we might be adding to the suffering of others.

Appreciating and Recognizing Brilliant Sanity

A final aspect of the third competency is recognizing and appreciating the brilliant sanity in each of our clients. Often this brilliance is obscured or covered over. In Contemplative Psychotherapy, we are especially attentive to not limiting our attention to what is wrong. In Chapter 5, I explore in depth how to recognize our clients' brilliant sanity.

THE FOURTH COMPETENCY: CONNECTING WITH OTHERS AND CULTIVATING RELATIONSHIP

What does it take to connect with others? Buddhist psychology suggests that connecting is not something we need to do deliberately; rather it is something we allow to occur by not creating obstacles to it. From a Buddhist point of view, we are already connected. Paradoxically, we are both inseparable and alone. We cannot find a separate self that is not affected by our environment and the other beings in it. At the same time, no one else shares our direct experience, and ultimately there is no way to fully convey it to someone else. In that sense, we are each alone.

Recognizing and Letting Go of Our Obstacles to Connection

The obstacles to recognizing and deepening our connection with others are the same as those which interfere with our being fully present: rejecting or ignoring uncomfortable feelings, trying to hold onto pleasant experiences, and clinging to a fixed sense of self.

Uncomfortable feelings often arise for us as therapists in the context of our work. If we are willing to be present with our clients, then we often do not know what to do next, and we may feel stupid, uncertain, and even anxious. Simply being present can feel quite vulnerable. When we are present we are not hiding behind a role, our expertise, or a treatment plan. We are just one person meeting another. We may, of course, still offer our expertise or create a treatment plan, but we are also willing to show up and be present in the moment. We may feel quite awkward. I sometimes tell my clients that feeling awkward is good news. It usually means that we are not falling into habitual patterns and are, instead, just present.

The biggest obstacle to genuinely connecting with others is our attempt to create and maintain a fixed sense of self. This activity of ego-clinging requires us to hang on to whatever supports it, to push away anything that threatens it, and to ignore anything that is irrelevant to it. In the traditional Buddhist language, we engage in the three poisons of passion or greed, hatred or aggression, and delusion or ignorance (Hanson with Mendius, 2009). This activity can be quite subtle.

One example of an ego activity that therapists might exhibit is what contemplative therapists call therapeutic aggression. It refers to our attempts to get clients to change when our motivation is the avoidance of our own discomfort (Wegela, 1988). A therapist I supervise confessed the other day that she had not confronted a teenage client about his alcohol use because she felt uncomfortable doing so. As we explored her reluctance more deeply, she uncovered a few layers. First, she did not want to look uncool. She was invested in being the new, young, with-it therapist at the agency. Going deeper, she recognized an old pattern going back to childhood. Questioning the behavior of anyone in her family was always met with teasing. She had learned not to share what were often clear insights. She had sought safety in pleasing others. When she explored her somatic experience of imagining confronting her client, she felt sadness and also fear. Being cool and pleasing was an identity that allowed her to avoid the more difficult experiences that arose when she was simply present. Maintaining that identity had interfered with her connecting in a genuine way with this client. Examining her own experience with this kind of precision was an expression of the wisdom associated with this competency: discriminating awareness wisdom (Trungpa, 1987).

The Healing Power of Relationship

In Contemplative Psychotherapy, we regard the therapeutic relationship itself as the primary vehicle for healing and change. Modern science has provided support for this view. As many writers have pointed out, our earliest relationships with others profoundly affect our neurological development as infants and children (Badenboch, 2008). As adults, the neuroplasticity of the brain means that our current relationships affect us and may even allow us to overcome deficits of our early development. The special relationship of psychotherapy can provide a powerful opportunity for such healing to occur (Watson, 2008).

Given the importance in a contemplative approach of being able to connect with others and to cultivate genuine relationships, I have chosen to devote all of Chapter 4 to this issue.

THE FIFTH COMPETENCY: ACTING SKILLFULLY AND LETTING GO

The first four competencies—being present, seeing clearly, appreciating differences, and connecting with others—lead naturally into practicing the fifth: acting skillfully and letting go. At this point, I would love to be able to say, "Here's how you do it," and present my readers with a set of Contemplative Psychotherapy techniques.

Unfortunately, that is not quite how it works. As we continue through the rest of the book, some strategies, and even techniques, will be introduced, but a kit of specific techniques is not what a contemplative approach has to offer. Instead, this approach relies on our ability to show up and to respond to what is happening in the moment and to tailor our actions to each therapeutic relationship. We might draw upon our training in a variety of approaches, or we might create an intervention on the spot. Our training in staying present with uncertainty is very helpful in being able to do this. Our willingness to let go of a fixed way of being frees us to become creative, spontaneous, and responsive.

What Is Skillful Action?

Our overall goals are to reduce our clients' suffering and to help them uncover their natural brilliant sanity. From the Buddhist point of view, skillful action or skillful means (Sanskrit, *upaya*) need to be balanced with wisdom in the same way that a bird requires two wings to fly (Trungpa, 1969). One without the other is not enough. Seeing what is needed but doing nothing does not really help, and taking action without clear seeing is likely to cause more harm than good.

Skillful action requires us to discriminate between what we believe will help us move toward uncovering brilliant sanity and relieving suffering and what will not. Of course, we cannot be sure that what we say or do will actually be useful to our clients, and that is why the fifth competency is also about letting go. Our willingness to drop an approach that is not useful is very important.

When I was a new therapist, just finishing my training in Gestalt therapy, I tried to use it with every client I saw—not unlike a child with a new toy. I remember my initial interview with one poor woman who resisted my efforts to get her to do an "awareness continuum." Despite her repeating several times that she did not want to do it, I kept pushing. She had the good sense never to come back. My insistence on applying only this one approach is, of course, an extreme example. I was not willing to be present, see clearly, or even connect with her. I did not take the time to appreciate what was going on with her, and I would not let go of my own agenda. My one-size-fits-all approach was a reflection of my inexperience and my desire to make something happen so that I could feel good about accomplishing something. It was a great example of therapeutic aggression. Needless to say, this was unskillful action.

Skillful action in therapy arises out of the spaciousness of mind in combination with clearly seeing what is needed and is associated with the wisdom of all-accomplishing action (Trungpa, 1987). It is based always in the context of a particular therapeutic relationship with a specific person at one moment in time. Another way to define skillful action is that it arises out of brilliant sanity and not out of a fixed sense of self and other. That may sound like a tall order, and it is. In fact, it may be better to hold that as an aspiration rather than as a plan. We do the best we can to let go of the obstacles to being able to manifest the first four competencies, and then we just go ahead imperfectly. Once again, our training in being gentle with ourselves can be invaluable in helping us to let go of any agenda about being a perfect therapist.

Being Responsive and Creative

All therapists respond to their clients in the moment to some degree. If they did not, their therapy would probably not go any-where and would fail to be useful to their clients. Sometimes therapy takes the form of applying an approach with a set of techniques that were developed by others. Certainly, these days a good deal of emphasis is placed on using evidence-based treatments, but even these approaches require us to determine on the spot what seems to be an appropriate choice. Some of my students are given actual scripts to use when applying some approaches in their internships, and I believe that often these go too far in not allowing for a sponta-neous and genuine response to individual clients' needs.

In my own work, I often draw on my training in Gestalt therapy, in the Trauma Resiliency Model (TRM), and in EMDR. Perhaps I should confess that I adapt even these approaches to the needs of the moment. For example, I was working with a man dealing with the aftereffects of a horrific car accident he had been in as a teenage driver. We began with some TRM work, and then I shifted into a Gestalt-based approach by asking him to identify with and speak as his older self to the younger self who had been in the accident. In this role, he was able to offer comfort and forgiveness to himself. This, in turn, led to weeping and letting go.

In other situations, I may just make things up on the spot. With a particularly articulate and often serious client, we noticed together that she often found herself at a loss for words as she struggled to find exactly the right word for what she meant in talking with me. I suggested that she use the wrong words and just keep going even if she made no sense at all. After a moment in which she acknowledged feeling a bit silly, she went ahead and playfully used not only wrong but nonsense words to describe a situation at work that was worrying her. The lightheartedness she tapped into let her take a larger view of the whole situation.

A young woman I was working with often called on the day of an appointment to cancel, usually because she "did not feel well." She was scrupulous about paying for the missed appointments, but it led her to miss still more appointments as she ate through the money she had set aside for therapy. She often mentioned how much she respected me and did not want to cause me inconvenience.

One day I brought this up as a problem not only for her but also for me. When she did not come, it threw off my own plans as well. My standing policy is that people need to call 24 hours before a missed appointment to avoid having to pay for it. This was clearly not working for her, I said, so I invited her to collaborate on a plan that would work for both of us. Together we came up with a strategy that acknowledged both of our needs. If she canceled by 8 P.M. the previous evening, she would owe me nothing. If she canceled after that, but before 8 A.M., she would owe me half of my fee. A cancellation after 8 A.M. would require her to pay my full fee. This worked well for both of us. Over time, she revealed that secret alcohol abuse was the main reason for her cancellations, and that my willingness to meet her halfway in a respectful manner had helped her to bring it out into the open where were able to work with it directly.

Sometimes being creative means something quite simple, like asking a client to look at me while he repeats something he just said. Other times it can become more elaborate, as when I helped a client create a ritual that helped him to let go of the guilt he felt for his former work in a laboratory killing small animals.[1]

Being Wrong

Giving ourselves permission to be creative and responsive goes hand in hand with allowing ourselves to be wrong. As noted above, many of us who become therapists have been rewarded for being right. Being wrong may require us to feel uncomfortable. If we can let ourselves have the physical discomfort that accompanies wanting to explain or trying to defend ourselves, and not give in to either of those impulses, then we expand our repertoire of ways we can be. When we let ourselves be wrong, we have the opportunity to make a fresh start. Just as we do in our meditation practice, we can ground ourselves in our bodies and notice what we are experiencing. We may realize that we have been holding tension or have lost our sense of connection with our client. Then we can bring a sense of openness and curiosity to what is happening in the moment with ourselves and with our clients.

It is not uncommon for me to say to a client something like, "Wait, I don't think that last question was helpful. Let me ask you this instead." Or I might ask, "Are we talking about what you want to be talking about or have I led you in a different direction from where you want to go?" Maybe the client wanted to bring up a sexual encounter he had with his partner, and I have gotten caught up in asking about the work situation that was on his mind last week. The issue with his partner is actually harder for my client to talk about, and he may have let me distract him into a more comfortable but less alive subject. Perhaps I have noticed the absence of liveliness in our conversation. Perhaps I have not. By checking in with him, I am showing that I am willing to be wrong and that I am genuinely interested in where he really wants to go. I demonstrate that it is all right to make mistakes and start over. If I am defensive and stick with my agenda, even a subtle one, I will short-circuit my client's process. When I do that, it is likely to create a sense of distance between us that will make it even more difficult for my client to bring up a vulnerable topic like sex.

Letting Go

In our meditation practice, we practice letting go each time we go out with our outbreath and let it dissolve into space. As therapists, we need to be able to let go again and again. We need to let go when we are wrong and when we are holding onto a mistaken viewpoint. Sometimes we need to let go even when we are right. To the extent that we grasp a particular theory or way of seeing, it may interfere with our ability to see what is happening in the present moment.

Another time we need to be able to let go is when we become caught up in an emotional response to what a client evokes in us.

Personally, I struggled with the idea of letting go for a long time. I remember an old boyfriend of mine saying, "Karen, you need to let go!" Of course, he meant I should let go of him, but it was still mystifying to me. Let go? How? As I wrestled with the idea of how to let go, I realized that for me, at least, letting go is not something to do. It is something I do not prevent. As the teachings on impermanence suggest, phenomena are constantly arising and passing away. It is only when we resist that natural occurrence that we fail to let go. Still, how do we go about it?

Now I think of letting go as being willing to allow the next moment to arise. Instead of focusing on how to let go of whatever has already arisen, I turn my attention—sometimes quite deliberately—to what is coming next. Opening to the next new moment automatically releases my grip on the last moment. Dr. John Rockwell, who used to teach in the Religious Studies program at Naropa, once described letting go as "letting it go along" (personal communication, 1986).

The Technique of Touch and Go

The technique of touch and go, mentioned in Chapter 2, helps us to train ourselves in this rhythm of touching our experience and then letting it go. We can practice this on the cushion and apply it in the rest of our lives, as well. It is particularly useful to therapists, who can use it on the spot as they meet with their clients.

The first half of the technique is touching our experience, whatever it is, fully and also momentarily. I sometimes ask students how long it would take to recognize the taste of their favorite food if they had their eyes closed and someone popped it into their mouths. Most of them say it would take a few moments at most. You can imagine this for yourself. It does not take long to recognize the smooth and creamy yumminess of chocolate or the spiciness and bite of a hot pepper. We can taste or touch our experience in the same way. Touching is a visceral experience—we touch with our bodies: we taste flavors, feel emotions, see sights, hear sounds, smell aromas. Another word for touch is "feel." We feel our experience from the inside. We let it in or, we could say, we let it come to us.

In a similar way, we touch or recognize our thoughts and mental images.

Then, having touched, we let go. Paradoxically, when we fully touch, letting go tends to happen naturally. We may find that a very similar experience arises in the next moment. This is especially likely with intense emotions or physical sensations. Still, we allow our experience to come and to go, bringing curiosity and mindfulness to whatever comes next.

The technique of touch and go may be clarified by doing it incorrectly. There are three ways to distort the technique, and most of us are quite familiar with all three. Doing them on purpose helps us recognize when we are avoiding touching or resisting letting go. I like to call the first one touch and grab (Wegela, 2011b).

To try this, sit in a comfortable seat. If you like, you can sit on your meditation seat, but staying in your reading spot is fine, too. Close your eyes and think of a situation in your life that has some emotional zing to it. It is probably best not to choose something that is too heavily charged. Then, as you think of it, do your best to keep the sense of stimulation going. In particular, notice what you experience in your body. If you notice it starting to lose intensity, rouse it again. Notice how you do that. Do this for as much as 5 minutes and then open your eyes and look around. Notice what you are experiencing.

The second distortion I call go and go (Wegela, 2011b). In this one, we do the opposite. We do not really touch. You can work with the same situation or choose another one. Once again, close your eyes and begin thinking of the chosen situation. This time, though, instead of leaning into your experience, back off. As it arises, avoid feeling anything. Notice how you do that. When you feel tempted to be mindful, do not be. Just keep pulling away. Again, practice this approach for up to 5 minutes. Then open your eyes and look around. Notice what you experience now.

The third mistake may be called push and go. In this one, practice in the same way as you did for go and go, but instead of pulling away, forcefully reject whatever arises. As you practice push and go, be aggressive in refusing to get into whatever comes next. Once again, practice this for up to 5 minutes, and then notice what you experience afterward.

Finally, try the technique of touch and go itself. Working with the same or a different situation, again close your eyes and bring the situation to mind. As it arises, touch into your bodily experience or, if there are thoughts or images, recognize them fully but briefly. Then, having touched or tasted your experience, allow it to go. See what arises in the next moment. Use this approach for up to 5 minutes, and then open your eyes and look around. Notice your experience at this point.

Some people find that they become lost in emotions or sensations when they practice touch and grab. Some find that despite their best efforts, they discover themselves letting go. Others find that they do not know how to touch at all. A few longtime meditation practitioners realize that they have never let themselves fully experience their emotions and thoughts. Still others recognize that they are experts in touch and grab and are even quite good at "touch and wallow."

In playing with touch and go, many people report that they feel dismissive and notice their minds becoming speedy. Some notice that it is quite familiar to them to turn away as soon as something with an emotional charge begins to arise. They see how they avoid any hint of intensity.

Others find that they are already familiar with pushing away forcefully. There may be tightness or heat in their bodies. They may recognize a quality of impatience that they recognize as common in their interactions with others.

Most people say that when they shift to touch and go that there is a sense of relief and ordinariness in their experience. Of course, not everyone says this, but it is by far the most common discovery. Many find that they can be present without losing track of the ongoing flow of their experience.

As we will see in Chapter 4, touch and go is a useful way to work with exchange, our experience of deep connection with our clients.

GUIDED EXERCISES: THE FIVE COMPETENCIES

The following exercises are designed to provide opportunities to experience each of the five competencies and then to try them out in your clinical work. The best way to do them is to read through each of the exercises first, and then try doing it, using the directions as a reference point as you go from part to part. There is no need to do all of them one right after the other. Do them at your own pace, however it works best for you. It is fine to skip any exercise for any reason.

Exercise 1: Being Present, Letting Be, and Seeing Clearly

The first exercise addresses the first two competencies, which are (1) being present and letting be and (2) seeing clearly without judging. For this first exercise, actually following the directions, which call for going someplace else, will be the most useful. However, if you want, you could try just imagining doing it. This exercise is based, in part, on a traditional Tibetan medical treatment for working with depression (Chagdud Tulku, personal communication, spring 1985). It is broken into Part A and Part B. For both, go to a high place where you have an expansive view. Here, where I live in the Rocky Mountains, it is easy to find such a place. If you are in an urban setting, try going to a high floor in a building where you have an unobstructed view. Seashores, lakesides, prairies, or desert landscapes are also good places to try this. You can also look up at the sky while leaning or lying back. You could even try bringing up a scene of vastness on your computer screen if nothing else is available. The idea is to be where you can tap into a sense of spaciousness.

Part A

Either sitting or standing, extend your awareness out into the vast sense of space in front of you. Rest your mind in the sense of spaciousness. Let yourself just be present with whatever this evokes for you. When your mind wanders, just return to the sense of limitless space that is inseparable from the nature of your mind. It is fine to move your eyes and your head if you like. Stay with this step for up to 5 minutes. Afterward, notice what you experience in your body.

Part B

Next, we work with seeing clearly, or we could say perceiving clearly. We will work with each sense perception in turn.

- Sight: Continuing to rest in a sense of spaciousness, begin with the sense of sight. Extend your gaze out toward whatever you can see and, as much as you can, attend to what you are seeing rather than yourself as the one who is doing the seeing. Explore the details of what you can see. Keep it simple as though you were a child seeing the world for the first time. If you find yourself beginning to evaluate whether you are dropping your sense of yourself, just return to the simplicity of seeing and let however you are doing it be good enough. Do that for a few minutes.

- Hearing: Notice what you can hear. Just let sounds come to you rather than reaching out to listen. Rest with whatever sounds or silence you notice. Do this for a few minutes.
- Smelling: Notice whatever aromas or odors you can smell. As above, let them come to you. If you do not notice any smells in the environment, that is fine.
- Tasting: Notice anything you can taste. Is there a taste in your mouth or a sense of dryness or moisture, for example?
- Feeling and touching: Turn your attention to anything you feel or are touching. If you can, continue to have a sense of spaciousness within which you notice any feelings on your skin or in your body. Note any areas of tension and relaxation. If there are areas you do not feel, just notice them. Notice the temperature, perhaps on your face, and feel the textures of your clothing where it touches your skin.
- Mind: Finally, we come to the last sense field in Buddhist psychology: the mind. Notice any thoughts that arise in the space of your mind. Note any images. Bring to this sense perception the same attitude of letting things come to you rather than reaching out toward them as you have done with your other sense perceptions.
- Finishing: When you are finished, notice again what you are experiencing in your body. Then, spend a few minutes thinking about what you learned doing this exercise.

Exercise 2: Recognizing and Appreciating Differences

For this exercise, on the third competency of recognizing and appreciating differences, begin by taking a comfortable seat, on your meditation cushion or in a chair. Start by doing a body scan (Kabat-Zinn, 1990). Begin by feeling your feet from the inside. If you do not feel anything, let it be that way. There is no need to try to relax; just notice what you notice. Then, move up your body noticing what you feel (or do not). Move to your ankles and legs, your knees and thighs. Notice what you feel in your groin, seat, and lower torso. Continue upward including your back and chest. Feel your shoulders, your arms, and your hands. Notice what you feel in your neck, the back of your head, your ears, your scalp, and your face. Add anything that may have been left out. Turn your attention to your breathing and notice whatever you might experience in your inner organs.

Then, having grounded yourself in your body, let it go and direct your attention to your imagination. What follows is a contemplation. Think of the things that have supported you in your life. You might include your parents, your class, your race, your gender. You might consider the opportunities you had for being healthy and educated. Consider the country and culture that you grew up in or moved into. Include any talents that you have and the ways in which these have been encouraged to flourish. Think of the specific people who have helped you: relatives, teachers, therapists, friends. Add any other people or situations that have been supportive to you. Spend some time with this and notice what you experience as you do so.

Next, think of the things that have challenged you. Again, think of the same kinds of things as you did before: your parents, your class, your race, your gender. Consider the challenges you had for being healthy and educated. Consider the country and culture you grew up in or moved into. Include any talents that were not encouraged to flourish. Think of the specific people who have been challenging for you: family, teachers, therapists, friends. Add any other people or situations that have been challenging for you. Spend some time with this and notice what you experience as you do so.

After you do these two contemplations, consider the possibility of how both the supportive and challenging aspects of your life have contributed to the richness of who you are now. See if you can find appreciation for these unique features of your life's journey to this point. If you find resentment instead of appreciation, let that be present. Practice touch and go with the different feelings that may arise.

Take a few minutes to think back over the exercise and notice what you may have learned in doing it.

Exercise 3: Connecting With Others and Cultivating Relationship

For this exercise on connecting with others and cultivating relationship, we will focus on imagining our own experience of being met by another person. In Chapter 4, our emphasis will be more on how we can extend out to others.

Once again, take a comfortable seat and begin by grounding yourself in your body. You might choose to follow the directions at the beginning of Exercise 2 as a guide in doing that, or you may come into a felt sense of your body in another way that you already know how to do. Take a few minutes to do this.

Then, think of a time in your life—a recent time or one in the past—when you felt compassionately met by another person. You might choose a time when you felt vulnerable or in pain, and the other person provided a supportive presence. Or you might pick a time of happiness when you felt connected with another person in a joyful or even blissful way. Remember the details of the situation as much as you can. Think of what was going on for you and why it was that you were with this particular person.

Notice what arises in your body and mind as you recall this time of connection. Where in your body do you feel something? You might feel a warmth or softness somewhere: for example, around your heart area or in your face. What images or thoughts are coming as you remember? What emotions are you noticing? You might have a feeling of tenderness or joy. Or you might feel something else altogether. There could be longing, nostalgia, or grief as you remember that person and your connection with him or her. Whatever arises, just include it, and as much as you can let yourself merge or melt into that experience. Take your time.

After a while, let it go, open your eyes, and look around the room. Allow whatever remains of this experience to be there. Practice touch and go with it. Consider what you may have learned from doing the exercise.

Exercise 4: Skillful Action and Letting Go

Acting skillfully and letting go is the fifth contemplative competency. Once again, we will do an exercise using our imaginations.

Start by taking a comfortable seat and grounding yourself in your body. Take a few minutes to do this.

Then, think of a task in your life that you know you need to do but that you are not looking forward to. Pick something that you regard as somewhat unpleasant. It might be related to your work or it could be something you need to take care of at home or elsewhere. In your mind, clearly define for yourself what it is you need to do. Then, imagine doing whatever it is, paying particular attention to those aspects of the task that you expect to be unpleasant. Allow yourself to notice what thoughts and feelings arise as you envision doing this. Spend a few minutes doing that.

Then, shift your focus slightly and think of the same task as something that needs to get done. Take yourself out of the equation for the moment. Now imagine the task being done, paying attention to those aspects of it which indicate that progress toward its completion are occurring.

For example, if you imagine cleaning the toilet, picture how the brush and the cleanser are making the bowl begin to shine. See how the water becomes cloudy and then how flushing drains the dirty water away and brings in clear, fresh water that swirls around and reveals the clean bowl. See how it sparkles.

Whatever task you have chosen, imagine how it gets completed and how the results of doing the task appear. Picture the successful completion of the project, whatever it is. Shift your attention back to yourself and notice the thoughts and feelings that arise now that the task is accomplished.

Think about what you may have learned doing this exercise.

Exercise 5: Applying the Competencies in Therapy

This exercise is more of an ongoing experiment than a guided exercise. As you go about your work with clients, notice when you experience the thoughts, emotions, and sensations that arose for you doing the previous four exercises.

When do you experience a sense of spaciousness and the ability to let things be as they are? Or does that never arise? Are there issues or feelings that you have a very hard time tolerating?

Notice the times of clarity when you are simply seeing and sensing but not judging. Notice the opposite times when you find you are judging your clients.

Identify when you feel appreciative of the uniqueness of clients' situations, both in the past and in their present lives. Notice the opposite: when can you not get past a sense of revulsion or resentment?

Track the experience of connection: notice when you feel you are meeting your clients and when you feel met by them. Notice, too, the times when you feel disconnected from clients.

And finally, notice the experience of accomplishment that follows upon choosing paths of action that are genuinely helpful to clients, and notice, too, the times when no matter what you try, nothing useful seems to happen. Note the experience of letting go of accomplishing what you hoped to be able to do.

All five of the competencies work together and can support our work as therapists grounded in a contemplative view and practice.

Chapter 4

CREATING GENUINE
THERAPEUTIC RELATIONSHIPS

In Contemplative Psychotherapy, the vehicle therapists and clients take on their journey together is the therapeutic relationship itself. The main concerns in creating a genuine relationship are the focus of this chapter.

GENUINE RELATIONSHIP

All therapists, no matter what their training, pay attention to their relationships with their clients to a greater or lesser extent. Since trying to maintain a mistaken sense of separateness is a major cause of suffering from a contemplative point of view, being in a genuine relationship and experiencing our connection with others is, in itself, an avenue to healing and reconnecting with our brilliant sanity.

Essentially, a genuine relationship is one that is free from any obstacles to authentic connection. If we are all already connected to each other, as Buddhist psychology suggests, then what prevents us from realizing and experiencing that connection? It is, once again, our belief in, and clinging to, a fixed and separate sense of self and phenomena. To the extent that we attempt to maintain those misunderstandings, we are unavailable to others.

None of us is always free from the confusion of trying to maintain these kinds of identities, but our ongoing mindfulness awareness practices help us to recognize and let go of them when they arise in our experience. Sometimes we will not notice at all; sometimes we will notice after a session is long over; and sometimes we will notice on the spot and be able to release our grip and open up again to our clients.

As contemplative psychotherapists, we do our best to show up and be present. We can work with our own obstacles to experiencing our connection with our clients, both on the meditation cushion and on the spot in our therapy sessions. Part of our work includes helping our clients to let go of their obstacles to connecting with others, as well. In the example of Martha (Chapter 3), we saw how I worked with recognizing my own discomfort with being fully present and how I supported Martha as she worked with the challenge of experiencing the awkwardness of intimate relationships.

Here is another example. I was working the other day with Josh, who often tells long stories. He had begun telling me about what happened when his in-laws came to visit over a holiday weekend. He had included a lot of details about what his wife had made for dinner and who was staying at his house and who was staying in a hotel. His story seemed largely irrelevant to me, and I wanted to get us back on track. The track was, of course, my idea of what the track should be. At some point I noticed that I was leaning forward in my chair, breathing shallowly, and clenching my jaw a bit. I have learned that when I fall into this posture, it is usually a sign that I am no longer fully present with clients. I felt impatient and wanted things to be different from how they were. When I noticed, I let myself touch the tightness and impatience. Then I sat back in my chair and breathed out. I turned my attention back to Josh, bringing curiosity to what was going on for him. I saw that he was holding his hands in his lap and clenching them even though the tone of his voice was quite matter-of-fact. I listened a while longer and began to wonder if he were experiencing some distress that he was not naming. I asked more about what this visit was like for him emotionally. Almost reluctantly, he said that it was bringing up a great deal of sadness about the absence of his own parents, both of whom had passed away. As we explored this further, it became clear that these family visits were quite difficult, but he believed that he needed to be a good host and enjoy his guests without burdening them with his own feelings. In fact, he should not burden himself—or me—with them either. Had I gotten us "back on track," we would not have tapped into the sadness and tenderness that underlay his hand-clenching. Nor would we have noticed the somewhat confused compassion within his desire to spare his guests, himself, and me from experiencing his pain. This habit of hiding his own experience was one he had mentioned to me before, and now we could explore it more directly in the moment.

Sometimes, of course, it is appropriate to interrupt a client's long story or bring a client's attention to the pattern of telling stories. What tipped me off that I was hanging on to my own mistaken view of what needed to occur in the session was my impatience and the tension in my body.

A mistake that beginning contemplative therapists often make is to think that being genuine means saying everything that arises in their minds. One still needs to apply the skill of discriminating between what might be helpful and what might not. This guideline applies as well to self-disclosure. Sometimes it can be very helpful, but self-disclosure is not, in itself, the same as being genuine.

On the other hand, sometimes new contemplative therapists think they need to be not only gentle, but passive. Being genuine means that we still respond in our own unique styles. For example, I tend to be fairly direct. For some clients, that is not only fine, it is what they are seeking. I can think of two clients who told me that it was my directness that led them to choose to work with me.

With one woman, I had asked her on the phone, when she first contacted me, if she were suicidal. With Brad, whom we will meet below, I asked him in our initial consultation what he meant by "it" in the sentence he had just said. "Oh good," he said. "You're not going to let me get away with that. My last therapist let me get away with too much."

For other clients, I am sure this would not feel like a good match for them. Being open does not mean that we can be a good therapist for every client. There is some maitri in accepting ourselves as we are with our own unique therapeutic styles.

At the same time, it is important to acknowledge that many therapists work in agencies and other settings where they do not have the luxury of choosing whom they will see in therapy. And some therapists work with clients who are court ordered into therapy with them, which can be even more challenging.

My preference is to work collaboratively with my clients. Not all clients will want to do so; some will want their therapist to tell them what to do. In some cultures, "the doctor knows best" can be a strong belief. In working with clients who are court ordered, or with some adolescents, it may take awhile to establish enough trust and perceived connection to do useful work. In those cases, as always, I try to meet my clients where they are and invite them to work together with me as much as they would like to. Doing our best, ourselves, to recognize our common ground of brilliant sanity and human suffering can help us see how we are connected.

THE ROLE OF THE CONTEMPLATIVE PSYCHOTHERAPIST

Being genuine also means not hiding behind our roles. It is not that we are not playing a role; we are. We are being paid for our services, and there is an inherent hierarchical difference in terms of power between us and our clients. We would be foolish to ignore that. In addition, our clients will project their thoughts and emotions onto us. Being genuine, though, means that we do create a false sense of difference and distance. We do not withhold our humanness in order to invite still more projection. Even being a blank screen is a role, and personally I find it one that is unhelpful to many clients who are seeking the healing that comes from experiencing real connection with another person.

Hiding behind a role might look like being an expert who dispenses advice and suggestions as a way to avoid the awkwardness of silence or the appearance of not knowing. It could manifest as maintaining a cool, objective stance. Given our interdependence, such a sense of separateness and objectivity is likely to be illusory. At the very least, whenever we respond to one thing instead of another, we are making a choice based on something. We are not really neutral. It is better, I think, to know what our preferences, goals, and biases are than to pretend to ourselves that we do not have any. Once again, it is our mindfulness awareness practices that help us recognize these things so that we do not mindlessly impose them on our clients.

Another role that is inconsistent with a contemplative approach is being a mechanic or fixer. As we have seen, at the heart of a contemplative approach is learning how to be compassionately present with what is already occurring and not rushing in to change anything. Another problem with the fixer identity is that it requires a client to have something that needs fixing. Built into that is the idea that the client has something broken. Given the view of brilliant sanity, we are more interested in recognizing the inherent wisdom and wholeness of our clients. Taking the role of mechanic easily falls into supporting clients' views of themselves as flawed or bad. We have already noted how such self-aggressive views can be the source of much suffering.

A metaphor that I do like for what we do is that of a midwife. Like a midwife, we help bring about the birth of something that we do not ourselves create. Traditional Buddhist metaphors for the discovery of inherent wisdom include things like waking up, dawning, and uncovering. These all point to the inherent nature of brilliant sanity. It is unconditional: it is present regardless of whether it is recognized. We can help our clients appreciate their natural wisdom and assist them in letting go of the obstacles to it that are in themselves the source of suffering.

Like a good midwife, we create an environment that supports such a birth. We can offer encouragement, warmth, support, and knowledge, but we are neither the ones in labor nor the ones who end up holding the baby. Perhaps I have pushed this metaphor far enough. It would be a mistake to make it too solid and turn it into yet another mistaken identity.

HOLDING THE SPACE

Part of creating such a genuine relationship is our ability to hold the space. This term is one that contemplative psychotherapists tend to use often. It requires the ability to practice the first skill: being present and letting be. The more present we are, the more there is a sense of spaciousness. This willingness to accommodate a wide range of experiences, in turn, creates an inviting environment for clients. If we are not flinching—literally or figuratively—when our clients bring up sensitive material, they are likely to feel welcomed. We can never guarantee that clients will feel or be completely safe, but we can aspire to create a therapeutic container that feels safe enough by being welcoming in this way.

A practical aspect of holding the space is creating predictable and reliable boundaries about policies, confidentiality, and starting and ending times.

What underlies our ability to hold the space for our clients in a compassionate and present way is our confidence in brilliant sanity. By holding the space, we help create the opportunity for clients to rediscover their innate wisdom and compassion.

CONFIDENCE IN BRILLIANT SANITY

If we regard or experience our clients as brilliantly sane, it affects all aspects of our work as therapists. If, however, we see our clients as basically flawed or bad, then we will direct our attention toward helping them curb or control their badness. When we see them as possessing the potential to realize their inherent wisdom and compassion, we do our best to nurture that. This does not mean that we become naive about how confusion and fear lead to harmful behavior toward oneself and others. As we saw above, the activity of clinging to and trying to maintain a fixed identity causes a great deal of suffering at individual and societal levels. Still, the view of brilliant sanity suggests that this is not our deepest nature.

For readers who have their doubts about this brilliant sanity idea, I would suggest that they could try on the possibility that there is goodness and the potential to realize brilliant sanity in one or more of their clients as a way to begin exploring this idea in the clinical setting. Again, please investigate these ideas for yourselves and see if they have value for you or not.

To whatever extent we believe that both we and our clients have brilliant sanity, it affects our relationship with them. No one's brilliant sanity is any better than anyone else's. Knowing this highlights the common ground we share with our clients and helps us to further recognize our interconnectedness.

INTERDEPENDENCE

As we saw in Chapter 1, our interconnectedness or interdependence means that we are not separate from our environment or from each other. As this idea of interdependence is increasingly being discussed by neuroscientists and psychotherapists, I find it amazing, and even reassuring, that the Buddhist meditators of the last 2,500-plus years came up with many of the same discoveries as modern science.

Interdependence is one of the ways that Buddhist psychology talks about emptiness. We exist interdependently, not independently. Family therapists understand this notion when they think of a family as a system consisting of parts that interact with each other. As one person in the system changes, it affects everyone else in the system.

An illustration of the idea of interdependence that I like to use is my own hair.[1] I have always regarded my hair as red or strawberry blonde. One day I was on a break while participating in a meditation retreat in upstate New York. I glanced in the mirror over the bathroom sink, and I was surprised to see that my hair looked brown. I quickly told myself, "No, no, my hair is really red. It is just the light in here." Then—perhaps because I had been meditating for some days already—I thought, "What color is my hair really?" I quickly realized that there is no "really" about the color of my hair. It depends on the light; it depends on the eyesight of the person doing the looking; it depends on how recently I have been to the hairdresser. Even if someone agrees with me that my hair is red right now, I cannot know what they are experiencing.

Similarly, there is no "really" about who I am. Like my hair, the I that I regard as myself is continually changing as well. It depends, as Thich Nhat Hanh has said, on nonself elements (Hanh, 2006). Buddhism has an elaborate system of the five *skandhas* for identifying these elements.[2] In any moment we are made up of changing experiences of body, emotions, thoughts, images, and mood. The point for us is that we are not solid, permanent, and separate.

If we are not separate, then we inter-are with our clients (Hanh, 1987b). There is no clear boundary line that we can draw. As I look at my client, my experience in the moment includes him or her. Where is the I that is separate from that experience? As I noted in Chapter 1 and explore further in the next section, we exchange with our clients. When they feel emotions, we may very well feel them, too.

EXCHANGE

In this section we look more closely at what exchange is and what it is not; then we go on to explore how to work with exchange in therapy.

What Is Exchange?

If one has not recognized the experience that contemplative psychotherapists call exchange, it can sound a bit strange. Exchange is our direct experience of another person. Not being separate means that we are often quite deeply touched by what others are feeling. Not being solid means we are permeable and may feel much the same thing as another person in whose presence we are. Experiencing exchange is generally available to us, though we are not always present enough to recognize our inner experience and thus our connection with our others.

For example, if I am sitting in a session with a client who is angry, I may very well begin to feel the bodily sensations I associate with anger. I may start to feel hot or tense. I may find that I am clenching my jaw or even my hands. I may begin to think I am angry about something myself and start to seek for a reason why I am feeling upset. The more I do this, the less present I am with my client.

I believe it is common for us, as therapists, to find some clients difficult because the exchange we experience with them is hard to tolerate. Those who are diagnosed with borderline disorders, for example, may be such clients. We might feel impulsive and wanting to escape pain, frightened of being abandoned, or intensely anxious as we meet with such a client. We might experience anger, threat, or hopelessness and find ourselves thinking that suicide seems like a good idea. Instead of being able to tolerate such intense discomfort, and in the absence of understanding that this may be exactly what it is like for the client, therapists may label clients as difficult, hopeless, or untreatable.

When we know about exchange, we may discover more compassion for clients with whom it is challenging to stay present. All of this points to the need for therapists to have some kind of mindfulness practice so that they are less likely to confuse their own desires, aversions, and preferences with clearly seeing and experiencing their clients.

What Exchange Is Not

Before we go any further, let us contrast exchange with some other possibilities. Exchange is not the same thing as empathy. In empathy we use our minds to put ourselves in others' shoes and to imagine what it would be like to have their experiences. In contrast, exchange is a phenomenon that simply happens and is not deliberately created by the mind.

Exchange is not countertransference. In countertransference, we respond to clients based on our own histories and habits. We project our own material onto our clients.

When I present exchange at workshops, participants often suggest it is the same as projective identification. In projective identification, clients are regarded as projecting some unwanted or unrecognized aspects of themselves onto another person. Perhaps exchange is one reason that projective identification can occur, but exchange is not a kind of pathology and does not require denying one's own experience. It is natural and goes on between people in all kinds of relationships.

Of course, we may very well experience any combination of empathy, countertransference, and exchange at the same time. We may also simply respond to a client without any of those things going on.

If we do not know about exchange, we will still experience it. I have met a number of conference participants who were relieved to hear about exchange. They had had supervisors tell them that they had bad boundaries or had not worked through their own countertransference issues.

Others' Descriptions of Exchange

If we have not heard of exchange, we may very well call our experiences of it empathy or countertransference. For example, Rollo May once described empathy as the "nonverbal interchange of mood, belief, and attitude between doctor and patient, therapist and client, or any two people who have a significant relationship" (1989, p. 108). Like two violins' strings which resonate if one violin's strings are plucked, he wrote, "human beings can resonate with each other to such an extent that they can exchange understanding at a subtle level" (pp. 108–109).

Others also have used the word "resonance" in writing about the experience of interconnectedness. Farrell Silverberg describes "a certain and identifiable resonance between therapist and patient; one that may be sensed only unconsciously by the patient, but is sensed consciously by the therapist" (2008, p. 239). He goes on to say,

> For many therapists, such a connection has palpable meaning, but it comes and goes with waves increasing and decreasing in intensity. From a Buddhist perspective, that deeper connectedness to the patient is always there and accessible, it is only our access to it that waxes and wanes giving the illusion that there are times of deep connection and times of surface interaction. (p. 239)

Silverberg uses the term "therapeutic resonance" to refer to the times when a therapist is "fully aware of such reverberation and intentionally remains open and calm in the face of it—welcoming it" (p. 239).

Daniel Siegel also uses the term "resonance." For Siegel, resonance follows attunement:

> Presence permits us to be open to others, and to ourselves. Attunement is the act of focusing on another person (or ourselves) to bring into awareness the internal state of the other in interpersonal attunement. . . . Resonance is the coupling of two autonomous entities into a functional whole. When such resonance is enacted with positive regard, a deep feeling of coherence emerges with the subjective experience of harmony. (2010, p. 54)

Siegel uses the same example of the strings of a musical instrument resonating with each other. He highlights how each person in such resonance is affected by the other. "This is the dynamic and interactive state of resonance. Two literally become linked as one. The whole is larger than the sum of its parts" (p. 54).

Exchange Goes Both Ways

Siegel points to an important piece of understanding exchange: it goes both ways. Not only do we pick up on the feelings, attitudes, and even thoughts of our clients, they exchange with us as well. This can be an unsettling discovery for therapists new to this idea.

We may find that our clients are picking up on how we are feeling. A few years ago I was working with a long-term client who began to talk about the experience of being with a dying relative. At some point she said, "I don't know why I'm talking about this. It really wasn't up for me today." She already knew about exchange since we had worked with it in different ways over the years. I told her that my dog Jackie had just that morning entered the dying process and might even have died while we were meeting. She had picked up on my grief.

Clients may or may not be consciously aware of exchanging with us, but it can certainly affect their experience of us and the therapeutic relationship. If we have a difficult time staying present and feeling what we feel with clients, they will pick that up. Perhaps we feel revulsion at something they tell us. They may exchange with our sense of struggle or the feeling of disgust. It is possible that they will add thoughts to their experience and conclude that not only are they feeling revolted, but they are themselves revolting.

A phenomenon that I have noticed a number of times is the difficulty experienced by some large frightened men. Ronnie was an ex-marine who had been in Iraq and was a student in our psychotherapy program. He was a big, muscular man with broad shoulders. One of my teaching colleagues, Stan, shared with me how scared he was of Ronnie. Stan found himself seriously worried that Ronnie might come to his house and harm him or his wife. Stan had his own history with an abusive father, so there was also some countertransference probably going on. Later, when Stan got to know Ronnie better, he began to see that Ronnie was not a scary man but a scared man. He was struggling with post-traumatic stress disorder and was often anxious and sometimes terrified. Ronnie's own meditation practice helped him to stay present with these waves of feeling, but Stan had not known about it. Instead, he had exchanged with Ronnie's fear and believed it was his own fear of a dangerous Ronnie.

In turn, Ronnie exchanged with Stan's fear and felt even more scared himself. He concluded that Stan, too, was a scary guy and avoided him. When Stan began to consider that exchange might be going on, he invited Ronnie to talk. They were able to acknowledge their mutual discomfort, which created some common ground that led to their getting to know each other better. Over time, they developed a friendly relationship in which Ronnie found a much-needed ally among the faculty.

As we will see below, knowing that exchange goes both ways opens up some interesting possibilities in therapy.

Labeling Exchange Is Always Tentative

Unless we are completely free from the confusion of trying to maintain a false, fixed identity, we filter our experiences through our expectations and habitual patterns. We may respond with passion, aggression, or ignorance. For that reason, we always hold tentatively the idea that what we are experiencing is exchange. Usually, there is some combination of accurate perception and distortion.

We cannot be certain that exchange accounts for our experience, but the more we know our own patterns, the more likely we are to have confidence in the possibility that we are exchanging with a client.

For example, I know that I am far more likely to get caught up in thinking than I am to just space out into a foggy state of mind. When I catch myself in a drifty, vague state, I have learned that it is likely that I am experiencing exchange with a client who is only partially present.

Teasing apart what is exchange and what is not is often not possible. Ultimately, once we are experiencing anything, including exchange, it is ours to deal with. It is our experience as much as anything is. Sometimes we will know, as I often do with the drifty state I mentioned, but often we not only do not know, we may not be able to find out.

WORKING WITH EXCHANGE

The basis of working with exchange is the same as working with our own minds during our therapeutic work altogether. Bringing attention to our ongoing experiences of body, emotions, and mind provides the ground for working with whatever arises in our awareness, including exchange.

Using Touch and Go

A very useful technique for working with our own minds is touch and go, already introduced in Chapter 2. We notice what we are feeling and thinking, touch it, and allow it to dissolve again. For example, when I was working with Josh, I felt the tension I was experiencing and noticed the impatient thoughts I was having and then let them go again before leaning back in my chair and taking a breath.

Employing a Shuttle

As we continue our meditation practice, we are able to increasingly track both our own inner experience and our awareness of the client at the same time. Our field of mindful awareness will become larger or, as Charlotte Joko Beck (1989) described it, we will have an ABC: A Bigger Container. Another useful approach is to make use of a common Gestalt technique, the shuttle (Yontef, 1993). In shuttling, we alternate our focus between two different things. In this case, we could go back and forth between noticing ourselves and noticing our clients. I have noticed that new therapists, especially, may become stuck in one place or the other. They may be so caught up with their own fears and self-consciousness that they forget about the client. Or they might focus so exclusively on the client and the client's words that they lose track of themselves. Using touch and go or employing a shuttle can be useful ways to become more present with the whole interaction.

Exchange Can Provide Information

Sometimes we find out a good deal about our clients through the process of exchange. I was listening to Francie in an early session, who was telling me about an abusive relationship she had been in years before. She simply reported what had occurred without much affect. As I listened, I felt quite flat. I was interested, but not terribly touched by the awful things she was relating. I noticed the disconnection I was feeling between my state of mind and the horror her words described. I speculated, in my mind, that she had dissociated during the abuse and that, even now, she was largely out of touch with her emotions, just as I was in listening to her.

I became curious about how else she might be disconnecting from her feelings. In telling me how she spent her time outside of therapy, it became clear that she had a number of ways of avoiding intensity in her life, including smoking marijuana, keeping extremely busy, and spacing out in front of the television when she was home. In later sessions we explored how she used these distractions to avoid dealing with the results of her abuse.

Another client, Chris, also had trouble tolerating intensity in his experience. In describing his sadness about a recently ended relationship, he told me he felt like he was drowning and had nothing to hang on to now. His former partner, he said, had been a poor buoy, but she was better than nothing. He started to tear up, and then to sob. As he did so, I felt a sudden jolt of terror through my body. It was extremely difficult for me to bear this very charged feeling of intense fear.

When, a few minutes later, I shared my experience with Chris, he confirmed that this sounded to him just like the terror that often arose for him and which he did all he could to avoid. It was all very well for me to encourage him to be present, but now I understood how much courage it was taking for him even to show up for our sessions.

Two-Way Exchange

Since exchange goes in both directions, what we experience in the presence of our clients is of critical importance. If we can work with our minds by bringing mindfulness, maitri, and courage to them, these qualities may be what our clients pick up on. We may create an atmosphere of spaciousness, curiosity, and warmth by how we hold our minds. Again, our meditation practice nurtures our ability to do so with any state of mind or body.

I have become convinced over the years that it is often their experience of exchanging with their therapists that forms a large part of what clients value in coming to therapy. My clients often tell me something like, "I don't know why this was so helpful today, but I feel much more like I can deal with things." If we hold the view that our clients are basically brilliantly sane, they can feel it even if they cannot put it into words or even consciously recognize it.

On the other hand, if we are having negative experiences like anger, revulsion, or judgment toward clients, they may very well pick up on those, too. What do we do then? If we try to ignore these feelings, pretend we do not have them, or try to aggressively push them away, clients may exchange with the sense of denial or aggression. I think we have to feel what we feel, and as much as we can bring curiosity, acceptance, and warmth even to these unpleasant and "un-therapist-like" experiences.

Sometimes these negative experiences are the result of exchange in themselves. Other times they may be countertransference. We still have the same task of working with our minds regardless of the source of our experiences.

Self-Disclosure and Exchange

How much do we share about our experiences of what may be exchange with clients? In the example with Chris, I chose to tell him of the sudden wave of terror that I felt. As he listened to my description, he felt heard or, to use Dan Siegel's term, he was "feeling felt" (2010, p. 34). This led to a few shared moments of wakeful connection before Chris pulled away again. We were able to talk together about both the sense of connectedness and also the discomfort he felt with staying with it.

I am more likely to share my experience with a client with whom I have an already established relationship, but I have sometimes done so even with a new client.

Sarah came to see me following a car accident caused by her partner, Barbara, who had been driving while intoxicated. In our initial session, Sarah reported that this had brought up questions for her about how to relate with Barbara about the incident. As she described their relationship, I noticed that I was becoming increasingly frightened. I felt tight in my belly, and I began to fantasize telling Sarah to get out of that relationship as quickly as possible. I wanted to shout, "Run, Sarah, run!"

Sarah described some arguments, which she always let Barbara win. "It's not really worth getting upset about," she told me. Of paramount importance to Sarah was finding a way to keep Barbara happy and to maintain peace in the relationship. She did not report any sense of being in danger, but that was what I felt as I listened.

First I asked about her feelings during the accident and then during the arguments she had with Barbara. While she did say she felt relief that no one was injured during the accident, she did not actually mention feeling frightened either then or while arguing with Barbara. If I were not having such a strong experience of fear myself, I might have let this go, especially during a first interview.

Instead, I chose to bring up my experience. I shared that I felt some fear listening to descriptions of the accident and of her disagreements with Barbara. I asked if she ever felt fear herself. Sarah told me that she did her best to push away fear whenever it arose, and that she had learned to do so growing up. "If I don't do that, I just get paralyzed."

She went on to tell me that she did not know how to turn her fear avoidance on and off, and so it had sometimes led her into situations that were not safe. We agreed that learning how to recognize her fear without becoming paralyzed might be a useful skill for us to work on together.

In fact, this turned out to be a key part of our work. It became increasingly clear that she and Barbara were actually engaged in a mutually abusive relationship. Over time, Sarah became better at recognizing the signs of fear in her body and assessing the degree of danger she was facing. She learned to leave the house and to find a safe place to be. Eventually, her increased confidence in her own judgment led her to leave the relationship.

Most often, instead of saying what I have experienced myself, I usually do what I did first with Sarah: I ask clients about their own feelings in the moment. Sometimes, if I notice an abrupt shift in my own body or mind, I ask, "What was that? Did something just happen for you?" More often than not, clients will share that they have had an emotion arise or a sudden shift in how they were viewing something. I may leave it at that, even if clients say that they did not notice anything.

Still other times, I may say nothing at all, though I might bookmark it in my mind as something that could bear keeping an eye on in the future.

79

Getting Stuck in the Exchange

Sometimes we find that we carry the experience of exchange with us long after our session is over with one client or another. We feel stuck in the exchange (Wegela, 2009). Often, working with our minds in mindfulness-awareness practice is enough to help us let go. Other times, we need something more. Tonglen, a compassion practice introduced in Chapter 9, can help us soften our hearts and assist us in letting go of whatever we are still carrying from sessions. Other times, using one of the mandala techniques in Chapter 11 or presenting the client in a body-speech-mind group, a supervision practice also introduced in Chapter 11, can help us work effectively with a difficult experience of exchange.

MUTUAL RECOVERY

As we have seen, in the contemplative approach to therapy, therapists practice mindfulness, awareness, and maitri during their work with clients. Their therapy work becomes part of their own personal contemplative path.

We use the term "mutual recovery" to point to this aspect of our work (Fortuna, 1987, p. 59). It is not only our clients who work to cultivate their mindfulness, maitri, and courage, it is also we therapists. I find that recognizing this adds to my feeling of gratitude for the privilege of getting to do this work and being allowed into the lives of my clients.

Chapter 5:

RECOGNIZING BRILLIANT SANITY—NOT ONLY PSYCHOPATHOLOGY— IN CLIENTS

In Contemplative Psychotherapy, we are particularly interested in helping our clients reconnect with their natural wisdom. When we orient ourselves toward recognizing our clients' brilliant sanity, or fundamental goodness, it can help us make a *shift in allegiance* in the therapy from focusing on what is wrong to cultivating brilliant sanity (E. M. Podvoll, personal communication, Summer 1979). As we make this shift ourselves, we are better able to help our clients do that as well. Both we and our clients will find that making such a shift is not something we do just once, but again and again. Still, when we notice that we have narrowed our attention just to tracking the history of pathology or to how the client is creating suffering for himself or herself, we can remind ourselves to reorient on the spot by taking a larger view.

In order to do that, as therapists we need to be able to recognize brilliant sanity not only when it manifests in a straightforward way but also when it arises in a confused or distorted way. This chapter explores some of the ways that brilliant sanity might appear. A summary of these markers of brilliant sanity appears in Figure 5.1.

I. Being present and letting be: the first competency
Signs of being present and letting be
Inspiration to enter therapy
Moments of letting go
Body awareness
Waking up through sense perceptions
Being present with emotions
Having a sense of sacredness
Feeling spacious
Humor

Distortions of the signs of being present and letting be
Mindlessness and numbness
Dissociation
Clinging to what's familiar and resisting change
Cultivating blissful ignorance

II. Seeing clearly and not judging: the second competency
Signs of seeing clearly and not judging
Being curious
Recognizing patterns and thinking logically
Clarifying meaning and values
Skillful use of the imagination
Recognizing thoughts as thoughts

Distortions of the signs of seeing clearly and not judging
Intellectualizing
Anger and aggression
Revulsion

III. Appreciating oneself and others: the third competency
Signs of appreciating oneself and others
Appreciating the richness of experience
Recognizing the richness of others
Maitri
Showing generosity

Distortions of the signs of appreciating oneself and others
Low self-esteem
Craving
Arrogance
Collecting
Idiot compassion and codependency

FIGURE 5.1. Summary of the Signs of Brilliant Sanity

IV. Connecting with others and cultivating relationship: the fourth competency
Signs of connecting with others and cultivating relationship
Discriminating awareness
Precise attention to the sense perceptions, especially in the arts
Compassion and empathy
Ongoing relationships
Solitude and aloneness
Experiencing exchange

Distortions of the signs of connecting with others and cultivating relationship
Pickiness
Perfectionism
Hanging on to dysfunctional relationships
Fear of intimacy
Desire for intimacy confused by having experienced sexual abuse
The Padma dance

V. Acting skillfully and letting go: the fifth competency
Signs of acting skillfully and letting go
Efficiency
Discipline
Setting and holding boundaries
Creative accomplishment
Cutting and pruning
Forgiveness
Playfulness

Distortions of the signs of acting skillfully and letting go
Mindless activity
Busyness and multitasking
Unable to complete or finish things
Worrying and obsessing
Self-doubt and paranoia

Figure 5.1. Continued

Please note that attending to our clients' inherent wisdom does not mean that we would notice the signs of brilliant sanity at the expense of hearing and respecting our clients' experiences of pain, discomfort, and confusion. Pointing out to clients that there is wisdom underneath their present suffering could easily become aggressive and disconfirming. Instead, we begin simply by noticing for ourselves where clients' wisdom may lie. Then, based on our experience of our clients, we can apply our best clinical judgment about whether to say something about what we have noted.

THE CHALLENGE OF RECOGNIZING BRILLIANT SANITY

Most of us were trained in how to recognize psychopathology and in how to use the technical language for discussing it. Few of us received much, if any, training in how to identify and talk about the signs of basic sanity. This does seem to be changing in some quarters as the idea of positive psychology is receiving more attention.[1] Nonetheless, it is actually more difficult, in my experience, to be as clear in describing how brilliant sanity might appear than it is to discuss pathology.

One reason for this, from a contemplative point of view, is that the nature of confusion and pathology is, in itself, characterized by grasping and fixation. In simpler terms, it tends to stick around. Brilliant sanity, on the other hand, is not graspable. We cannot hold onto it, and so it tends to appear in brief flashes and then disappear again.

When we ask clients about their history, it is usually easier to track with them the various events that added to their suffering: various kinds of trauma, family dysfunction, losses, physical and mental challenges, and so on. We can look up definitions in the current *Diagnostic and Statistical Manual of Mental Disorders* (American Psychiatric Association, 2013) and use its lists of symptoms to arrive at a diagnosis.

On the other hand, when we try to identify a history of sanity, as Dr. Edward Podvoll, the founding director of the MA Contemplative Psychotherapy program at Naropa, suggested we could do, we have quite a different task before us. Clients do not know how to tell us about this history, which is characterized by "subtlety and evanescence" (Podvoll, 1983, p. 11). Like the rest of us, they have been well trained in focusing on what is wrong. Adding to the difficulty is, as noted in Chapter 1, that moments of brilliant sanity cannot be captured in words. Clients need help from us in identifying the times when they are in touch with their underlying natural wisdom.

As therapists, we need to listen closely for this less obvious history. In addition, in the context of our ongoing work, we can pay particular attention to the sanity that clients express and show us both directly and indirectly when they are in the room with us.

GUIDELINES FOR RECOGNIZING BRILLIANT SANITY

Given these difficulties, how do contemplative psychotherapists recognize brilliant sanity? The five competencies, explored in Chapter 3 as qualities of a good contemplative therapist, can also provide us with useful signposts to follow as we look for our clients' own natural wisdom. They can assist us in recognizing the often fleeting appearances of brilliant sanity and also point us in the direction of where it is presently being covered up or expressed in a confused way. And so, here we revisit these competencies and see how they can be applied as helpful sanity indicators in our therapeutic work. As you read this chapter, you might try applying these guidelines to one or more clients or to other people you know.

Finally, even though the various manifestations of brilliant sanity are organized into the five competencies in this chapter, it is not essential that we know in which category a particular behavior or quality belongs. It is more important that we are open to recognizing our clients' natural wisdom in whatever form it may take. This listing of the ways in which brilliant sanity might manifest is not meant to be exhaustive. Therapists who attune themselves to the idea of brilliant sanity will discover other signs of it in their clients. Figure 5.1 summarizes all these signs of brilliant sanity.

BEING PRESENT AND LETTING BE: THE FIRST COMPETENCY

The ability to be present and to let one's experience be what it is shows up in a number of different ways in our clients. First I discuss how it may look when it appears without distortion. Then, as for each of the competencies, I go on to explore some of the ways it might appear in a disguised, hidden, or confused form. These distorted versions of the competencies are based on the Buddhist teachings on the six realms or classes of existence (Sangharakshita, 1977). The six realms can be understood as descriptions of different psychological states, and I unpack them further under each competency below (Trungpa, 1976).

Let's begin by looking at how brilliant sanity may manifest in an uncomplicated way in the first competency.

The Inspiration to Seek Therapy

Often clients seek a counselor or therapist when they recognize in themselves a longing to be free from ways of behaving and being that are no longer working for them. They may say something like, "I used to be calmer and not so caught up in being busy all the time. I wish I could relax." Or they might say something like, "There has to be a better way. I am so tired of worrying all the time. I'm stuck in my head." Most clients arrive at therapy because of this longing to go beyond their own confusion and suffering.

Mary came to see me after going on a backpacking trip by herself. While she was in the wilderness, she found a sense of peace and relief that were lacking in her ordinary life. The sense of contrast, once she was home and again getting caught up in habits like compulsive texting and drinking alcohol, was painful. She felt a deep longing to tune in once again to the state of mind she had glimpsed in the mountains.

Being Present in the Moment

One of the ways that clients find out that it is possible to awaken from the suffering of their lives is that they have experienced moments in which they have let go of confusion and are simply present. Like Mary, they have glimpsed their own brilliant sanity and, for many of them, there is a stark contrast between their usual way of being and the relative relaxation and clarity of such moments. Sometimes clients experience this kind of letting go during their sessions with us. If we show interest in these moments, clients may become more interested in them, too.

Brad described a morning when he woke up and felt free of his usual urgent need for a cigarette. He told me that he just felt okay, "kind of good, really. Everything seemed all right. I lay in bed a little while longer than usual." Once he got up and moved into his day, the sense of relaxation disappeared. He became speedy and found himself craving a cigarette. He wondered how he could connect again with that sense of things being workable.

In one of our later sessions, after I had invited him to pay attention to what he noticed inside his body, he reported that he was feeling a bit like he had on the morning he had described to me a few weeks earlier. We became interested together in how that sense of being present and okay seemed to come out of nowhere, linger awhile, and go away again. Over time, Brad became increasingly interested in being more mindful of his body and emotions, and he learned to notice the breaks in his mind's speediness.

Body Awareness

Since the body is always in the present, bringing mindfulness and awareness to it is one way that people come into the present moment. A recent client, Connie, who had been a star athlete in high school and college, told me about the sense of pleasure she felt in the simplicity of swimming. She contrasted it with the aggressive striving that drove her when she was preparing for competitions. When she could just go swimming for its own sake, she felt present and good. The difference between "just swimming" and "driving herself" became a useful metaphor in our work together.

Waking Up Through Sense Perceptions

Closely related to body awareness is attending to one's sense perceptions. They, too, are always available in the present moment, and their potential wakefulness often goes unnoticed. We can listen for and highlight for our clients when they describe vivid experiences of sight, sound, taste, touch or feeling, and smell. Enjoying a tasty meal in a restaurant or recoiling from the awful noise of a nearby train whistle in the middle of the night may be experiences during which clients are actually present on the spot.

Sense perceptions are often the easiest way for clients to contact their direct experience, and they can help clients to let go of distractions of all kinds. I often invite clients to notice what they can see, hear, and feel during sessions. Many clients find that they also use their sense perceptions outside of sessions as a way to come back into the present moment.

Being Present With Emotions

In the same way that clients come into the present through their sense perceptions, they can contact direct experience through their emotions. I often ask clients how they know that what they are feeling is anxiety or anger or some other emotion. Most people experience emotions through bodily sensations. They may feel a tightness in their belly with fear or heat on their neck with anger, for example. Other clients report that they know they are feeling a particular feeling because of the thoughts that arise. Still other clients notice colors or imagery. Whatever ways clients recognize emotions can provide gateways into the present moment when they bring their attention to their experiences.

Having a Sense of Sacredness

Another sign of this competency is the experience of sacredness. No matter what spiritual or religious tradition clients feel a connection with, they may recognize a sense of sacredness, blessing, or holiness in their experience. Such experiences may provide a sense of opening beyond a fixed sense of self. They may feel panoramic and vast. Often they allow for a sense of letting go of worry and pettiness. I always listen carefully and show curiosity when clients bring up their experiences and beliefs about the sacred, whether they are theistic, nontheistic, or atheistic.

Several clients have described to me their sense that "whatever happens is meant to happen." Sometimes clients refer to their "higher power" or "wise mind" or "God." Having confidence in the absolute can give clients powerful ways of letting go. A conviction in brilliant sanity or basic goodness may do the same.

Feeling Spacious

I am always interested when clients describe the times in their lives when they have felt a sense of freedom, relaxation, peacefulness, relief, or slowing down. Often they are pointing to experiences of having a sense of space. They have felt a gap in their usually cluttered minds. Many times, when clients experience such a gap, they quickly fill it with thoughts. Staying with such moments of openness, for many people, feels unfamiliar and anxiety provoking.

Many people experience a sense of space when they are in transition. Verónica was about to graduate from school, and she did not yet have any plans for the future. As she described what this was like for her, she struggled to find words for the sense of vast open space that she was confronting. At one point, she actually forgot what she had been talking about and said so. Rather than reminding her of what she had been saying, I suggested that she just notice what it was like right now to experience this moment of forgetting. As she let herself simply be present, she noticed the urge to escape from it. She noted that she was starting to feel a bit shaky and wanted to find something specific to talk about. We talked about how this unstructured moment was a common experience for her now as she tried to figure out what to do after graduation. She did not want to rush into something just to have a plan, but she was also quite uncomfortable hanging out with not knowing. Acknowledging this brought some relief. Forgetting what she had been talking about was not a sign of something wrong; it was just a time in which the openness of her situation and her mind became vivid to her.

Humor

Having a larger or spacious view may manifest as seeing the humor in a situation. Brad and I had worked for some time with the variety of ways in which he cultivated the opposite of mindfulness: mindlessness. Among two of these activities, both of which he found embarrassing and painful, were smoking cigarettes and biting his nails. He had tried many different strategies to help him stop both.

Brad mindlessly bit his nails everyday, and they often bled as he nibbled them down below the quick. Only then would he notice what he was doing and stop. With smoking, too, he could reach for a cigarette and only after smoking most of it realize that he had done so.

One day, I asked him about where in his home he smoked. He described how he would settle in his favorite chair, read, drink coffee, and light up a cigarette. I asked him to fill out the picture a bit more so that I could get a better sense of his smoking experience and perhaps why it was so hard to give up. "What sort of ashtray do you have?" I asked, wondering if perhaps his smoking accessories were special in any way.

He began to laugh so hard, he could barely speak. "I don't have an ashtray at all," he gasped through his laughter. "But I have a really fancy manicure kit for my nails!" I began to laugh with him at the absurdity of the manicure kit for which he had no purpose and the absent ashtray that would have acknowledged that he really did smoke. Soon tears were rolling down both our cheeks as we connected through his humor and his insight into his situation.

We also noted that both the missing ashtray and the unused manicure kit reflected his aspiration to let go of his harmful habits.

When Being Present and Letting Be Are Distorted

As we saw with Verónica, momentary times of being present can go unrecognized. At other times, aspects of natural wisdom may appear only as potential. What are the clues that we can look for that suggest when a sense of being present or letting be is being covered up but could possibly be invited to reveal itself? This competency is associated with two of the six realms of existence: the animal realm and the realm of the gods (Ponlop, 2006).

Mindlessness and Numbness

The confused psychological state associated with the animal realm is mindlessness, numbness, or stupidity. I hasten to add here that this is an ancient metaphor, and, as a dog person myself, I am well aware that this does not describe all actual animals. As I describe further in Chapter 7, all of us have ways of leaving the present moment and losing touch with our bodies, emotions, and mind.

Francie often talked about the ways in which she got lost in the fog of numbness. Sometimes she called it "spacing out," echoing the wisdom quality of spaciousness. Her favorite mindlessness practices included smoking marijuana, zoning out in front of the television, and staring off into space. All of these activities brought her a temporary sense of relief, and that was what she was seeking. She was trying to find a sense of peace and spaciousness, but these activities, lacking a sense of mindfulness or awareness, tended to perpetuate or postpone her difficulties, not relieve them. Still, underneath was the healthy longing to find peace and relaxation.

Dissociation

Similarly, dissociation, losing track of one's sense of the present, is an attempt to escape from pain. For many clients, dissociating began at a time in their lives when finding a way to cut themselves off from an intolerable present situation was actually an expression of brilliant sanity. Many therapists are well aware of how clients who suffered childhood physical and sexual abuse learned to dissociate as their best option.

One client of mine who was sexually abused by her father throughout her childhood reported that she no longer wanted to "miss her life" through habitually "checking out." Her longing to be present was an expression of the first competency.

Clinging to What's Familiar and Resisting Change

Another way in which the animal realm approach may show up is in resisting any change to familiar routines or patterns. There may be much comfort in following the same routine day after day. At the same time, moving through one's life with blinders on can narrow one's world down to a predictable, but sterile, existence. Still, underneath this sort of stuckness may be a wish to be free from unnecessary suffering—the same desire that leads some to seek a spiritual path.

Cultivating Blissful Ignorance

The realm of the gods points to a different way that the spacious qualities of the first competency may be expressed in a confused way. In this realm, or psychological state, we seek to escape our suffering by cultivating blissful ignorance. Clients may try to find peace and bliss through the abuse of drugs and other addictive substances like cocaine, crack, or heroin. They may use LSD or marijuana (now legal where I live in Colorado) to pursue altered states. Or they may misuse their meditation or contemplative practices to avoid painful emotions, unpleasant circumstances, or difficult states of mind.

When clients talk about any of these sorts of things, I become interested with them in what states of mind they are trying to attain. Once again, we usually uncover a longing to be awake and have a sense of peace. Recognizing that these yearnings are aspects of natural wisdom may relieve clients' feelings of shame and shift our focus toward ways that they can express these same longings in a less harmful way. We return to this, too, in Chapter 7 as we explore the skillful uses of mindlessness practices.

SEEING CLEARLY AND NOT JUDGING: THE SECOND COMPETENCY

Recognizing when clients express the qualities of seeing clearly and not judging helps therapists identify the second competency in their clients.

Being Curious

Showing inquisitiveness and interest is a sign of the second competency. Clients may be interested in all kinds of things, and when we join them in being curious we invite them to tap more deeply into their natural wisdom. Their interests may include various pastimes like photography, sports, music, collecting film recordings, or reading novels. Or they may be fascinated by how their own minds work. When clients are interested, as they often are, in how their own patterns of behavior affect their experience and their relationships, we have a wonderful basis for exploring these things together.

Martha and I were able to explore together how her patterns of avoiding intimacy through drinking alcohol resulted in her feeling isolated within her marriage. She was able to engage her curiosity in moving toward the uncomfortable feelings of awkwardness that arose when she let herself be more present with me and with her partner.

Bringing curiosity to these unwanted experiences also helped her to let go of judging herself. Increasingly, she could simply feel what she felt without adding the extra layer of self-criticism. In fact, she even became curious about the experience of negative self-judgment.

Recognizing Patterns and Thinking Logically

As in my work with Martha, when we help our clients to recognize their patterns of behavior and how they lead to particular results, we are inviting their inherent clarity and ability not to judge. Of course, many times clients demonstrate this ability without any help from us. In addition to recognizing patterns in their own behavior, they may also recognize patterns in other domains.

I have worked with a number of people, mostly men, who work in the fields of engineering or computer sciences. They have cultivated their ability to recognize patterns and the interplay of the different elements within their own fields. Rather than regarding their explanations of nonpsychological patterns as a possible distraction from the work of therapy, we can show interest in how they manifest this aspect of their brilliant sanity and invite them, perhaps, to apply their well-trained minds to exploring the patterns of mind and behavior that may have brought them into therapy.

James, an engineer at a nearby technology company, brought his curious mind to the question of boredom. He had ended a series of relationships and did not understand why. We worked to identify the pattern that repeated itself in these failed relationships. He described how he began with a sense of excitement and fantasy, and then would become bored. That was the point when he would leave. After we had spent some time exploring whether his expectations were realistic, I asked him, "What's the problem with being bored?" Together we examined what he meant by boredom, how it arose, and what it meant. Bringing his inquisitive mind to these questions opened things up for him. He began to explore the physical sensations of boredom both in our sessions and out of them.

Eventually he found that he could tolerate the sense of not knowing, absence of control, and spaciousness that were the experience of boredom for him. This, in turn, freed him up to explore relationships and not leave them prematurely. He could stay present with boredom and see what happened next. Some time after we finished our work together, I ran into him at a local store, where he introduced me to his fiancée.

Closely related to recognizing patterns is the ability to think clearly and logically. We can show interest in whatever area in life our clients have applied their ability to plan and to reason things out for themselves. For many, this may be in their work lives. Understanding the financial markets, for example, requires the application of the intellect. Others may study something that interests them like the history of baseball or the Elizabethan period. Still others may bring logic to understanding how to plan their vegetable gardens so that they have fresh vegetables available through the growing season. Wherever clients' curiosity takes them and where they apply their critical minds may be the places in which they display the wisdom of seeing clearly.

Clarifying Meaning and Values

One issue that brings people into therapy is the need to sort out and clarify what matters to them. Both the longing to do so and the actual process of discovering what holds meaning and value for them are reflections of this competency.

I often work with clients who bring up some version of the question, "What do I really want?" One client and I joked that at the age of 50 she was ready to ask, "Who do I want to be when I grow up?" Many people have simply gone along with what they were taught growing up. When clients question those values, they may feel very disoriented and even frightened.

Jillian, the client who laughed about discovering what she wanted to be when she grew up, was contemplating leaving her husband of many years. She had followed the script she was given by her family, and now she was questioning if this was really the life she wanted to lead. She described what she wanted as "clarity." It required a good deal of courage to look at this question straight on, and I was impressed at her determination to do so. After she and her husband did some couples counseling with another therapist, she decided that she would stay in the marriage. Leaving would violate deeply held values. At the same time, some of her other values had been neglected, and she decided to add additional activities to her own life, including returning to practicing the piano and going to music workshops out of town by herself.

Skillful Use of the Imagination

In the Tibetan tradition of Buddhism, visualization is used as a part of some meditation practices to tune in to the wise and compassionate aspects of our being. Similarly, many approaches to working with trauma invite clients to resource themselves by evoking positive experiences such as real or imaginary people, places, and memories (Leitch & Miller-Karas, 2010). In recognizing our clients' strengths and competencies, we can listen for how clients already make use of their imaginations to access their innate brilliant sanity.

I had a client who had an "inner wise woman," whom she pictured as an elderly ancestor to whom she could go for counsel and support. Sometimes in a session she would take a few moments to think of this figure and imagine a conversation with her. She might do this aloud or silently, and she usually felt confidence in the messages she received in this way. She knew she was accessing an aspect of herself, yet when she turned her mind toward her inner wise woman, she was able to let go of her usual, smaller outlook and tap into something more open and, I would have to say, wise.

Recognizing Thoughts as Thoughts

When clients see that thoughts are thoughts and not reality itself, they are expressing the competency of seeing clearly. Tim described to me how he was able to sometimes recognize that his thoughts about himself were just thoughts, and that he did not have to believe their messages about his being a loser or hopeless. We may teach clients to do this when we apply various kinds of cognitive therapy, yet clients may also exhibit this quality of clarity on their own.

Recognizing Clear Seeing When It Is Distorted

When the competency of seeing clearly is distorted or covered up, it may appear as anger, aggression, or misuse of the intellect. It tends to show up as negative judgments directed toward others or oneself. The realm associated with this competency is the hell realm, which may manifest in the psychological states of either the hot feeling of anger, rage, or hatred, or the cold feeling of distance, disdain, or intellectual superiority (Ponlop, 2006).

Intellectualizing

When clients engage in intellectualizing, they avoid their direct experiences of body, sense perceptions, and emotions. Sometimes they have had enough of a taste of these direct experiences to know that they do not want to have them. Usually, however, these tastes are so brief that they are not even noticed.

A client I worked with tended to get into long-winded explanations. For example, he once drew on his training in physics to offer me a thorough explanation of how he saw the cause and effect of his losing a job recently. I suspect that there was a great deal of accuracy in his description, but he was not discovering anything new in this well-plowed ground. I invited him to notice what he experienced as he told me his story. Over time he came to recognize a quality of sadness and even tearfulness. Both of those were frightening for him, and we worked with touch and go to titrate the intensity of his exploration. He began to be curious when he found himself in the midst of long explanations, especially in therapy, where his stated goal was to go more deeply into his experience.

Anger and Aggression

Anger and aggression are often based on a clear perception of something that is not right. What happens, though, is that that moment of clarity is quickly co-opted by the habit of clinging to a fixed sense of self. We might, for example, see that someone is being injured or treated without compassion, and we see that this is wrong. Instead of keeping our attention on what needs to happen to remedy the situation, we quickly attach to it with a thought like, "I don't like it."

Rita described a situation that arose in her family. She had said something thoughtless to her brother, and he had felt hurt. As she told me, her focus was on how angry she felt because, as she saw it, he took what she said too personally. She had seen his hurt—a moment of clear seeing and empathy—but she quickly blamed him for being too sensitive. Then, on top of that, she was mad that now she felt guilty for hurting him. Both in her anger and in her guilt, she had lost track of her initial perception of her brother's pain and her own brief tenderhearted response to it.

Even rage often has its roots in the perception of a genuine injustice. Perpetrators of domestic violence, for example, have often been the recipients of violence themselves in childhood. People who suffer as the target of racism, sexism, homophobia, and other forms of oppression and discrimination may clearly and accurately recognize that harm has been done. On top of this clear perception, however, confused anger and rage may become misdirected or internalized. It is important that therapists recognize both the wisdom and the confusion that may be part of rage and deep anger.

Revulsion

Rita's sense of guilt led quickly to a sense of self-revulsion. She fell seamlessly into an old pattern of self-aggression. There must be something wrong with her that she was so mean, so thoughtless. She felt fed up with herself and disgusted. Such experiences of revulsion are extremely valuable, and I explore them more deeply in Chapter 10 when I return to the issues of anger and aggression. Here, let us note that below the sense of revulsion is clear seeing into how one has harmed oneself or another. This points both to our inherent clarity and to our innate compassion. We do not want to be harmful, and so we may reject ourselves when we see how we are lacking in kindness. Moments of revulsion are pivotal points. We can continue turning the revulsion into self-aggression, or we can make use of the glimpse of clarity to cultivate a greater sense of clarity and compassion.

APPRECIATING ONESELF AND OTHERS: THE THIRD COMPETENCY

While the third competency for a contemplative therapist focuses on the appreciation of differences, when we apply it to our clients it can be expanded to include a wider range of experience.

In whatever areas our clients express appreciation for the richness of life, we may see a reflection of their natural wisdom. Additionally, when clients extend generosity and hospitality to themselves and to others, they are expressing this aspect of their brilliant sanity.

Appreciating the Richness of Experience

Clients express appreciation for the richness of experience in innumerable ways. They may show admiration for art, music, or dance. It does not matter if they prefer Renoir to body art, Bach to rock, or classical ballet to the latest dance craze. They might appreciate an elaborately prepared meal in a fine restaurant or love McDonald's French fries. Often the sense perceptions are engaged in such activities, but clients may also show appreciation for the beauty of a well-reasoned math proof or a well-written novel. As therapists, we are interested in the brilliant sanity we see when clients open up and allow themselves to be touched by their experiences. At such times they may show the qualities of letting go, letting be, and going beyond self-absorption.

Recognizing the Richness of Others

As we saw in the description of this competency as it applies to psychotherapists, its wisdom aspect, equanimity, can be extended to an appreciation of people from cultures and traditions different from our own. It means appreciating differences instead of rejecting them.

As we become curious about how our clients recognize the richness of others, we may find deeply felt convictions in the basic goodness of all beings or we may find only a love of ethnic food. In either case, we can listen for the sense of appreciation and openness to differences that underlies both.

Maitri

We have touched on this key element of Contemplative Psychotherapy before. Being able to be present with one's experience and let it be what it is while having a quality of warmth toward oneself is maitri, the opposite of self-aggression. It is also an expression of the third competency. I pay attention to even the smallest hints of maitri in my clients. I may not say anything or make a big fuss, but

I am deeply interested in any way they express increasing kindness toward themselves.

Sonya, for example, is well practiced in self-deprecation and self-doubt. Having recently experienced a breakup with a longtime boyfriend, she quickly concluded that he ended the relationship with her because she was not good enough and was probably unlovable altogether. Recently, she told me that she had applied for a promotion at work. She shared that she was feeling more confident at work and felt that she deserved a better position. In this, I saw an increase in her sense of appreciation for herself.

When clients express an interest in taking better care of themselves, it is also a possible sign of increased maitri. Clients who finally get around to going for a physical checkup, begin a healthier diet, or start going to the gym may be demonstrating a growing appreciation for themselves. They may, on the other hand, be using the same activities to express a feeling that they are not good enough as they are. Still, I listen closely and become interested in the potential maitri in such choices.

Another way of helping clients experience maitri is through the mandala of strengths technique, introduced in Chapter 11.

Showing Generosity

Being generous is another way in which clients may express this aspect of brilliant sanity. In Buddhist teachings, being generous is regarded as extremely important. It has been described as the "virtue that produces peace" (Simmer-Brown, 2002) and is the first stage of a set of teachings about the cultivation of awakened, compassionate actions (Sanskrit, *paramitas*; Wegela, 2009). Serving as a therapist may be an expression of generosity in itself.

In attending to how our clients express generosity, we can see a wide range of behaviors. First, we may recognize the generosity in giving actual things to others. This might include giving gifts to friends and family, donating to charities and homeless people on the street, or lending books or clothing to others. In addition, clients express generosity when they offer services to members of their families like looking after children, listening to the sometimes tediously repeated stories of the elderly, picking up the family's dry cleaning, shoveling the snow on the sidewalk, and doing the grocery shopping. Or they may extend their generosity through service to those beyond their families. I have had clients who have served Thanksgiving dinner at a nearby homeless shelter, walked dogs at the local humane society, and read to the blind at the library. Some show generosity through their work as first responders, medical personnel, caregivers, and psychotherapists.

Some clients express generosity by providing hospitality to others. This can range from inviting a friend over for a cup of coffee to caring for a sick or dying relative in their homes.

A form of generosity I find particularly inspiring is what in Buddhist teachings has been called the gift of courage or fearlessness (Wegela, 2009). This is providing a sense of comfort and safety to those who are afraid. I believe that this is a large part of what we offer to clients: creating a safe enough space in which they can explore their experience. We can recognize that our clients make this gift, too, when they serve as good people to talk to, perhaps providing a sympathetic ear or a shoulder to cry on for family or friends. Many clients do even more through their volunteer and work activities.

Recognizing Appreciation When It Is Confused or Distorted

The common threads in the confused and distorted versions of this competency are craving and never feeling satisfied with oneself, others, or circumstances.

Low Self-Esteem

Many clients say that what has brought them into therapy is a feeling of inadequacy or low self-esteem. They believe that they need to be improved, fixed, or changed in a fundamental way. These feelings are a distorted version of this competency. Underneath this personal poverty mentality may be the accurate sense that they are basically workable but presently confused. If they had no hint of the possibility of feeling better about themselves, they would not have come to therapy. Still, they have a confused idea about how that feeling better is to be accomplished. They think they need to get rid of something or acquire something else, while a contemplative approach would be interested in changing their relationship to who and what they already are.

Craving

One way this sense of not being good enough can manifest is as a sense of insatiable hunger or craving. In turn, this may lead to confused attempts to feel full or better. For many, the misuse of food or addictive substances or behaviors may be attempts to get enough. This is a different motivation than what we saw in the first competency with clients who turn to addiction in order to attain a sense of spaciousness or bliss. The realm associated with this competency is the hungry ghost or preta realm (Maté, 2008). A hungry ghost, or preta, has a big belly and such a small neck that its big belly can never become full .

A client with whom I worked had an eating disorder in which she not only ate her own food but also stole that of her housemates. She frequently went on starvation diets or indulged in punishing exercise in order to control her weight. Then she would again give in to the craving to feel full, and the cycle of eating and self-recrimination would repeat itself. We worked together on bringing mindfulness to the feelings that preceded the bingeing and to the experience of eating itself. What she found was deep sadness and loneliness as well as the conviction that she was never good enough, no matter how she looked. Over time, she became more able to tolerate and soften to these feelings. She slowly made friends with her body as it was and began to trust her sense of hunger when it was belly hunger and not her "hungry heart" (Roth, 1982).

Arrogance

The other side of the coin of a poverty mentality is an inflated sense of self or arrogance. Instead of regarding oneself with kindness and acceptance, a client may cling to a mistakenly overblown sense of his or her abilities and qualities. This, too, is regarded as a distortion of the wisdom of the third competency. Usually, not far below the surface is a sense of impoverishment and a sense of not being good enough. I had one client who was very overweight, which gave him a sense of solidity that he otherwise felt he lacked. It was as though the bigger he was, the more okay he was, and if he was really large, he was correspondingly more important. Losing weight would be, he feared, becoming less substantial, both literally and psychologically.

Collecting

Sometimes clients express the same fear of not being good enough or having enough through the acquisition of material things. Collecting things in a mindless way is one way this might appear. An extreme version would be hoarding. Less obviously, a client who collects fine art, for example, and displays a good deal of discrimination in the process may also be doing so in order to feel more full and satisfied with himself. He may be showing the wisdom of clarity in his choices and at the same time expressing a sense of poverty mentality in the fear he may show at the possibility of losing his collection or his status as a discerning collector.

Idiot Compassion and Codependency

A distortion of generosity we may recognize in our clients has been termed idiot compassion or, as I sometimes think of it, idiot generosity (Wegela, 2009). Instead of being generous by providing what another may need, the practitioner of idiot compassion provides what is not only not needed but may actually be harmful. A classic example of this is providing heroin to an addict so that she will not have to experience the pain of withdrawal.

A common expression of idiot compassion is codependency. My client Jack had a series of relationships in which he was always the provider of comfort, money, and attention. Many of his partners were emotionally unavailable and most were struggling with addiction. What he got in return was the feeling of being needed and important as well as the opportunity to hang on to a particular story about himself as a helpful and caring person. He denied his own needs and rarely received back the kindness and love he craved. He was terrified of being alone, and so he continued to put up with relationships that did not meet his needs.

In both idiot compassion and codependency there is some genuine compassion and appreciation for another person, but it becomes misdirected in the service of maintaining a particular fixed identity as a helpful, generous, or kind person.

CONNECTING WITH OTHERS AND CULTIVATING RELATIONSHIP: THE FOURTH COMPETENCY

We can recognize the degree to which our clients are able to access this relational aspect of their brilliant sanity not only through what they tell us but also through our own experience with them in the therapeutic relationship itself.

Traditionally, two aspects of wisdom are associated with this competency: discriminating awareness and compassion (Trungpa, 1987). Both are important elements in relationships.

Discriminating Awareness

In Buddhist teachings, discriminating awareness (Sanskrit, *prajna*) can refer to the attainment of enlightenment, the full realization of one's inherent wisdom. It can also refer to a more worldly level, and in therapy we are usually working with this more mundane level of it: the ability to tell the difference between what is beneficial and what is harmful to oneself or to others. Being able to make such distinctions is the necessary ground for taking compassionate action (the fifth competency), and it underlies good clinical judgment. For our clients, too, it is the prerequisite for being genuinely helpful to others.

Discriminating awareness is more akin to intuition than it is to reasoning out a decision based on applying the intellect. Clients sometimes talk about how a particular choice feels right or tell us, "This is the right thing to do even though it's not really what I want for myself." Often such discernment is a reflection of the wisdom of discriminating awareness.

A frequent dilemma that contemplative psychotherapists have to address for themselves and with their clients is choosing between letting things be and seeking change based on compassion. Buddhist psychology teaches the importance of both, but how does one decide which one to emphasize in any moment? In Dialectical Behavior Therapy (DBT), too, the "central dialectical tension" is between the same things: acceptance and change (Linehan, 1993, p. 98). It is with the wisdom of discriminating awareness that we penetrate this difficulty. In general, unless we can see things as they are with some clarity, we do not know how to act compassionately. It is through discriminating awareness, too, that we can recognize the impulse to indulge in idiot compassion.

I sometimes think of discriminating awareness as the ability to tell the difference between the wheat and the chaff: this is food and will be nourishing; this is inedible and needs to go in the compost.

Frank needed to make a decision about how to relate to his nephew, Bryce. After Bryce had successfully completed a drug rehabilitation program, Frank invited his nephew to live in his own home. This extension of hospitality, a reflection of the third competency in Frank, had seemed like a good decision, and perhaps it was to begin with. It gave Bryce a place to land and the live-in support he needed as he made the transition from a highly structured program to ordinary life. For a few months it seemed to be working well, and then Bryce began to use drugs and drink alcohol again. He once again fell in with his old buddies and began to neglect his commitments to Frank. He came home late, or not at all; he neglected his share of the chores around the house; and he made it difficult for Frank, a recovering alcoholic, to maintain a stable home environment.

Frank brought his dilemma into our ongoing therapy: should he keep trying to provide a home for Bryce or should he tell his nephew to move out? Frank felt some urgency about getting this decided as soon as possible. What was the compassionate and wise thing to do and how could he tell? After listing the pros and cons of each choice, he was still unclear. Finally, he asked me to help him to ground himself in his body instead of continuing to go around and around in his head. As we had done in some previous sessions, I invited Frank to feel his feet on the floor and to tune in to the rest of his body, area by area, with a body scan. As Frank settled into the present moment, anchored in his bodily sensations, he let himself relax and let go of the urgency he had felt to make a decision. Then he had an insight. "I need to sit Bryce down and restate the boundaries we agreed on. Then, I'll give him a specific time period, say a week, in which to get back on track. If he can't do it by then, then he'll have to move out." Frank felt relieved that he had found what felt like a good path forward. As he described it, his insight had not come from his internal mental wrangling, but had arisen when he relaxed and let go.

Recognizing discriminating awareness in clients can be expanded to include good judgment not only about what actions to take, but also discernment in other matters. Deciding what habits, relationships, activities, and values to cultivate and which ones to discard requires the application of discrimination. It is often just such issues that clients wrestle with in their lives and in therapy. As we seek to recognize our clients' natural wisdom, we can pay attention to the areas in their lives where they already make good choices and demonstrate insight.

Renee worked as a vice president in a corporation. Called upon to make decisions all day long, she was quite comfortable in that role and reported feeling a good deal of confidence in her choices. When it came to deciding about how to proceed with her teenage son's desire to attend a college 2,000 miles away, though, she felt at sea. I asked her how she would address this problem if she were at work. "Well, first I would gather more information. I would talk to my colleagues and staff and get more input. I wouldn't close out any possibility without exploring further." While this was not all she needed to explore—there were her feelings about her son being so far away, for example—recognizing that she had some skills that she could apply to this situation helped her feel more grounded and less overwhelmed.

Precise Attention to Sense Perceptions

The fourth competency also includes precise attention to sense perceptions, especially in the arts. It may appear as an appreciation or practice of various art forms. Once again, it is the quality of discrimination that is at play here, in contrast to the mindfulness of sense perceptions referred to in the first competency.

I have worked with many clients over the years who have been musicians, singers, painters, sculptors, writers, or dancers. Some have been professional artists, but most were dedicated amateurs. I am always interested in the state of mind they experience while they practice their particular disciplines. How do they think about what they do and how do they choose how to proceed? Often they describe a nonconceptual sense of knowing or perceiving that seems to be an expression of discriminating awareness.

One professional fiction writer told me how she knew when to keep what she had written. "I keep working with it, changing the words slightly, until I know it's right. It's hard to describe, but at some point I just know. Then I leave it alone."

At a more prosaic level, most clients have areas in their lives where they apply precise attention to sense perceptions. Perhaps they cook and use their senses of smell and taste to decide how to prepare dinner for their families. Or they create a visual feast by combining different colors in a salad. Other clients show this competency in how they put together their clothing, combining interesting textures and colors of tie, jacket, and shirt. Still others are discriminating in their choice of music to listen to as they commute to work. If we are curious, we will find limitless opportunities to note our clients' precise appreciation of the senses.

Compassion and Empathy

The other important aspect of this competency is compassion and its relative, empathy. In the fifth competency, compassionate action, the emphasis is on doing and acting. Here, in the fourth competency, compassion is about the longing, and sometimes the commitment, to relieve suffering that precedes taking action. Often, empathy forms the basis of this desire. Our ability to put ourselves in someone else's place and imagine what it is like to be that other person is empathy.

Margaret described an incident to me in which her sons, her husband, her sister and her two children, plus her husband's mother had celebrated Christmas together at her home. Margaret's sons were not getting along with each other, and everyone else felt ill at ease as a result. As she told me about it, Margaret was able to imagine what each of her sons was feeling and could readily see why they were having a hard time with each other. She could also put herself in the place of her other family guests and see how awkward and uncomfortable this had been for them. Empathy and warmth toward others came easily for Margaret. What was missing from her description was anything about her own experience. I acknowledged her ability to be empathetic and invited her to explore the possibility of extending the same kind of kindness and understanding to herself.

In general, I make it a practice to keep the focus in therapy on the client with whom I am working and do my best not to get caught up in trying to figure out what might be going on with others in their lives. For example, when Sean blamed his partner, Steve, for his own feeling of disconnection in their relationship, I asked about Sean's experience and did not pursue his list of complaints about how Steve treated his parents. However, I did ask him, "What do you imagine was going on for Steve when he left the table and slammed the door?" I was asking about Steve, but I was actually interested in Sean's ability to empathize. Could he put himself in Steve's place and imagine what it was like for him when Sean had once again complained about his cooking?

If we listen for it, we can often recognize compassionate longings in even our most dysfunctional clients. Bob, whom I worked with in a residential program for people suffering from extreme states of mind, often spoke of his desire to teach yoga. He was not actually able to engage in much yoga himself since his mind was too wild to work with the breathing, postures, and chanting practices he aspired to share. Instead of dismissing his desire as merely an unrealistic idea, I showed interest in the longing to serve that inspired it.

Another client I worked with, Arlene, had recently been released from a 2-week stay on a ward in a mental hospital. She struggled with depression and feelings of powerless, which, as she described it to me, had to do with the state of the earth itself. The increasing scarcity of food and water, global climate change, and destruction of the rain forests were topics she returned to again and again. When she talked about them, her focus was on the suffering these phenomena caused ordinary people, especially those without the privileges she had been born with. There was, of course, a great deal going on that was about Arlene's tendency to avoid working with her own immediate difficulties, but the compassion that she felt for the suffering of others and her desire to alleviate it were also important to recognize.

Many times the struggles that clients bring into therapy reflect their desires to be compassionate to others and also kind to themselves. Gail wanted to divorce her husband, but she worried about how this might be harmful to him and their children. They had already tried both couples and family counseling to no avail. She hated the idea of the children becoming caught up in what might be a messy custody battle. At the same time, the relationship was actually detrimental to her, and it had taken a good deal of courage to face this reality. How could she be compassionate and still take care of herself too?

Marvin's 14-year-old dog, Stormy, was ill with untreatable cancer. Marvin struggled with the decision to have Stormy put down. Stormy had been Marvin's longtime companion and had been there for him through many hard times. The thought of letting him go was not only sad, it was frightening. Yet the most important thing to Marvin was to do the compassionate thing for Stormy, who was starting to suffer.

Ongoing Relationships

The ability to engage in and cultivate ongoing relationships is a clear reflection of this competency. This does not mean that clients' relationships are smooth and easy, but their willingness to work with the everyday give and take of relationships demonstrates this competency.

I am interested in my clients' relationships not only with family, friends, coworkers, and others but also with pets: dogs, cats, birds, and even reptiles. Many times, as was the case with Marvin, clients' closest relationships may be with their animals.

The longing to be in relationship and intimacy are common reasons people come into therapy. They come when relationships have ended, when they have recently begun, when they have never happened, and when they have been going on so long that they have become stale and lifeless. All of these are reflections of our underlying recognition of interconnectedness and the need for others in our lives.

One ongoing relationship that we, as therapists, have direct access to is the one clients have with us. I pay attention to simple things like clients' eye contact and posture. I may ask about a client's experience of our relationship in the moment. Finally, I might comment on my own sense of how we are or are not connected.

In working with Sam, for example, I noticed how he leaned back into his chair, crossed his leg away from me, and looked down whenever he began to talk about his emotionally charged relationship with his former wife, Naomi. His voice became somewhat flat, and I had the sense that he was no longer with me. I was especially struck by it because it was in sharp contrast to his more customary posture of look-ing at me and leaning forward as he spoke. Once, I asked him what his sense of connection with me was as he talked about Naomi. "I didn't have a sense of you just then. I was pretty much off the air, actually. I guess I'm still not very able to stand the pain." This gave us an oppor-tunity to acknowledge our more frequent sense of connection and how its absence gave us information about what was happening for him.

Solitude and Aloneness

Being able to be alone is another aspect of this kind of wisdom. One of the benefits of meditation practice is making friends with oneself, by oneself. Being able to experience aloneness is important in being able to connect genuinely with others. Without it, it is all too easy to fall into unhealthy, overly dependent relationships. An appreciation of solitude can thus be a reflection of the competency to engage in and cultivate relationships. Loneliness, on the other hand, may be a rejection of aloneness, yet it too is a reflection of the desire to be in relationship.

Experiencing Exchange

As we have seen in Chapter 4, exchange is an aspect of our con-nection with others. In recognizing this competency in clients, I listen for their experiences of exchange. I may explain what exchange is when it becomes apparent that such clarification would be helpful. It can be especially useful to clients in understanding the emotional climates in which they may have grown up. Clients may then see that exchange is a sign of their brilliant sanity and not the reflection of something wrong with them, as some of them may have concluded.

Donald grew up with a depressed mother who could barely make it through the day. One aspect of his childhood was exchanging with her feelings of hopelessness and sadness. Donald now struggles with depression himself. Of course, we can point to a number of factors that may contribute to his depression, including what he may have learned about becoming lost in negative thinking, a possible biological predisposition, and the pathways that may have been formed in his brain; but another strong factor could be his exposure over many years to the experience of depression through exchange with his mother. Donald picks up easily on the emotions of others in his current life as well, and he fears it is evidence of something missing or broken in him. He was relieved to hear of the idea of exchange, and we worked with how he could deal with his talent for so readily exchanging with others, including how it could even be an asset.

Recognizing Distorted and Confused Expressions of the Fourth Competency

When discrimination is inappropriately applied and when the longing for connection is misdirected, they can cover up the wisdom of the fourth competency.

Pickiness

A distortion of discriminating awareness is being overly picky or fastidious. Wanting things to be exactly how one wants them can reflect the desire to avoid change—as we saw in the animal realm associated with the first competency. It can also be an attempt to hold on to a fixed view of oneself or reality. I exemplify this particular distortion whenever I order a club sandwich, a dish that is usually served as a triple-decker. I want the bacon to be extra crisp, but not burned; I want the bread to be rye or whole wheat but not plain white; I want it to be toasted, but not too much; I want the middle piece of bread to be left out; and I want mayonnaise but only just so much. The problem with this misplaced precision is that it is all about controlling and maintaining reality exactly the way I want it without being open to the novelty available in the present moment.

Perfectionism

Discriminating awareness may be distorted beyond usually harmless pickiness into perfectionism. Many of my artist clients struggle with this problem. It often leads to procrastination, followed by self-recrimination about the art, music, or writing that they have failed to create. Not being able to begin or to complete these creative projects often is an expression of discernment that is being held hostage to the desire to be a person who produces such perfection. In other words, instead of letting one's natural wisdom manifest as creative discriminating awareness in the service of one's art, it gets turned into self-criticism and dissatisfaction with oneself. We can listen for their discriminating awareness when our clients become stuck in this pattern.

Hanging On to Dysfunctional or Dangerous Relationships

As we have already noted, codependent relationships contain both confusion and genuine compassion and connection. Other relationships that our clients are engaged in may show other kinds of dysfunction.

Some clients may have grown up in families where no one was allowed to talk about their feelings, or they may be members of such families now. Often these clients do not know how they feel or have a very limited range of allowed emotions. It is common for many men to grow up being allowed to show anger but not softer feelings like sadness or tenderness. Women, on the other hand, may be permitted to express sadness but not anger. Sometimes these clients long to engage in genuine, open relationships but feel that they do not know how to go about it.

Similarly, clients may be in relationships in which genuine communication is minimal. They may fear being dismissed or humiliated if they were to open up. I have worked with many men and women who were told growing up that they were "too sensitive" or that they were "making a big deal over nothing." Their fears of expressing emotions may be well founded, reflecting some clarity, while at the same time their longing for communication reveals the fourth competency.

Other clients stay in relationships in which they experience either physical or sexual abuse. Their longing for connection keeps them in such relationships despite what may be quite dangerous circumstances. Even the perpetrators of such abuse may fear losing connection. Listening for clients' desires for connection, even when they are deeply buried within such relationships, can help us see their brilliant sanity.

Some people stay in abusive relationships out of misguided compassion. They may very well feel love for their partners and hope to relieve their suffering. Others stay because they fear the consequences for their children if they leave their breadwinning partners. As therapists, we need to hear and reflect not only the obvious danger and dysfunction but also the confused compassion and clarity.

Fear of Intimacy

Many of my clients both long for and fear intimacy. Clients who enter relationships with a person who is not really available may be expressing this particular ambivalence. This dynamic may also be at work in codependency. Ginny's marriage provided her with a sense of security and identity, but there was little intimacy in it. She and her partner, Chuck, had stopped having a sexual relationship years ago, and she more recently developed a crush on her massage therapist, Jason. It was especially confusing to her because Jason often complimented her and seemed to regard her as special. The physical contact of massage further complicated the situation. She thought of him longingly and imagined scenarios in which she and Jason could be together. At some point Jason mentioned his own partner, and Ginny realized that she had created a fantasy relationship with yet another man who was not actually available to her. She felt rejected and hurt.

As we explored her relationships with both Chuck and Jason, Ginny began to see how she was blaming the men for not being available for intimacy when, in reality, she too was not really available. As she imagined being fully present sexually and emotionally with either her husband or with Jason, she realized how frightened she was of being so vulnerable. When she looked back, she was embarrassed to realize that she had been the one to pull away from sex with her husband. She had complained about how he touched her and was frequently "too tired" to engage with him. She wondered now if he had felt rejected and had given up. Perhaps he, too, was uncomfortable with intimacy? At the same time, she genuinely longed for the closeness that she had helped to short-circuit. She decided to invite Chuck to join her in couples therapy to see if they could kindle a genuinely intimate relationship.

Desire for Intimacy Confused by Having Experienced Sexual Abuse

Many clients have suffered sexual abuse in childhood, perpetrated by one of their parents or caretakers. As they work with the current effects of their past abuse, many of my clients have been especially confused and distressed to recognize that their natural desire for affection and connection was at play as well. Their abusers may have actually felt warmth toward them, and these clients can see that. Sometimes it was the only parental affection they received. They may have yearned for this warmth and attention while also being terrified and hurt by the inappropriate, painful, and sometimes dangerous sexual contact. They may wonder if they invited the abuse through their need for affection. Was there something wrong with them? Was it their fault?

This is a difficult topic for many clients and their therapists to negotiate. What I want to point out here is that clients' natural, brilliantly sane longing for connection needs to be recognized by therapists and perhaps pointed out to clients directly. Helping clients to tease apart the confused tangle of emotions they may still carry about their experiences of abuse requires discriminating awareness as well as compassion for their own suffering.

The Padma Dance

The Buddhist name of this competency is Padma, "lotus" in Sanskrit (Trungpa, 1987). Contemplative psychotherapists sometimes call a particular pattern the Padma dance. For example, one person (let's call him Rob), pursues another person (let's call her Amy). He chases Amy, showering her with attention: texts, e-mails, phone calls, gifts, compliments. Won't she please be his partner? He will give her anything she wants. In response to this outpouring, Amy feels overwhelmed and pulls back. The more she draws away from him, the more Rob pursues her. Finally, Amy, who has been hesitant to become involved, lets Rob catch her. They enjoy fabulous sex for a week or so. Amy feels joyful and happy.

Then Rob stops being so attentive. Over a few days or weeks, he pulls away from Amy. She becomes distraught and feels abandoned. She pursues him, taking the role of showering him with attention while he continues to be unavailable. Finally, he becomes interested again. They connect for a short while, and Rob feels happy and believes that he has at last found his one true love.

Then Amy pulls away, and the dance continues. With brief exceptions, often characterized by passionate sexual contact enhanced by alcohol, the distance between these two dance partners remains fairly constant. In the surprisingly common Padma dance, the longing for connection and the fear of genuine intimacy is acted out again and again.

ACTING SKILLFULLY AND LETTING GO: THE FIFTH COMPETENCY

The fifth competency is about being able to act in the world and also about being able to recognize when it is time to let go and then actually to do so. In order to act skillfully, all of the competencies are brought into play. One needs to be able to be sufficiently present and able to let things be as they are (first competency) in order to see clearly (second competency) what needs to be done. Recognizing and appreciating resources (third competency) and the ability to relate to others as well as discerning what needs to be done and what does not (fourth competency) are also usually involved in taking actions that benefit oneself and others. Moving from the first four competencies into the fifth involves actually doing, and no longer just seeing or contemplating what needs to be done.

Efficiency

Being able to efficiently perform the actions of beginning, following through, and completing tasks in an orderly way, while making good use of one's time, is one way in which the fifth competency is expressed.

When I think of this competency, I sometimes think of watching a server at a breakfast café I used to go to. Judy seemed to effortlessly keep track of everyone's orders without writing anything down, provide coffee refills just as patrons were ready for them, pick up orders as soon as the cook placed them on the counter, and supply the check when it was needed but not before. She did all these things while keeping up a lively conversation with everyone. It was like watching a dance. She never rushed, yet everything got done.

My client Marcia was an administrator for a large university. One of the ways that she manifested this competency was in her skillful delegation of work to her staff. Drawing upon the other competencies, she could hold in mind all that needed to be accomplished; she could clearly prioritize what needed to happen and in what order; she could identify the human and material resources available to her; she could discern who was the best person to complete each task; and she had the interpersonal skill to communicate to her staff members what she needed them to do. Marcia herself did not do many of the things that needed doing, but she saw that they got done.

Discipline

One way to understand disciplined action is as the ability to do what needs to be done and to refrain from what does not need to be done. It is discriminating awareness that lets us see which is which, but it is the fifth competency that actually takes the next steps.

Sometimes skillful action means not doing something. For many clients who struggle with addictions, being able not to act on the impulse to indulge their cravings is a noteworthy expression of this competency. Gloria was a recovering alcoholic. She had been sober for many years and yet the craving to drink continued to arise. She exercised discipline in choosing to avoid places where alcohol was served, especially when she was feeling stressed by other things in her life. When things were going well, she knew she could handle the temptation that having alcohol around presented, but she had learned that there were times when it was too difficult to be around others who were drinking. When her mother was ill and dying, for example, she knew she had to be especially careful not to put herself in the way of temptation. I recognized this as an expression of her brilliant sanity and showed interest not only in the craving but also in her ability to tolerate it without taking action.

Setting and Holding Boundaries

Closely related to this kind of discipline is the ability to set and hold appropriate boundaries. Once again, it is discriminating awareness that brings us the understanding of what boundaries to set and when we need to set them, but actually setting them and holding them is the work of the fifth competency.

Many of the clients I work with who have experienced sexual or physical abuse in childhood have made decisions to set boundaries with family members. Janine chose to cut off contact with her abusive father and also with other family members who denied that the abuse had ever occurred. It was painful for her to make that decision and also difficult to hold it. Her sister, in particular, kept trying to reach her and criticize her choice as selfish and immature. Janine took practical steps like changing her phone numbers and cutting off her sister's access to her through social media. She felt many painful emotions including fear, guilt, and anger. Moreover, Janine's hope that her mother would finally become nurturing and protective continued to arise despite Janine's intellectual certainty that her mother was extremely unlikely to become now what she had never been before. Janine felt heartbroken as she recognized and acted on this knowledge. It involved not only holding the boundaries she had established but also letting go of her wish that things might be different.

Over time, Janine chose to change the boundaries. As she worked through her trauma history, she became ready to communicate first with her mother, then her sister, and finally with her father. She set new boundaries about how and when she would communicate with them. This ability to set and also to appropriately change the boundaries was an expression of her skillful action.

Creative Accomplishment

The fifth competency is also expressed through creative endeavors such as playing a musical instrument, painting, writing, and other arts. Similarly, it applies to any occupation that requires a beginning idea or vision, doing the actual work of following through, and then reaching completion.

One of my clients, Rebecca, is a writer. She spends a great deal of time, months and sometimes years, working and reworking her prose. It requires that she be disciplined in finding time to write and then sitting down with her notebook or at her computer even when she does not feel inspired. Then, even after she has completed a manuscript, she has the further work of presenting it to others who will take it to market. Working with her agent, editor, and publishers, among others, is all part of the task of getting her book into the hands of readers.

Finally, letting go of one's project, allowing it to be finished, is the last step in creative accomplishment. In Rebecca's case, it means that at some point she stops reworking and tinkering with it: no more corrections, no more edits. Actually, she finds this one of the most challenging aspects of her work. She knows it can always be improved, and yet she knows she also has to let it go.

Cutting and Pruning

Eliminating what is not needed is also an expression of the fifth competency and a reflection of brilliant sanity. A big part of writing is taking out what does not work. I am doing that over and over as I write these words right now. I have noticed that it is often more difficult to let go of phrases that I personally like even though my editors over the years have been gentle and clear about why such phrases may need to go. For example, I was quite attached to a title I had come up with for an article some years ago, but it was pointed out to me that it would not mean anything to anyone else. After a bout of internal resistance, I let it go.

A metaphor associated with this competency is pruning plants. A skilled gardener knows when to cut plants back, removing the portions that are retarding the healthy growth of the plant.

Our clients, too, may recognize that they need to let go of certain habits or activities so that their health can flourish. For example, Ellie showed this kind of wisdom when she chose to give up her beloved, but stressful, mental health job working with acting-out adolescents at the suggestion of her doctor when she was having difficulty becoming pregnant.

Clients who recognize and give up addictive behaviors are also showing this kind of wisdom. For many of them, giving up smoking or drinking is not only difficult because of its addictive nature, it is also hard because it feels like letting go of one's most familiar and always available companion.

Forgiveness

A special case of letting go is being willing to forgive. I have been very touched by clients who have been able to let go of their resentment and anger toward others who have harmed them. We saw above how Janine was able to change the boundaries she needed in dealing with her family. Her father, toward whom she had felt deep anger, became increasingly fragile and demented as he aged. Until that time, she had opened communication with him only in writing. She had attended one family event where he was present, but had not spoken with him. Janine found that she wanted to see him one final time. She was not sure yet if she would speak with him.

She told me about seeing him in hospice care and how she recognized that he was no longer the same man who had hurt her. As she told me, she began to feel a softening and a letting go. She identified that what she was feeling was a sense of forgiveness.[2] This did not mean that she in any way condoned what her father had done, but she realized that her anger had dissolved and that she was willing to release both of them from its pain and heat.

Playfulness

Being playful and engaging in delightful activities are other ways that the wisdom of the fifth competency can manifest. I sometimes tell my students that I believe that "rampant earnestness" is one of the world's biggest dangers. The opposite of playfulness, taking everything seriously, is usually a reflection of holding tightly to a fixed version of oneself or the world. Being able to see oneself with some humor or not to take oneself so seriously can open things up—as we saw in the first competency.

Playfulness does not mean ignoring the real and important issues that require compassionate attention. Rather, it means that we can relax, take a break, and play. I am always interested in what kinds of recreation my clients engage in. Often they provide a useful resource for them as well as a way for us to connect in the moment.

Polly loved to hike and mountain climb. She went on a trip with her parents to a national park where they could all hike together. Their relationships had never been easy, yet she was curious to see if the work she had been doing in therapy and elsewhere would let her be less tense and judgmental with them. When she returned from the trip, she showed me photos of herself and her parents. They were taking silly poses and smiling. I asked about what the photos showed, and she proudly reported that they had been able to play together. It had been a relief to all of them.

Richard likes to swim. Usually, he swims inside at a gym, but he loves most to swim in the sea. He told me that he taps into a sense of childlike delight when he can wiggle his toes in the sand and surf the waves. In those moments, he experiences the brilliant sanity of letting go and being fully present.

In a session when he was experiencing difficult emotions, he was able to moderate the intensity of what he was feeling by using the memory of his toes in the sand and the sensation of clean water pouring over his skin as a mental resource. As we worked, he went back and forth between the present pain and the happy memories. This gave him a way to be more present and explore the pain without having to shut down. Instead, he could mindfully choose to leave the present moment until he was ready to return again. Recalling a memory in that way also supported his sense that he was not permanently stuck in pain, but that he did also feel happy at other times.

Confused and Distorted Expressions of Skillful Action and Letting Go

When the energy that could go into skillful action and letting go becomes confused, clients may be just as busy as they would be if they were actually accomplishing something. Their activity may be physical or mental, but it does not lead to a beneficial outcome for themselves or for others.

Mindless Activity

Playing video games, working crossword puzzles, jogging while listening to music, becoming lost in fiction, drinking alcohol, and an unlimited number of other things may be activities in which we engage mindlessly. Body and mind may be desynchronized: the body is running down the path while the mind is listening to a recorded talk by Pema Chödrön about how to be mindful.

None of these activities are necessarily mindless in themselves. What makes them mindless is the state of mind that they produce. We lose track of the present moment and tend to speed up. Alternatively, we become spaced out or lost in thought. I look more closely in Chapter 7 at how mindlessness can be harnessed to cultivate mindfulness. Here let us notice that when our clients fall into mindlessness, either out of habit or in an attempt to avoid a painful experience in the present, they are revealing a distorted version of the fifth competency. They are able to do things, but they are not able to maintain awareness while they are doing them.

Busyness and Multitasking

It is sadly common these days for clients to feel overwhelmed with being busy. It seems to me that we have lost the in-between time that I enjoyed growing up in the mid-twentieth century. Mail correspondence took longer and a reply might not appear for a week even if the other person responded promptly. There was no assumption that we would hear a response to our missives the same day or the same hour. What we used to think of as a long-distance phone call was reserved for only the most crucial things.

Now, things are different. With texting, smartphones, e-mail, social media, and who knows what else in the next few years, it is not only possible, but often expected, that we will hear back from others very quickly. We may even feel slighted if we do not receive instant acknowledgment of our attempts to make contact.

As a result, clients are often quite busy. There is a constant flow of communication, much of it lacking in importance. However, clients still need to look to see if something rises to the threshold of requiring attention. We, too, may be caught up in this painful flurry of activity.

Or clients are multitasking: checking e-mails while working on something else on the computer, looking at their smartphones instead of talking to the person across from them, or talking on their cell phones while driving. Their attention is interrupted again and again as they try to do more than one thing at a time. This usually leads to not doing things well or feeling stressed and burdened. We can, perhaps, help them to turn their available energies into useful activities that lead to a sense of satisfaction and confidence instead of feeling that nothing is ever quite adequately finished.

Melanie described to me how she had a long list of things to do, all of which seemed essential or desirable. She often arrived late and breathless to our sessions. Occasionally, she canceled at the last minute. When a close family member became ill, she dropped all unnecessary activity in order to care for him. The seemingly essential things proved to be less urgent than they had appeared before. She reported that it was something of a shock to realize how overscheduled she had made herself and how little pleasure she had taken from even the things she thought she would enjoy. When the crisis passed, she noticed how tempted she was to fill her time again. We were then able to turn our attention to prioritizing how she truly wanted to use her time, and we became curious together about what arose when she refrained from being overly busy.

Of course, not all clients have a choice. Some report that between their responsibilities at work and at home, they feel overwhelmed. In such cases, we may still recognize that their ability to manage as well as they do is a reflection of their ability to act skillfully.

Inability to Complete or Finish Things

Having difficulty finishing what one starts is another distorted way in which the fifth competency appears. There may be many reasons why this might occur, including the perfectionism we looked at in the fourth competency. Failing to prioritize, organize one's materials, or usefully schedule one's time may be involved. Or clients may have a hard time letting go, like Rebecca, who wanted to keep editing her writing. Another factor at play may be the hesitation to let go of one's identity as the performer of a particular activity.

Hank had enjoyed being the head of a faculty search committee. It had been hard work, but he was proud of how well he had performed it. The committee had already brought in wonderful candidates for interviews, but Hank, alone among the committee's members, wanted to bring in a few more. He found himself reluctant to let go of his role. As we explored it, he realized that the position had carried a certain amount of power and prestige. Returning to the relative anonymity of his usual role was a blow to the new identity he had enjoyed.

Worrying and Obsessing

Instead of being able to act, some clients become busy in their minds, and this is also a distortion of the fifth competency. Running the same thoughts over and over in one's mind or obsessing about something reflects the same qualities of speed and mindlessness as other distorted forms of this competency.

Peter broke up with his long-term girlfriend, Merry, after he discovered that she had been seeing another man without telling him. Over and over, he returned to imagining Merry and her new lover together. He spun stories about how happy they were and how he would be alone forever. He worried over memories from his time with Merry and tried to identify exactly when things had begun to go wrong. He easily fell into self-aggression, blaming himself for not being a better partner. Although he was already suffering, he shied away from directly feeling sadness and anger. He was every bit as busy as if he were actually doing something physically.

Recognizing that all this mental activity was a misuse of the fifth competency, I invited Peter to find ways to ground himself in the present moment by becoming more active physically. Sports that required his full attention, like mountain biking on dirt trails and getting into a pickup basketball game at the gym, brought some respite from his misery-making mind. We also worked in our sessions with bringing mindfulness to his body and to gradually touching into the emotions that arose when he settled physically.

Self-Doubt and Paranoia

Finally, the experience of self-doubt or paranoia is a distortion of the fifth competency (Trungpa, 1987). The same kind of mental activity that occurs with worry and obsession can readily become thoughts of doubting oneself or distrusting others. Peter's self-aggression took the form of self-doubt as well. He turned his doubts about himself into a solid conviction that he was basically unlovable. This conviction was maintained with still more negative thoughts. Peter felt some relief in escaping from the uncertainty of not knowing exactly why Merry had sought out a new lover now that he had come up with his own shortcomings as the reason, but his new fixed sense of self came at a high price. Helping him to return to uncertainty and not knowing was a path toward recognizing that he was a decent person and maybe even lovable.

When these same kinds of beliefs are turned outward, they become a sort of paranoia. Expecting the worst from others provides a distorted sense of certainty, and it, too, is the fifth competency

other words, they help us to become more mindful and aware, more in touch with natural wisdom and compassion. "Negative" refers to actions that increase suffering or add to confusion about our nature, promoting a mistaken sense of self as fixed and permanent. "Actions" may be overt behaviors or they may be our inner thoughts and emotions, since they lead to outer actions in the world. Thich Nhat Hanh (1992a, p. 97) uses the expression "planting good seeds" to describe how we can help our clients by understanding this phenomenon.

How Seeds Are Planted

According to Buddhist psychology, whenever we engage in any action, seeds are planted in the aspect of mind known as the storehouse consciousness (Sanskrit, *alaya-vijñana*; Hanh, 1992a). It is like planting seeds in the soil, hidden from our view. The right causes and conditions can be thought of as the sunlight and water that nurture those seeds and cause them to grow and become experienced in consciousness. These causes and conditions are circumstances, or even details, similar to the ones present when particular seeds were originally planted. Therapists commonly call such things triggers.

In other words, whatever we experience sows the seeds of our experiencing it again, or something very similar to it. The more times we plant the same sorts of seeds, the more likely we are to experience the same states of mind and body. As we continue to experience the circumstances that trigger these seeds to sprout, those sorts of experiences will continue to arise in us. If we react to the new experiences in the same way we did in the past, we will replant similar seeds. If, however, we meet these experiences with mindfulness and openness, we can plant different seeds: the seeds of mindfulness and openness. Still, there are likely to be many similar seeds in the storehouse consciousness that may become activated and arise into awareness because we will have been replanting them for a while.

It can be very helpful to clients to have this explained to them, especially when they find themselves experiencing old feelings that they thought they had already taken care of. The appearance of such old feelings is not a sign that clients have not properly dealt with them. It is just that not all of the seeds have been used up. It can take quite awhile before all the seeds are exhausted. This is another reason why being able to bring mindfulness to whatever arises in the moment is so important.

I explained this metaphor to one client who found it so comforting that she asked me to tell it to her again each time she came to see me for a few weeks. "Tell me again about the seeds!" she would say. What she found in the metaphor was reassurance that simply experiencing familiar painful feelings was not evidence that she was bad or doing things wrong. The idea of cause and effect softened, and sometimes even eliminated, the sense of guilt and self-blame she had been perpetuating.

This ancient system of thought is notably similar to what we have learned about how the brain works in creating new neural pathways. It is saying much the same thing as "Neurons that fire together, wire together" (Hebb, 1949, cited in Hanson with Mendius, 2009, p. 5).

As Thich Nhat Hanh (1992a) describes it, we can purposely plant positive seeds, for example, of peace and happiness. He suggests that we can practice smiling as a way to plant good seeds. And perhaps most importantly, we can practice mindfulness and kindness toward ourselves. Similarly, we can refrain, as much as possible, from planting negative seeds by not cultivating negative states of mind and body.

Trauma and Planting Negative Seeds

This understanding has special significance for our work with survivors of abuse and other kinds of trauma. When a person experiences trauma, many seeds are planted in the storehouse consciousness. Circumstances and details that seem similar to the original situation can easily lead to the arising of sensations, emotions, thoughts, or images like the original trauma. These, in turn, plant further seeds of similar suffering. Therapists are familiar with this as the idea of retraumatization.

Methods of working with trauma that invite clients to reexperience their trauma, without adding any new seeds, will keep the cycle of planting and replanting going.

Instead, contemplative therapists work with their clients to plant something new and beneficial. For example, by bringing mindfulness to their somatic experience while telling their story, clients can plant mindfulness along with the seeds of whatever else they might experience in the telling. They are less likely to activate their sympathetic nervous systems as they did during the original traumatic experiences. By being in relationship with their therapists, clients also may be planting a sense of relative safety, warmth, and confidence.

Thich Nhat Hahn (1992) suggests that we do not need to bring everything into awareness; sometimes, he says, the good seeds in the storehouse consciousness can take care of the bad ones without our having to process everything.

This may be what happened for Pamela, with whom I worked over a period of years. She had come into therapy with no clear memories of having been abused, though she had a good deal of other evidence that she had been. Her father was known to have sexually abused other children in the family; she was fearful and revolted by sex; she was very uncomfortable being watched by others in any situation; she was unable to access her feelings; and she often turned to alcohol to numb herself out. Sometimes she was quite dissociated, and the rest of the time she was barely in touch with any of her bodily sensations. We worked together to gradually bring mindfulness to her direct experience of her sensations and perceptions, working also with her potential mindfulness practices (discussed further below). Over time, she began to feel her emotions and became more grounded in her body. Even though she discovered a good deal of anger and fear toward her father, she never did recover any specific memories of abuse. However, she became able to enjoy sex with her husband and felt more present and content in her life altogether.

Helping to Plant Good Seeds

Like other therapists, contemplative psychotherapists draw on models that are specifically designed for working with trauma and that are less likely to retraumatize their clients. I especially like the Trauma Resiliency Model (TRM) because it combines somatic awareness and mindfulness with a gradual and gentle approach. Moreover, it teaches basic skills that clients can use on their own.

Let us look at an example drawn from my work with Emily, in which I used elements of both the TRM model and my earlier Gestalt training as a way of helping her to plant beneficial seeds. Needless to say, this is not meant to be a full presentation of either Gestalt or TRM.

Emily had come into therapy having identified some issues she wanted to work with, none of which were obviously abuse related. Only after she felt some comfort and trust in our relationship did she begin to talk about a time when she had been badly beaten by a former partner some years earlier. She felt a good deal of shame that it had happened and told me that she had never talked to anyone about it in detail. She was scared to explore it and tended to become numb when she remembered it. I explained to Emily that I wanted to work with this painful memory in a way that felt supportive and that did not just make the situation worse. I was concerned that simply telling me the story of the abuse would be planting still more negative seeds and would not only not change anything but would also make it more likely that she would need to shut down even further to keep the memory at bay.

We began by working with cultivating skills that are basic to many trauma-related approaches and that plant good seeds: grounding and resourcing (Leitch & Miller-Karas, 2010). I asked Emily to take a comfortable seat and to turn her attention to what she noticed inside as she felt her feet on the floor and her back against the sofa on which she was sitting. She reported a tight place in her belly and a shaky feeling around her heart area. She took a few minutes feeling into that.

Then I asked her to think of a real or imaginary place, person, or occasion that she found pleasant and good. After a little while, Emily described a time when she was on a ski lift. I asked her to fill in some more details of this resource, and she described the cold wind on her face, the spacious and vividly blue Colorado sky, and her sense of feeling relaxed and excited as she anticipated skiing down the mountain. I invited her to notice what was going on inside her body as she imagined being on the ski lift. She reported that her belly had relaxed a bit and the shaky feeling was gone. Now she felt "kind of grounded" even though she was "up in the air on the lift." As I watched, I noted signs that she was no longer feeling activated and that her parasympathetic system seemed to be calming her down: her breathing, which had been somewhat shallow, had deepened; she was no longer feeling shaky; and she had started to yawn. Enhancing the resource memory with more details was a way to plant still more good seeds in her storehouse consciousness.

Based on those signs and her own report of feeling more relaxed, I invited her to remember a little bit about the assault. I suggested that she just touch into it gently and then return to the resource of being on the ski lift. Working back and forth between the memory of being assaulted and the resource of the ski lift, in the context of our relationship, Emily was able to tap into feeling more in control and empowered.

In another session, drawing on the Gestalt approach, I invited her to have a conversation with the man who had beaten her. Again, she tracked her inner experience as she expressed her anger and fear to him. We continued to work with alternating between the negative emotions that arose and the relative safety of her resources. Over time, she identified other traumatic memories as well as other resources, and she practiced grounding and resourcing as homework between sessions.

Using these techniques helped Emily to plant seeds of mindfulness, curiosity, confidence, and maitri. As we have noted, memories and negative emotions still arose from seeds in the storehouse consciousness. Now, though, instead of pushing them away and replanting not only the seeds of fear and helplessness but also the seeds of mindless ignoring, she felt more able to stay present and join those difficult experiences with mindfulness and maitri. She was on her way toward using them up, exhausting them.

CULTIVATING MINDFULNESS AND AWARENESS WITH THE FOUR FOUNDATIONS OF MINDFULNESS

Drawing on some early teachings of the Buddha, contemplative psychotherapists make use of the four foundations of mindfulness to help their clients cultivate mindfulness and awareness. The four foundations are just what their name suggests: four aspects of experience that can be foundations for sowing the seeds of mindfulness. All four of these foundations are already present in our experience; all we need to do is to pay attention to what is already happening.

Different Buddhist traditions present these basic teachings in different ways. One well-known way identifies the four objects of mindfulness as the experiences of body, feelings, thoughts and emotions, and mind (Epstein, 1998). Since we have already noted these bases of mindfulness in previous chapters, let us look at another approach to the four foundations here, one I have found to be especially relevant for psychotherapists. This one is drawn from the Tibetan oral tradition as presented by Chögyam Trungpa. As Trungpa (2005) presents them, the four foundations are mindfulness of body, life, effort, and mind.

Mindfulness of Body

Mindfulness of body invites us to pay attention to the sensations of the body, including our breathing. In presenting mindfulness of body, the Buddha said that "a practitioner remains established in the observation of the body in the body" (Hanh, 1990, p. 3). Cynthia, the swimmer who noticed the difference between "just swimming" and "driving herself" in preparing for competitions, noticed another difference as we worked with bringing mindfulness to her sensations and her breathing. Somewhat surprisingly to me, she pointed out the difference she felt between "noticing from the inside," as I had suggested she do during one session, and the sense of experiencing her body somehow "from the outside" that she felt in competitive swimming. This was another useful reference point we returned to again and again. Noticing from the inside was noticing "the body in the body."

Body-Body and Psychosomatic Body

Trungpa (2005) identifies another distinction between the experience of the body in the body, which he refers to as body-body, and what he calls psychosomatic body. Body-body is an enlightened person's sense of body and is free from any conceptualizations or projections. Psychosomatic body, in contrast, is our thoughts, concepts, and fantasies about the body, and it can be quite subtle. In body-body there is no sense of a separate self experiencing the body. Instead of watching ourselves, we are fully embodied.

While neither contemplative psychotherapists nor their clients are likely to be fully enlightened beings, the difference between experiencing our bodies realistically and merely conceptually can be a useful one to make. An extreme version of the difference is seen in clients struggling with eating disorders. Clients suffering from anorexia who starve themselves in a quest to be thin enough and others who binge and purge or abuse exercise often have very distorted senses of their bodies. They rarely experience their bodies as the Buddha suggested: as the body in the body. To the extent that we can invite these clients to bring mindfulness to aspects of their somatic experience, we may be able to help them to become more realistic about their bodies.

When I first began working as a counselor, I worked with Marjorie, who struggled with bulimia. It was in the late 1970s, and I had never heard of eating disorders. I was astonished at the behavior she described to me, and my colleagues at the time were equally bewildered by it. I suppose there was one advantage to my ignorance: I had no preconceptions. My client knew no one else, either, who indulged in eating and then throwing up.

Together we simply brought curiosity to her experience. When did she feel like bingeing? Did she feel hunger? Where in her body did she feel it? Or did she not feel it? What was her experience in the moments when she ate her way through bags of marshmallows and pints of ice cream? Did she taste the food? How did she feel after she binged? What was going on before she would make herself throw up? And then how did she feel? How often did this happen? It became apparent that she was not very present at all when she binged, and she was not in touch with any sense of hunger. She was, however, able to track her experience afterward. She felt a burning pain in her throat and a tightness in her belly. Emotionally, she felt shame and revulsion once she binged. Then she would feel fear, though she could not say of what, exactly.

It soon became apparent that the cycle of binging and purging was tied closely to her difficult relationship with her boyfriend, Phil. It took longer for her to reveal to me that he often hit her than it had to tell me about her eating behavior. She did not tell me until one day she arrived for our session with a black eye and her injured wrist in a cast. In that session she described how she had begun to binge the moment her boyfriend left the house after beating her up. She felt both comforted and revolted by her behavior, and the revulsion led her to throw up. It was also a way to keep secret from her boyfriend that she had been bad by indulging in overeating. He insisted, she told me, that she remain slender and attractive. She identified that she was afraid he would hurt her more if she gained weight or if he knew about her eating behavior.

I invited Marjorie to notice how she felt when she was with Phil. How much of the time was she happy? How often was she frightened? Based in part on the work we had already done bringing mindfulness to her sensations and emotions after bingeing, she was able to track her experience at home with Phil. She reported that she only rarely was happy when she was with him. This let us begin to explore what kept her in the relationship and whether she wanted to continue in it.

We may also want to bring curiosity about how brilliant sanity may underlie eating disorders. Some who suffer from sexual and physical abuse take control of their bodies as a way of exerting control somewhere. Of course, not all people with eating disorders are abuse survivors.

Seeking the Psychosomatic Body Beautiful

Both men and women are exposed to strong cultural pressures to look certain ways. Sadly, there is much prejudice against people who are obese or unattractive. Research has shown that teachers, employers, and voters have a bias toward physically attractive people (Shahani-Denning, 2003). Overweight children are often bullied; the beauty products industry is booming.

I see many clients who unquestioningly expend a good deal of money and time on their physical appearance. Some opt for painful facial treatments and even plastic surgery. How much do they experience their bodies from the inside? Often a good deal of self-aggression underlies their quest for beauty. Working with clients to bring mindfulness and, most importantly, maitri to their experience of their bodies is often an important part of our work together.

Mindfulness of the Aging Body

Another aspect of mindfulness of body comes up with clients as they age. Being able to accept how we look and how our bodies behave as we grow older is an important part of therapy. To do that, we need to cultivate mindfulness of body. We cannot make friends with how we look now, the ailments we may have now, and with what we may no longer be able to do if we do not first bring mindfulness to body and sensations.

One of my clients, Bert, a man in his mid-70s, struggled with his diminished capacity to do the heavy gardening work he had enjoyed for most of his life. He knew he could afford to hire someone else to do the lifting and digging that were now causing him neck and back pain, but accepting the meaning of his declining abilities was more of a challenge. Losing his sense of himself as a strong man who could do physical labor without help was a blow to his notion of who he was. Moreover, for Bert, these changes were harbingers of death. One way we worked with his situation was by bringing mindfulness to his experience of psychosomatic body. That is, we worked not so much to change his experience as to notice it and bring mindfulness to it as it was. As it happened, this did lead to his noticing his direct experience more and to acknowledging the fear he had about dying, but it was important not to become aggressive about pushing for some specific experience. In this way, he planted more seeds of mindfulness, self-compassion, and curiosity.

Mindfulness of Breathing

One other way that mindfulness of body enters therapy is through the use of the breath as a grounding technique. Sometimes I invite clients to take a few deep breaths and to arrive in the room. Often, I do this when clients have just arrived and are especially speedy. Many clients find breathing into their bellies a useful way to ground themselves in the present moment.

I have become somewhat careful about using this technique for a few reasons. First, a client may hear it as a request to stop feeling the way he or she already does feel. Second, I like to notice how clients are breathing as a clue to what is going on with them, so I often refrain from interfering with it. And finally, I once had an experience with a client in which noticing her breath was actually problematic.

Nastaran was an Afghani woman I worked with at a mental health center that provided services to Asian and Pacific communities in Denver. Her husband had been taken away from their home by Soviet soldiers and had never been seen again. She had no idea what happened to him. Although we struggled to understand each other's language, we made a good connection with each other. From her point of view, the problem was that her arm hurt. She did not show much emotion, generally just smiling at me and waiting for me to ask her questions.

At one point, I invited Nastaran to take a few deep breaths. As soon as she began to do that, she began to hyperventilate and became extremely frightened. Coming into her sense of her body in this way was, in itself, retraumatizing. Clearly, this was not helpful. I invited her just to look at me, and I smiled at her. Then I invited her to notice what she could see and hear in the room. I often invite clients to notice their sense perceptions when asking them to attend to their inner body experiences is either too triggering or just unavailable. Nastaran looked around the room and came back to looking at me. She smiled shyly at me and returned to her usual shallow breathing.

Mindfulness of Life

The second foundation in this version of the four foundations of mindfulness is mindfulness of life. Like the other foundations in this approach, we bring mindfulness to what is already going on, including things that we might otherwise regard as a distraction from becoming mindful. Using mindfulness of body, for example, we might pay attention to psychosomatic body without trying to change it. Here, we bring mindfulness to our tendency to cling to life itself and to preferred states of mind. Often this means bringing attention to experiences of wanting, longing, and fear. The specific practice we apply in the second foundation is touch and go, the same technique we explored in Chapter 3.

Paying Attention to Wanting and Longing

Being alive means that something is always arising. Often, what arises is the desire for things to be different. It might be something minor like wanting a cookie or a cup of coffee; or it might be the longing to be in a meaningful and committed relationship. Maybe we want a new car, a better job, the recognition of our peers, good health. There is no end to the list of things we want.

Every time we get caught up in wanting and longing, we tend to lose track of the present moment. Our thoughts are about the future and how it would be better if only we had X. The second foundation directs us to pay attention to the actual felt experience of wanting or longing. Those desires are happening in the present moment, and we do not need to get rid of them. In fact, they can be very helpful to us in cultivating mindfulness.

My client Sonya, whose boyfriend had recently broken up with her, often felt the longing to be in a committed, romantic relationship, preferably with her ex-boyfriend, Justin. As she talked about this longing, she was likely to dwell on thoughts about the past or fantasies about the future. I invited her to tune in to the experience of longing itself. As Sonya brought her attention to what she was sensing in her body and feeling emotionally, she tuned into the texture of longing in the present. She reported that feeling longing was actually less painful than the busy and nearly obsessive mind states that she tended to generate when she was thinking about Justin. Instead she felt softness and relief. She was able to use longing as an object of mindfulness, which helped her cut through the painful thoughts about Justin.

Although we did not use the words "touch and go," that is what Sonya had done. She had touched the texture of her experience of longing and then she had simply been present for what came next. In this case, it was a sense of relief and softening. A couple sessions later, we had a shared moment of tenderness when she described how she had realized that she had named the longing feeling "Justin," but that it was just the feeling of her own heart and did not really need to be about Justin at all.

Mindfulness of Fear and Anxiety

Being afraid that one is not going to survive or being anxious without a clear sense of what one is afraid of can be brought into the practice of mindfulness with the teachings of the second foundation. Instead of trying to get ourselves to calm down, we can bring our mindfulness to the experiences of fear or anxiety themselves. When we do this, we drop the sense of struggle, and may find the confidence that we can actually work with our minds as they are. As noted earlier, this was an important part of my own introduction to mindfulness practice.

Evan often felt anxious and awkward when he met a woman whom he found attractive. He hoped we could find a way to make those uncomfortable feelings go away and never come back. When I suggested that he go toward those feelings instead of trying to get rid of them, his first reaction was that I had not understood him. I explained that part of what fed his anxiety was trying to push it away. I invited him to experiment with noticing what he experienced in his body and mind when he felt nervous or awkward. Evan tried it out both in our session and then when he met a new woman at work. He reported back that he was able to do it. He did not become comfortable exactly, but he felt like he could show up and be okay.

Katrina was told by her physician that she needed to have open heart surgery. She was understandably quite frightened by the whole idea. Knowing that her heart was not working properly, having her chest cut open, and being under anesthesia were all alarming. She feared that she would not survive the surgery, and even talking about it with me was terrifying.

The suggestion of the second foundation teachings is to recognize that one has already survived to this moment, and to touch and let go of one's thoughts about the future. Beyond making a practical plan for how to take care of her needs postsurgery, the most helpful thing for Katrina would be to come back to the present moment again and again. Sometimes this meant returning to the sensations of fear itself. She would notice her tight belly, her shallow breathing, and her dry mouth. Other times, when she noticed that she was gearing up to indulge her fearful thoughts, she practiced coming back to her hands on the steering wheel of her car, the feeling of the fur of her beloved cat, and her sense perceptions altogether. In both approaches, feeling the fear and tracking her sense perceptions, she was touching into the present moment and cutting her future-oriented thoughts. Kristina found that practicing touch and go with her sense perceptions was more helpful than coming back to her inner experience since the latter was a reminder of the upcoming surgery.

Both Kristina and Evan told me that it was helpful to have a way to practice with their fear. Just knowing they had something they could do was, in itself, useful.

Clinging to Mindfulness Itself

Another application of mindfulness of life has to do with trying to hold onto one's mindfulness. It can be quite tempting to try to perpetuate a particular state of mind, in this case mindfulness itself.

True mindfulness is an open and fluid state of mind. The kind of mindfulness that we try to hang on to, in contrast, is a distortion of mindfulness. It is more like fixation. For example, Kristina found that when she cut through a worrisome thought about her heart surgery by feeling her hands on the steering wheel of her car, she wanted to keep feeling the steering wheel in the hope of preventing any unwanted thoughts from arising. If that could work, it would be great, but that kind of clinging is counterproductive. It requires so much attention that we lose track of the next unfolding moment—certainly not a good idea while driving. Even at home on the sofa with her cat, she really could not keep her mindfulness from slipping away. The present moment is always changing into the next moment, and clinging to any experience is trying to keep the present from becoming the past. It cannot be done. One of my colleagues, Antonio Wood (personal communication, 1982), has even suggested that not letting the present moment die is one cause of depression. Kristina learned to practice both touch and go. Once she returned to the present moment through any of the techniques she employed, she chose to practice letting go by asking out loud, "Now what's coming?" The awareness and curiosity in that question helped her let go and be open.

Mindfulness of Effort

The third foundation is mindfulness of effort. The kind of effort we pay attention to in this foundation is not our usual sense of effort. Most of us usually think of effort as trying hard, exerting ourselves, or even straining to accomplish something difficult. Of course, when we practice mindfulness, we need to exert ourselves, but trying too hard becomes an obstacle to mindfulness. To the extent that we push for results, we short-circuit our ability to be present with the moment as it is.

Instead of this kind of deliberate effort, we practice bringing our attention to the mind's natural tendency to return again and again to the present moment (Trungpa, 2005). Paradoxically, we bring mindfulness to the times when we are suddenly, without any deliberate effort on our part, awake in the here and now.

This is easiest to recognize when we practice formal meditation. We may be lost in thought, rerunning an incident from the day before, and then we just wake up and realize that we are not having a conversation with someone who is not here. We are sitting here on our cushion. It is a very ordinary experience, but we do not usually notice it. It is a key point in meditation and may show us how reliable our minds actually are. When we return in this way, we simply note that we have been gone, and we may use the label "thinking" as further acknowledgment. By the time we add the label, we are often beginning to get caught up again in thinking and leaving the moment. We may even be indulging in self-aggression about having left the present. In any case, the moment of returning is a glimpse of brilliant sanity: without concept or choice, we have simply awakened.

Minding the Gap

In the London Underground, there are signs that tell passengers to "mind the gap." Instead of being careful about the gap between the train and the platform, here we can mind the gaps in the stories we perpetuate.

In our work with clients, there are often moments when they lose track of their stories. They have a gap. Usually, they quickly try to pick up the thread of their stories again and smooth over any awkwardness of not knowing what they were talking about.

In the same way that the first two foundations make use of experiences that we might regard as obstacles to mindfulness, here we bring attention to what we might mistakenly think of as a moment of not being present. Clint had been telling me about his week at work when he forgot what he was talking about. He began to apologize and to struggle to remember what he had been saying. I invited him to notice what he was experiencing right now. "I feel stupid. Awkward. You probably think I'm dumb."

I asked if he could remember exactly what he noticed before he started telling himself he had done something stupid. He took a few moments, and then he said, "Well, I found myself looking at the doohickey on the top of the fountain. What is that anyway, a hummingbird?"

In other words, he had come into the present moment with his sense of sight. He had noticed the hummingbird shape feeding on the metal flower sitting on the small fountain in my office. As we talked about what had happened, we noted the contrast between telling me his workday story and his direct experience of sight. We explored the questions of when was he more present and what felt more familiar. Telling his story was both more familiar and comfortable. "But," he said, "I was less present with you when I was telling it." Clint became curious about how often he had similar moments and whether he usually missed them as he quickly returned to his stories. He decided to track these interruptions in his stories as homework.

For both meditation practitioners and clients, recognizing that the mind does return again and again and again to what is occurring in the present moment can bring a sense of relaxation.

The Abstract Watcher

A technique associated with the third foundation is the cultivation of what Trungpa (2005) has called the abstract watcher. The abstract watcher is simply the function of recognizing that we have been lost in thought. In meditation practice, this is the technique of labeling "thinking." Other terms for the same thing might be "witnessing" or "observing." The main point is that no judgment is attached to catching ourselves. In fact, once we have noticed, we are no longer caught up; we are already back in the present moment. Such moments are often fleeting, so having a way to acknowledge them can be useful.

Clients often seek this kind of nonjudgmental noticing from their therapists. Katrina, for example, often commented to me about how important it was to her that she experienced me as not judging her. One day as she was relating her embarrassment to me about her messing up her checkbook, I asked her what she thought my reaction to what she had told me might be. She said, "Oh, you would probably just say something like, 'Yeah, that kind of thing happens. It's not a big deal.'" We talked about how she had attributed this nonjudgmental response to me and how it had come from her own mind. Working with her projections about what I might think became a useful tool for her. Over time, she was able to own the projection again and ask herself, "Is there a kinder way I could look at this?"

Mindfulness of Mind

Mindfulness of mind, the fourth foundation, has two main aspects. The first has to do with finding a sense of balance and light-handedness (Trungpa, 2005) and the second is attending to the ever-changing flow of moments of nowness.

Not Too Tight, Not Too Loose

As noted in Chapter 2, we are most able to develop mindfulness and awareness when we hold our mind neither too tightly nor too loose. We can help our clients work with this idea of the shifting balance between tightness and looseness. At its heart, this balance is about cultivating gentleness.

Sometimes clients become frustrated when they try to work mindfully with their experience. Sonya, whom we met above, struggled to work with her habit of obsessing about Justin and other men in her life. She would vow to herself that she would not get caught up in still more stories about the past and the future, and then she would find herself doing it again. Often she would judge herself harshly for this lapse. If she made no attempt to tame her wild mind, she would spend many hours each day entertaining these stories. If she tried really hard to keep them at bay, they seemed to rebound even more. What could she do?

We talked about trying to bring awareness to the present moment when she caught herself running her internal stories, but seeing if she could find a gentle way to do it. I asked if she had any ideas about how to do that. One way, which we had already identified, was to notice the longing that underlay these thoughts. Another way, which she came up with, was to say herself, "Okay, then. Where are my feet and where are my toes?" She could ground herself in her body in this way, and for Sonya the whole idea of toes was a bit silly. Coming back to her toes let her lighten up and the "Okay, then" felt friendly.

Recognizing the Uniqueness of Each Moment

Whatever experience or story my clients and I may explore, I am always interested in noting that every moment dissolves and is replaced by whatever arises next. After clients describe an experience, I often ask the brief question, "And now?"

This invites them to notice that something may have already changed and may be recognized. For example, in working with trauma survivors, after they spend some time imagining a resource, they may report that their breathing has slowed down a bit or their belly feels soft now.

When we invite clients to bring their attention to the uniqueness of each moment, it can bring a quality of freshness into their experience. Moreover, it helps them to recognize the impermanence of their thoughts, emotions, and bodily sensations. Both of these approaches can bring the mindfulness and the light-handedness to which all of the four foundations point.

Chapter 7

WORKING WITH CLIENTS' EXISTING AND POTENTIAL MINDFULNESS AND MINDLESSNESS PRACTICES

Many clients already have mindfulness practices when they enter therapy. Most clients, like the rest of us, also have mindlessness practices: methods of distracting themselves from the present moment (Wegela, 2009). In this chapter we begin by looking at how contemplative therapists can draw on clients' existing mindfulness practices in our therapeutic work with them. Along with that, we will explore the question of whether and how therapists should teach their clients how to meditate. Finally, how to make use of mindlessness practices in the service of cultivating mindfulness is presented.

MINDFULNESS PRACTICES

Clients may have formal practices like yoga, prayer, meditation, tai chi, or other martial arts. They may also have what I call informal mindfulness practices: everyday activities that require them to have mindfulness but that we would not usually regard as mindfulness practices per se. For example, they might play a musical instrument or engage in various sports or take care of children. By drawing on what we know about the four foundations of mindfulness, we may be able to help clients turn their already existing activities into opportunities to cultivate mindfulness and awareness.

Formal Mindfulness Practices

Somewhat arbitrarily, I have included only traditional mindfulness practices in this category: meditation, prayer, yoga, ikebana (Japanese flower arranging), and traditional martial arts like aikido, tai chi, karate, and so on. These are practices that clients have learned from a class or that have a spiritual lineage of some sort. Typically, clients practice them in a group setting and may engage in them on their own at home as well. In class, their teachers are usually explicit in talking about the need to be mindful of one's physical and mental experiences in these practices.

When clients have ongoing formal practices, contemplative therapists have the opportunity to draw on what clients already know about mindfulness in working with them in therapy. Daniel, for example, came into therapy to work with feelings of depression. Since I usually ask about clients' formal mindfulness practices in our initial meetings, I knew he had a yoga practice. As part of my interest in identifying how he connected with brilliant sanity, in one of our early sessions I asked him about his experiences doing yoga.

In describing his yoga practice, Daniel noted a contrast between how he usually felt doing yoga and how he felt in the rest of his life. He was calmer and less likely to feel depressed on his yoga mat. I became curious with him about what was different. As we explored his physical and mental experience doing yoga, Daniel said that he could interrupt any thoughts that were not about the particular posture he was working with and bring himself back to the direct experience of holding a pose. When I asked how he felt when he noticed that he was not paying attention to the asana he was holding, he told me that often he gave himself a hard time but not always. Sometimes he could just gently bring himself back without much commentary. Not only was he practicing mindfulness of body and mind, he was also doing a version of touch and go when he gently brought himself back.

In our work together, we explored how he could use what he

knew from yoga to work with the proliferation of negative thoughts that fueled his feelings of depression. I invited him to bring his already well-developed sense of mindfulness to the thoughts that arose in his mind and especially to his negative self-talk. In addition, we talked about seeing if he could bring gentleness to his nonyoga experience as he could sometimes already do in yoga.

Evan had a prayer and mindful breathing practice. Every evening before bed, he would think about how his day had gone and then offer thanks to God for the blessings he had received and ask for guidance and help with the difficulties he had in his life. Then, he would practice mindful breathing for 10 or 15 minutes. As he thought over the day, he would do his best just to see what had happened and to let go of any judgments about his own or others' behavior. In doing mindful breathing, he brought his wandering attention back to his breath. In doing these practices, he cultivated important aspects of mindfulness: precise attention and nonjudgmental awareness. In addition, he aspired to forgive himself and others for being less than perfect. In that way, he also planted seeds of maitri and compassion. Finally, feeling gratitude for the blessings of the day tended to open his heart and bring relief and tenderness.

In our work, Evan could sometimes bring these same attitudes of nonjudgmental awareness, maitri and compassion, and openness to whatever issues we were exploring. For example, although he was a college graduate, he could not find work commensurate with his education. He finally found a job doing menial work at a high school. At first he struggled with the low status of the position, but when we looked at how he might bring this struggle into his prayer practice, he was readily able to see that there was much to be grateful for in his situation: he had a steady job that paid the bills, he liked the people he worked with, he did not need to bring the job home with him, and it gave him the free time to play his saxophone and listen to the music he loved.

Evan could also bring his curiosity and nonjudgmental awareness to other problems. He and his ex-wife, Carla, often disagreed about how to raise their two daughters. From his point of view, she was too controlling, and she thought he was too lenient. The girls lived with her most of the time, and she complained that she ended up being the unpopular enforcer of rules while he got to be the good daddy who let the girls do whatever they wanted. He felt angry, believing that she dismissed his opinions in the same way as she had when they were married.

As we tracked his experience while he talked about their conflict, he noticed that he was "feeling small." He felt belittled and as though she were treating him like a child. He identified echoes of how his mother had treated him and became curious about how much of what he experienced with Carla was really about Carla and how much was an old reaction to his mom. As he continued to explore these questions over time with a nonjudgmental mind, and to track his inner experience as he did so, he felt less anger. Instead, he noticed sadness. The whole situation was painful for everyone: for him, for Carla, for the girls. The question shifted for him to what really mattered to him in his role as father to the girls. How could he be consistent with his own values and also support Carla in her role as their mother without fomenting unnecessary conflict? His ability to take a step back and view the whole situation from a larger and nonjudgmental point of view came in large part from his daily formal practices.

Informal Mindfulness Practices

Everyone does activities that may be used to develop mindfulness. Some of these things do so by their very nature: sports and the arts are especially rich in their mindfulness potential. Other activities can become opportunities to further clients' mindfulness with the assistance of their therapists. Therapy itself may become a mindfulness practice, too.

Therapy as Mindfulness Practice

As we have noted, serving as a psychotherapist is often a mindfulness and awareness practice for therapists themselves. Tracking our own bodily experience, our emotions, and our thoughts and images requires precise attention. In addition, we attend to our experience of clients: noticing their facial expressions, gestures, and postures; listening to their words and tones of voice; and following their stories and their descriptions of emotions, sensations, thoughts, and images. Furthermore, we pay attention to the overall qualities of the relationship and the environment. In that way we not only bring mindfulness to details but also awareness to a larger sense of what is happening.

For our clients, too, therapy is an opportunity to practice mindfulness and awareness, and participating in therapy may be their main mindfulness practice. In therapy, especially with a contemplative therapist but also with others, they are invited to bring mindfulness to all of the aspects of their unfolding experience. In the context of a nonjudgmental relationship with their therapists, clients may learn to be both curious and accepting of their inner and outer experience.

As we have noted above, the four foundations of mindfulness may be practiced in the context of the therapeutic relationship itself. In that way, therapy is a kind of shared mindfulness practice for both parties.

Mindfulness and Awareness in Sports

Engaging in solitary and team sporting activities can be a wonderful support for cultivating both mindfulness and awareness. The need to pay attention to how one is using one's body as well as how one holds one's mind are already a part of many sports.

Solitary Activities　Many clients' workout routines provide rich opportunities for developing greater mindfulness and awareness. Jogging, biking, swimming, hiking, skiing, golfing, kayaking, horseback riding, rock climbing, bowling, skiing, and lifting weights all can be mindfulness and awareness exercises. No doubt readers can add to this list. While all of them could be engaged in with others, they can also be done alone.

I have worked with clients who have engaged in all of these activities. I become curious with them about what they experience in their bodies and in their minds as they run, swim, or lift weights. Where is their attention: On the muscles they are using? On their breath? Or are they noticing their surroundings? What do they do when their minds wander? Or do they use their workout time to worry about their problems or catch up on the TV news while they walk on a treadmill at the gym? Simply asking these sorts of questions helps clients who are interested in becoming more mindful to bring more precise attention to their experiences.

The same principles that guide meditation practice can be applied to informal mindfulness practices. They can include working with the breath, feeling one's body and posture, applying touch and go, noting when one is lost in thinking or mental imagery, and striking a balance between not too tight and not too loose. Repeating the same motions again and again provides an opportunity to notice the subtle changes in one's mind from one repetition to another.

My father was an avid golfer, and, beginning in my childhood, he gave me golf lessons. He would tell me how to hold the club and how to take a good stance and so on. But, most importantly, he would point out how I needed to hold my mind. "Keep your eye on the ball, concentrate, but not too much. Hold the club gently but firmly, and just imagine that you are throwing a baby out the window. Easy does it." The wisdom of throwing babies out windows not withstanding, it was my first lesson in "not too tight, not too loose."

Heather was a jogger who got up every morning, rain, shine, and sometimes even snow, and ran her route before breakfast. In response to our conversations about it, she identified some runs as times to practice mindfulness. She would particularly notice the feeling of her feet hitting the ground and the sensations of breathing. After a while, she added paying special attention to the colors and sounds of the neighborhoods through which she passed. This naturally expanded into awareness beyond the details she was already noticing mindfully. She reported a kind of panoramic sense of the landscape with herself running through it. In turn, we were able to draw on her increasing mindfulness and awareness in our work together by bringing those qualities to her in-the-moment experience as we discussed the relationship issues that had brought her into therapy.

Many of my clients are swimmers. I, too, swim on a regular basis, and we sometimes talk about what to do with one's mind while swimming lap after lap. It is very easy to become distracted and fall into mindless stories while swimming. Angie and I talked about how she could train her mind as well as her body by attending to the sensations of the water as it flowed over her back, her arm muscles as she pulled water in her crawl stroke, her sense of the water's temperature changing as her body warmed up, and the glimpses she got of the pool area as she turned her head to breathe.

Team Sports　Participating in team sports like basketball, baseball, volleyball, tennis, and rowing are especially good for helping clients to develop the kind of panoramic awareness that is the expansion beyond simple mindfulness. Team sports require that players pay attention not only to themselves but also to their teammates and to the larger environment as well.

Basketball is a good example. Skillful players need to know where their teammates are and also where they are likely to be in the next moments if a pass is going to reach them. Moreover, that awareness needs to extend to where the five players on the opposing team are and will be. Having that kind of large view is awareness.

One of my favorite stories of mindfulness and awareness in team sports comes from my work as a member of a team who worked with Dennis, a 32-year-old client who had experienced extreme states of mind on a regular basis since he was 19.[1] Dennis was often preoccupied, listening to threatening voices that no one else could hear. He was unable to take care of himself in even the most basic ways like tidying up his room or washing his body. He had been a star football player in high school, and during one of our shifts together, he asked me to take him to the tryouts for a local intramural softball team. I was doubtful that this would work out, but I was willing to go with him.

I was surprised to see how comfortably he picked up a glove and ran out to third base. Once there, he punched his hand into his glove a few times and turned his attention to home plate, where a batter had taken his stance. Soon Dennis was picking at his beard and staring into space. He began talking in a soft voice and looked like he was having a conversation with someone I could not see. "There he goes," I thought. "That's that."

As another batter hit the ball toward third base, Dennis swiveled his head toward the crack of the bat, made a neat catch, and tossed the ball to the pitcher. He was soon engaged again in pulling at his beard hair and talking to the unseen listener. When it was his turn to bat, he again showed up completely and hit a grounder that was picked up by the shortstop. Although Dennis was not invited to join the team, I was impressed by the glimpses of his brilliant sanity that were revealed as his mindfulness and awareness came and went.

In the same way in which I become curious with practitioners of solitary sports, I ask team players to tell me about their experiences. Then, we apply what they already know how to do, as much as we can, to their therapeutic work. Another baseball player, Gary, struggled with getting lost in obsessive thoughts about how he could get his former girlfriend back. She had already made it quite clear that she had no interest in doing that, but he would spin fantasies of how he could entice her to return. He spent an enormous amount of time coming up with such schemes and imagining how they could work. When he would come back to himself in the present moment, he often felt hopeless and depressed.

Gary was the pitcher on a team that played in an intramural league. He told me how could pay attention to his own body as he would wind up for a pitch and hold a sense of the whole field at the same time. Clearly, his pitching required both mindfulness and awareness. When he pitched, he never became caught up in his habitual fantasizing; he never felt hopeless or depressed on the field—except sometimes about how the game was going. I asked him if he ever thought of his ex-girlfriend while he was playing or if he thought of her but dealt with it differently when he was playing. He described how he might occasionally think of her but would cut those thoughts by paying close attention to the game and what he needed to be doing. When he was on the bench waiting his turn at bat, he was more likely to think of her, but even there, he could let go and bring his attention back to the game.

We began to explore how he could carry those skills over into the rest of his life. The first thing he considered was the question of what to bring himself back to if he noticed he was caught up in thinking or fantasizing. During a game there was a lot going on, and it was easy for him to turn his attention to that. What was an equivalent in his nonbaseball life? The first thing he thought of was coming back to the tasks he had at work. As he worked at his computer, he could bring attention to his weight on the chair. Then he could notice the computer screen's contrasting colors. When I invited him to make use of his ability to take a larger view, he added noticing a sense of the whole room in which he was working. That strategy seemed to work for him.

Next, what could he use when it was the middle of the night and he was lying in bed unable to sleep while he spun out fantasy after fantasy? He could interrupt his thoughts, but he quickly started them up again. I agreed that this was one of the most challenging times to interrupt thoughts. He took that question home with him. Then he reported that he had found a way that worked for him some of the time. He had begun to use the body scan practice, which we had practiced in one of our sessions, as he lay in bed. He would slowly and mindfully feel each part of his body, not trying to change it at all, but just tuning in to whatever he found there. Many times, he would be able to sleep after that. If not, he found that he was better off getting out of bed and reading a novel in another room. Then, when he grew drowsy again, he would return to bed. More often than not, he could then fall asleep. Sometimes he just had a poor night's sleep.

In this way, Gary was making use of all of the four foundations. He brought mindfulness to his bodily experience, applied touch and go, recognized when he was back in the present moment, and worked with not holding his mind either too tightly or too loosely. There were qualities of mindfulness, awareness, and also maitri in his approach.

Mindfulness and the Arts

When clients practice an art form like playing a musical instrument, dancing, singing, painting, sculpture, or writing, they are likely to have learned a good deal about working with their minds. It is especially true for those clients who have engaged in an art form for many years. They may know how to bring their attention back into the present moment by returning to their bodies and sense perceptions; they may know how to interrupt the flow of distracting thoughts; and they probably know a good deal about how to hold their minds without becoming too tight or too loose.

Edward Podvoll (1983) described his work with a music teacher. When this client became frustrated with his own difficulties,Podvoll asked him what advice he would give one of his music students. He said, "I would tell him to start again and take it very, very slowly." (p. 22)

As mentioned earlier, many of my clients over the years have been professional or amateur artists. Often painters bring their work, or digital images of it, to show me. One of the ways that my client Sylvia cultivated mindfulness was through her precise attention to color. She would work with different combinations of pigments until she got the exact shade she wanted. At the same time that she worked with a small portion of a painting, getting the color right, she was also holding in mind the overall effect of the painting as a whole.

As Edward Podvoll did with the music teacher, we can ask our clients how they would bring what they know from their artistic disciplines into other aspects of their lives. With Sylvia, I asked her to describe a feeling in terms of a color. What color did her present anger feel like? When she told me it was red, I asked what sort of a red. And what colors were in her confusion or disquiet? Sylvia found that she could be quite precise in describing her feelings this way. She had a language that allowed her to track her feelings and how they changed.

I was curious about what she did when a painting was not going well. She described to me how sometimes she could repaint over an area and how other times she had to let the whole thing go and start over from scratch. I asked how she might apply this approach to her difficulties with her overly critical mother. With this approach as a metaphor, Sylvia worked with learning to discriminate between the times she could repair what had occurred with her mother and when she could not. Sometimes she could respond to her mother's concerns in a way that seemed reparative, and other times she needed just to note them and let them go. Having made that choice, she often needed to set a boundary with her mother. We worked together on how to set those boundaries and even how to take a communication break for a few days or longer.

Day-to-Day Activities

With their therapists' help, clients may use nearly any activity as an opportunity to practice mindfulness and awareness. The more concrete the task, the better it is for helping clients bring body and mind together. Many ordinary activities present good opportunities.

I might ask clients to tell me how they decide what to wear. Do they choose their clothing for the day based on texture, color, comfort, or something else? How do they put an outfit together?

We can invite clients to pay attention to how they brush their teeth, blow-dry their hair, make their breakfasts, taste their food, wash the dishes, or drive their cars. What do they notice? What do they do when they notice that they are distracted by thoughts? Can they come back to the small details of whatever task they are performing? What thoughts do they have when they come back; can they remind themselves kindly or do they fall into self-criticism?

I often talked about daily activities with Nastaran, whom we met above. She loved to cook, and I asked her what she made and how she went about it. I realized that this was one arena in her life where she was often fully present and had a good deal of confidence. One day she brought me a small plastic bag with a combination of spices that she liked. As we smelled them together, we connected over our different experiences of the pungent spices. It was a time when she was generous with me and took the role of mentor, loosening up the fixed roles she had previously assigned to each of us.

Work offers other opportunities for us to be curious with our clients. Where are their minds when they are at work? Are they out of touch with their bodies, sitting at their computers? Or are they focused tightly, working with their hands? Are they juggling many demands, like elementary school teachers who have a classroom full of children all wanting their attention? Can the out-of-touch computer people build in a way to remind themselves to feel their backs against the chair or their hands on the keys? Can the ones doing manual work remember to look around at the environment? How about the ones who are interacting with many customers or a classroom full of youngsters all day? Can they find a way to pay attention to their own inner experience and not have their attention always on someone else?

Bringing attention to their bodies and their sense perceptions as they do their usual tasks can also help clients to ground themselves when they are experiencing difficult times. One of my colleagues, Sharon Conlin, often responds to clients who are feeling overwhelmed and anxious by asking them to do basic household tasks. I once overheard her talking with a client on the phone, saying, "I'd like you to do the laundry. Well, if you already did it, you can do it again." The point was to give the client something concrete to do that would require her to pay attention to something other than her overactive mind.

Many clients find it particularly challenging to maintain mindfulness and awareness when they are interacting with family members at home, especially with teenage sons and daughters. Inviting these clients to come up with ways to come back to their bodily experience and their sense perceptions can be useful. At whatever point they notice they are caught up, they can practice coming back to themselves. Linda would drawl "Okaaaaay" in the middle of a verbal tussle with her 15-year-old son, and it would remind her to feel herself breathing. That would give her the chance to come into the moment, take a step back, and take a fresh look.

Thich Nhat Hanh (1987a) describes an ongoing practice that he learned as a young monk in Vietnam. The monks used a series of short verses called *gathas* to turn the most ordinary of activities into mindfulness practices. Thich Nhat Hanh has written a number of gathas for his modern students to use, for example, when the phone rings, when they are sitting at a red light in traffic, or when they start their cars:

> Before starting the car,
> I know where I am going.
> The car and I are one.
> If the car goes fast, I go fast. (p. 66)

Therapists and their clients can come up with similar reminders or short phrases that clients can use in their own lives. Linda's "Okaaaaay" worked like a sort of gatha for her.

SHOULD THERAPISTS TEACH THEIR CLIENTS TO MEDITATE?

I have struggled with this question for a long time, and I still feel torn. Let's take a look at both sides of this issue.

Problems With Therapists Teaching Clients to Meditate

The first concern I have is that very few therapists have been trained to teach meditation. When I received meditation instructors' training years ago, it followed a model not unlike clinical training. We were required to study, listen to lectures and engage in discussion, conduct practice interviews, and pass an experiential examination before being authorized to serve as meditation instructors.

For the past few years I have given a talk to the meditation instructors' class taught by Acharya Dale Asrael at Naropa University about the differences between psychotherapy and meditation instruction. These differences can actually be quite subtle and tend to be mostly a question of emphasis, especially for therapists informed by a contemplative approach. As a meditation instructor, or MI, I am interested in helping my students to connect with the unconditioned aspects of mind, what we have been calling brilliant sanity. Of course, I am also interested in this as a therapist, but there my emphasis tends to be on conditioned existence, the relative aspect of experience. In other words, we usually focus on clients' personal issues and especially on how to relieve suffering.

When I did demonstrations of both kinds of interactions recently in the meditation instructors' class, the students noted that I tended to pick up on different things and to respond even to similar things differently. As an MI, I was most likely to ask how a meditation student was bringing a personal issue into his or her meditation practice. Furthermore, since I was in the role of instructor, I offered a good deal of advice and guidance about how to proceed. As a therapist, I tended to ask a practice client about the details of his or her emotional experience and issues, and I refrained from stepping into the teaching role except for the relatively minor amount of teaching I might normally do as a therapist.

Serving as an MI is an aspect of a meditation instructor's own meditation practice and is intended to help those practitioners cultivate interpersonal mindfulness and compassion. From a contemplative point of view, this is not unlike serving as a psychotherapist, with one important difference. As a therapist, I am paid, and in private practice I am paid fairly well. As an MI, I am not usually paid at all, or I receive just a nominal amount. I feel uneasy about being paid for meditation instruction in the context of a paid therapeutic session. It could even be regarded as a dual relationship for me to serve both as a client's therapist and also as his or her MI.

Another issue is that if I introduce meditation to clients, it is easy for them to mistake it for just another therapeutic technique instead of a spiritual practice. Perhaps a good comparison would be to liken it to a therapist teaching a client how to pray. Both might be quite beneficial to the client, but I am not sure it is really a proper role for a therapist.

A further concern is that I want my clients to be free to feel a full range of feelings toward me in the context of our work together. I would be unhappy to have clients reject meditation because of negative feelings they might have toward me. Since meditation is a life-long practice, unlike therapy, I would not want to abort their meditation practice in that way or any other.

At the same time, though, I find that I cannot just rest on this side of the issue.

Benefits of Teaching Clients to Meditate

In my own experience, there is nothing better than meditation practice for cultivating mindfulness, awareness, and maitri. Through meditation practice, we learn how to settle down with ourselves and cut through a good deal of unnecessary suffering. Why would we not share with our clients this practice that so many of us find beneficial in our own lives?

From the contemplative point of view, we suffer because we confuse what is really happening with our own version of what is happening. As discussed above, we mistake our thoughts and opinions about ourselves, others, and the phenomenal world for reality itself. Meditation is a powerful tool for penetrating exactly that kind of confusion.

Moreover, meditation gives us the opportunity to recognize our brilliant sanity, our fundamental wisdom and goodness. It uncovers our natural compassion for ourselves and others.

Teaching our clients to do simple forms of meditation like counting their breaths or following their breathing as it goes in and out are such ordinary human things to do that it is hard to imagine any way these things could be a problem. In fact, they are similar to many other things we already ask our clients to do.

I have, on occasion, taught clients simple meditation techniques. Usually, though, if possible, I tell those who are interested in sitting meditation practice how to find a qualified MI. Where I practice, in Boulder, Colorado, a great many different traditions are represented, and clients have a wealth of choices if they want to explore meditation. Most therapists, though, do not have this luxury. If they do not teach clients to meditate, then their clients may have no other way to receive meditation instruction in person. There are, of course, books and Internet sites, but they are not interactive and responsive to clients' questions in the same way another human being can be.

Practices to Teach to Clients

I teach clients what I sometimes call mindfulness exercises, and, when possible, I do the exercises with them in therapy. Then, if they like, they can continue them at home. I openly tell them that these are methods for developing mindfulness and awareness.

One exercise I introduce to clients is counting their breaths (see Chapter 9). Another exercise is simply to follow the breath either at the nostrils, the chest, or the abdomen, noting how it comes in and out without changing.

A variation of walking meditation practice that I tell my clients about as something to do outside of therapy is aimless wandering or mindful wandering. It is best to do this exercise outside in a place that feels safe. I tell clients to set aside about half an hour (or any other period of their choosing) and then just walk wherever they feel drawn to go. The particular instruction is to notice their sense perceptions: what do they see, hear, smell, taste, and touch? If they want to stop and pay attention to something specific, that is fine. Many clients report that wandering in this way shows them how much of their experience they usually miss. Some continue it as an occasional awareness practice or as a way to relax when they feel stressed.

Another mindfulness practice that many teachers present is mindful eating practice. I suggest to some clients that once a day they might try paying attention to all the details of their experience as they eat a meal. I describe how they can bring their attention to the movement of their hands, arms, and mouth as well as the processes of chewing, tasting, and swallowing. I suggest that they imagine that this is the first time they have ever tasted this particular mouthful of food. Of course, this is actually true; each moment is a first time.

With all of these exercises, I emphasize that there is no wrong way to do it. If they become distracted, I encourage them to gently return to the exercise.

If clients are interested in learning formal sitting practice, I refer them, whenever possible, to qualified MIs or meditation centers. I refrain from introducing more advanced meditation techniques. I try to walk a line between being interested in clients' developing practices on one hand and advocating for their having any particular relationship with their practices on the other hand. For those who ask, I sometimes recommend books on meditation.

When I have clients who practice meditation, either because I have introduced it to them or because they have a practice already, I show interest in it the same way I would about anything else in their lives that helps them to cultivate mindfulness, awareness, maitri, and courage.

An incident that happened many years ago, when I lived in rural Connecticut, still serves as a kind of wake-up call to me about not being stingy in letting clients know about meditation. As a still-new therapist, I was working with a middle-aged, stay-at-home wife and mother who had issues of anxiety. In those days, the local Buddhist meditation group of fewer than 10 people met weekly in a group space in the suite where I had my therapy office. One of the members had posted a flyer for an upcoming meditation class near the front door, and my client had noticed it. She asked me about it, and I dismissed it with some vague answer. I was sure she would not be interested, and I feared that knowing I was interested in meditation might be off-putting or too out of the mainstream for her. (This was well before the current interest in mindfulness.) For several weeks in a row, she asked me about the poster. Finally, the light went on: she was actually interested. I told her about the class, and she began to attend it. She developed a meditation practice that was quite helpful to her in working with her anxiety.

Some Suggested Guidelines for Therapists

Just as in the rest of our therapy work, as therapists we do not use techniques for which we have received insufficient training. At the same time, if therapists have some kind of ongoing mindfulness practice themselves, either a formal practice or an informal one, they probably know enough about working with mindfulness and awareness to be able to assist clients in working with them as well. In general, we should only introduce mindfulness exercises and practices with which we are already familiar ourselves.

In determining which mindfulness practices to suggest to clients, I pay particular attention to clients' ability to be embodied. If clients have difficulty being present because of past trauma, for example, I have learned to tread slowly and carefully in inviting them to practice mindfulness of their internal bodily experiences. Like Nastaran's reaction to my invitation to breathe deeply, sometimes coming into one's body abruptly can be overwhelming and even retriggering. With clients for whom that may be an issue, I prefer to begin by inviting them to pay attention to their sense perceptions. Attending to what they can hear is a good beginning. Sound is always in the present and is often neutral—especially the sounds in a therapy office. Then, as that becomes comfortable, I invite clients to bring their attention more to their inner bodily experience.

Ronald Siegel (2010) has made some helpful suggestions about how to approach mindfulness practices. He points out that even though we may aspire to bring mindfulness into all aspects of our lives, we cannot do so all at once. He points out the need to pay attention to pacing.

In the same way that we generally help our clients to proceed at a pace that is neither too dangerous nor too boringly safe, we need to introduce mindfulness practices that help our clients go deeper in a way that feels workable. When clients feel overwhelmed in their lives, it may be helpful to offer them grounding practices that bring their attention to one focal point, like their breathing or the sensation of their feet on the floor. When they are too inwardly focused, we can offer them a balance by inviting them to notice the objects in the room or practice attending to a particular sense perception. In Chapter 9 we look into practices that cultivate compassion and loving-kindness, which may be helpful grounding practices as well. Ultimately, therapists need to feel their own way with what, if any, meditation practices they introduce to their clients. As Ron Siegel has put it, "figuring out which form of meditation to favor at a given moment is something of an art" (2010, p. 88).

MINDLESSNESS PRACTICES

I often ask clients how they spend their time, and among the things I listen for are mindlessness practices. Knowing about clients' mindlessness practices can provide another avenue of approach to the cultivation of mindfulness. Essentially, mindlessness practices are ways of desynchronizing mind and body, usually in an attempt to escape from discomfort. They split our awareness between two or more objects of attention. Usually, our bodies are doing one thing while our minds are doing another. For example, while eating lunch and listening to a recorded book at the same time, we probably do not taste our food very much. When we engage in mindlessness practices, we may have more or less awareness, but we are not fully present. We may be thoroughly dissociated and no longer aware of where we are, or we may be just slightly out of touch.

There is a wide range of such practices, some of which may be dangerous and others which may be mere distractions. Another kind of practice that desynchronizes mind and body is visualization in the service of art, culture, or spirituality. We have already noted in Chapter 5 that there are healthy ways of making use of the imagination. For the purposes of our discussion here, let us restrict ourselves to ordinary mindlessness practices that are engaged in as a way of leaving or diluting the present moment.

Some practices are based on the body, others on the use of speech, and still others are performed entirely within the space of the mind.

Mindlessness Body Practices

A classic example of a body-based mindlessness practice is the twiddling that Bruno Bettelheim (1972) described in autistic children. These children made use of repetitive movements of their fingers or other parts of their bodies as a way of disconnecting from their surroundings. I have seen a young man, Shawn, who used rocking back and forth between his back foot and his front foot in the same way. He tended to use his rocking practice when he was scared, and it was his way of calming himself.

Like children who hang on to transitional objects (Winnicott, 1992) such as teddy bears or the corner of a blanket, we all have mindlessness practices in which we might indulge when we feel overwhelmed, frightened, or in need of a bit less intensity.

I sometimes tell clients that I collect mindlessness practices. One of my favorites in that collection is a chalk-rolling practice that a professor of mine had.[2] At the beginning of class each week, he used a piece of chalk to write one or more words on the blackboard. Sometimes he referred to those words in his lecture, but usually he did not. Instead, he walked around the front of the room or perched on a desk and talked. Often, he looked up at the ceiling or out the window while he rolled the piece of chalk back and forth in his fingers. He sometimes ran his fingers through his hair, pushing it away from his face. His hands, his jacket, and his hair all became chalk covered. As a student in the class, I had the sense that he was repeating a lecture he had given many times before. He was palpably absent from the room.

My students delight in pointing out that I have a paper clip practice. I remove the paper clip from my notes and roll it between my thumb and first two fingers of my right hand. When I notice, I put it down but soon find it has jumped back into my hand somehow. Now that I have my class notes on my iPad, I have escaped from my paper clip practice. No doubt I will soon enough replace it with something else.

Biting our nails, fiddling with worry beads, playing with our pens, and twirling our hair are all common mindlessness practices. I have only to look around a classroom, or anyplace else, to see people engaged in a rich variety of body-based mindlessness practices. Most times, like my professor, people are not aware of what they are doing.

Addictions are another form of body-based mindlessness practice. Drinking coffee, smoking tobacco and marijuana, consuming alcohol, and abusing prescription drugs and illegal substances all have their body elements. There is the ritual of acquiring and manipulating the paraphernalia of the addiction, but most importantly, as with all mindlessness practices, there is the mindless state of mind that is cultivated. There is quite a range. Frank had to have his coffee in the morning before he felt normal. Pamela had to have her two glasses of wine every night to take the edge off her day. Jerry would go on a drinking binge every few weeks and end up behaving in hostile ways that he regretted and sometimes did not remember. Of course, addictions have other important aspects, not least of which are the physiological aspects of the addictive process. When we explore with our clients, though, we often find the desire to attain some kind of mindlessness in either their initial or ongoing motivation. They were, or are still, trying to escape some circumstance or state of mind they find undesirable or even intolerable. At an even deeper level, they might be seeking a peaceful or blissful state of mind, as noted in Chapter 5.

Mindlessness Speech Practices

Speech practices make use of the voice as a way to dilute one's experience. A beautiful example of a mindlessness speech practice is the character Raymond's recitation of the Abbott and Costello "Who's on first?" routine in the movie *Rain Man*. When Raymond, who was autistic, felt anxious, he began to rock and to recite this routine.

Recently, I met with a prospective client who spoke rapidly and without pause. I could follow what she was saying, but I also noticed that I was not feeling much as I listened to her description of quite painful events. I suspected that I was exchanging with a dulled state of mind, possibly cultivated and maintained by her speech. When there was finally a gap in her spate of words, I asked her how it was for her to tell me all of this. At that point, she turned to look at me. She seemed to wake up; her tears began to flow; and her speech became slower and had more gaps in it. I knew that if we were to work together in the future, I would be curious to see how she used her speech and whether it was a mindlessness practice she used elsewhere in her life.

Mindlessness Mind Practices

As anyone who has ever meditated for even 5 minutes knows, we easily become lost in our thoughts and fantasies. Such mind-based mindlessness can manifest as painful obsessive thinking, as pleasant daydreaming, or as anything in between.

When Lillian was first referred to me, she described how she became absorbed in thinking about her lover, Will, who had died only days before in a sailing accident. Remembering him with tender thoughts and appreciation led quickly to wishing he were still alive. She might feel a moment or two of what she described as intolerable longing, and then she would quickly spiral into thoughts of suicide so she could be with him still. She fantasized about how she could kill herself and how wonderful it would be to be together with him again. As she did so, she would lose touch with the painful present where she was alone without him. I return to Lillian below.

Other mindlessness mind practices include leaving the present moment by doing things like fantasizing, reading mysteries, or obsessing. We become engrossed in the experiences of our minds. We may easily forget about our bodies until we realize that we need the bathroom or are interrupted.

Another way mindlessness can manifest in the mind is in the cultivation of a sense of absence or blankness. I have worked with a number of abuse survivors who knew how to dissociate and not feel anything much at all. They might have a sense of watching from a distance or just be gone. They had cultivated this ability at a time when it was extremely useful to them, but now they might find themselves disconnected when they do not want to be.

Any mindfulness practice can be misused in the service of mindlessness. Instead of using one's meditation practice, for example, as a way to support one's ability to be present with all of one's experience, some meditators use their practices as an opportunity simply to space out or daydream. More problematically, some people engage in spiritual bypassing, misusing their contemplative practices as a way to avoid the emotional nitty-gritty of their lives (Welwood, 2002). On the cushion they may practice "go and go" or they might ignore their emotions in the name of emptiness. They may deny that they ever feel anger, jealousy, or pride, and they may be correct. They may not feel them because they have cultivated mindlessness instead.

Hallmarks of Mindlessness Practices

How can we tell if an activity is a mindlessness practice? In the same way that the four foundations of mindfulness help us identify mindfulness practices, we can notice some distinctive features of mindlessness practices. In particular, these features point to states of mind produced by engaging in mindlessness.

The first hallmark of mindlessness is a loss of aliveness in the person. Like clients who numb out by watching television while stoned on marijuana, practitioners of mindlessness may find themselves feeling tired, diminished, or just out of touch with themselves, others, and the environment. Sometimes, this is exactly what they are seeking. Other times, it is simply the result of indulging in habitual mindless activities.

This loss of vividness may be accompanied by an absence of curiosity about oneself and others. Lack of interest in others manifests as a second important hallmark: losing touch with one's heart or one's compassionate impulses. Mindlessness practices generally are ways to withdraw from whatever is going on around one, and that includes other people. There may be a quality of self-involvement as well.

Addicts, for example, are well known for putting the satisfaction of their cravings above their concern for even those whom they love. When Jerry was on one of his periodic drinking binges, he gave no thought to the welfare of his family. All that mattered to him was making sure he got his next drink.

A third hallmark which I see as a key give-away of a mindlessness practice is that the person is irritated if they are interrupted while engaging in it. Instead of expressing gratitude for being awakened into the present moment, even those who are otherwise committed to cultivating mindfulness are likely to experience or express impatience and annoyance if they are interrupted. "Leave me alone, can't you see I'm busy," is more likely than "Oh, thank you dear, I was getting caught up there, wasn't I?"

Using Mindlessness Practices in Therapy

There are three main ways that I draw on my clients' mindlessness practices in therapy: using them to increase mindfulness, substituting a relatively benign practice for a potentially dangerous one, and mindfully applying a mindlessness practice as a way to titrate intensity.

Bringing Mindfulness to Mindlessness Practices

As noted, most of us have mindlessness practices. When our clients tell us about their mindlessness practices, they give us an opportunity to help them cultivate more mindfulness. Telling us about what they do and how it affects them brings mindfulness to the very activities designed to desynchronize body and mind.

I ask about the details of how they engage in whatever their practice is. I often ask them to teach me their practice and tell me about its advantages.

For example, with Brad—the smoker and nail-biter who had no ashtray but did have a nice manicure kit—I asked him to tell me what he actually did when he bit his nails.[3] How did he know which finger to begin with? How did he know when he was done? Was he aware of when he started? If not, when did he notice? Where was his mind when he bit his nails? Did he only do it when he was alone, or did he also do it when others were around? If others were present, what was his relationship like with them when he was practicing nail-biting? What did he feel if he was interrupted?

When did he do this practice? When he was anxious? When he was relaxed? How did he feel about doing it? What was it about biting his nails that he did not like? What would he lose if he stopped?

In asking all these questions and genuinely being interested in his responses to them, I was inviting him to bring mindfulness to the nail-biting, which he usually began without noticing and did not stop until he felt pain. To whatever extent he was able to notice what he was doing, he was bringing mindfulness to his experience and planting seeds of wakefulness. In subsequent sessions, we checked back in on what was going on with his practice. I emphasized that I was not trying to get him to give up his practice but instead to bring curiosity to it.

Like many clients, Brad felt a good deal of self-disgust and embarrassment about his mindlessness practice. He easily fell into self-criticism and self-aggression. By bringing my own nonjudgmental curiosity to the practice, and inviting his, I also hoped to help him feel more maitri and compassion toward himself.

Another way that I work with bringing mindfulness to mindlessness practices is by encouraging clients to play with the timing and details of their practices. Pamela described how she would mindlessly reach for a glass of white wine as soon as she got home in the evening. She drank only two glasses each night, but she was increasingly aware that she relied on them to ease her transition home.

To begin with, I suggested that she not change what she was doing at all but bring her attention to the state of mind the wine produced. She reported back that she felt just slightly dulled and more relaxed after she had her first glass of wine. What would happen, I wondered, if she delayed that first glass? I was not suggesting she not have it, but I was curious about what she would feel during, say, a 5-minute delay. Pamela was curious too, and she agreed to give it a try. When she came in the next time, she said that she had noticed a couple different things. First, she noticed that as she waited for the 5 minutes to pass, her mind was somewhat speedy and her body was tense. Once she had the wine, her mind tended to slow down a bit, and her body also began to breathe more easily. Second, she was surprised to find that when she delayed by 5 minutes, sometimes she no longer wanted the wine. She was intrigued by discovering that her craving was not as solid as she had thought. Bringing mindfulness and curiosity to her experience had already begun to change it.

Replacing Harmful Practices With Less Harmful Ones

Like all therapists, contemplative therapists take whatever steps are necessary to prevent clients from harming themselves and others when there is an imminent threat. Some mindlessness practices can become dangerous. Addictions, for example, have much potential to harm oneself and others. Drunk drivers, for example, cause accidents that injure and kill not only themselves but also others. Obsessive suicidal thinking is another potentially dangerous mindlessness practice. Sometimes therapists can help their clients replace dangerous practices with relatively benign ones. All mindlessness practices exact a price: they reduce our aliveness and lessen our experiences of compassion. Edward Podvoll (personal communication, July 1979) used to say that they cost us our dignity. Still, some mindlessness practices are safer than others, and we can use them to help our clients.

Lillian, whose lover Will had died, was often absorbed in suicidal thinking. Although she was willing to contract for safety, she was still having a very hard time. We worked together to identify other activities that would let her find respite from the intolerable grief she experienced in the present moment but which would not be as risky as creating suicidal plans in her mind. She liked to become lost in science fiction novels, and she agreed to read them instead of planning her own death. As time passed, she described how the window of opportunity to join Will was no longer open. She was willing, now, to turn her attention back to life, but she found herself still having unwanted suicidal thoughts. Lillian was also an avid mountain biker, and we agreed that this sport, which required a great deal of mindfulness, might be another good activity for her. When she was riding on the many mountain trails near her home, she could not also indulge in obsessional thinking. At night she continued to read novels. In our work together we gradually approached her grief, and as she was able to increasingly feel her sorrow over her loss and acknowledge her anger at Will for dying, the suicidal thoughts subsided.

Using Mindlessness Practices to Titrate Intensity

Sometimes clients who are dealing with difficult situations or intense emotions need a way to back off and rest. Mindfully choosing to use a mindlessness practice offers them a way to do that. What often happens to clients who do not make that choice is that they will mindlessly fall into a mindlessness practice anyway. Janet's partner had been diagnosed with breast cancer and was having a series of procedures as a result. Her prognosis could change with each set of results, and this meant that Janet and her partner were both feeling anxious and stressed as they waited helplessly to hear the extent of Fran's cancer. They decided to have a film festival at home. They gathered their favorite movies and settled in for a marathon of mindless movie watching. Janet reported that it felt empowering to be able to make that choice, especially at a time when she was feeling that she had so little control over events.

Clients who are working with past trauma, too, sometimes find that they need a way to take a break from what may feel like overwhelming emotions. Making use of the imagination in resourcing, as described in Chapter 6, can be the mindful application of mindlessness. Usually when I work with clients using resourcing, I invite them also to notice their inner bodily experience so it is actually a mindfulness practice. Other times, though, being able just to go, for example, to a beautiful and serene landscape in one's mind, without trying to pay attention to anything else, can provide a welcome time out.

A time when many clients find that they need this kind of break is during small and large transitions. The transition between work and home has been challenging for a number of the clients I have worked with. Often they feel that they go directly from the demands of work to the demands of family. We have come up with a variety of ways to ease that transition including the use of mindlessness practices.

Whitney would tell David that she was to be left alone for 20 minutes after she got home. She would use her "me time" to lie down and drift off listening to music over her earphones. A lawyer I met some years ago in Australia told me that when she came home, she played computer games while chatting with her young children. The kids knew not to interrupt her too much. She was not entirely present with either her games or her children, but she felt this let her ease into her evening. When she did not play her games, she felt that the transition was just too abrupt, and she was likely to snap at her children and her husband.

Larger transitions like packing up to move from one home to another, being in the middle of a divorce, or grieving the death of a loved one are other potentially stressful times when having permission to go off the air for a while can be helpful.

Helping clients to increase their options for developing mindfulness through the use of both mindfulness and mindlessness practices is an ongoing part of the ordinary work of a contemplative therapist.

Chapter 8

EXPLORING EMOTIONS

Like most psychotherapeutic approaches, Contemplative Psychotherapy places a good deal of emphasis on emotions. In working with emotions, the contemplative approach draws on Buddhist psychology, especially the teachings of Tibetan Buddhism. In general, emotions are regarded as part of our humanness and are seen as containing much richness. Contemplative therapists are interested in helping their clients to tap into this aspect of their brilliant sanity. Let us begin by looking at what emotions are from this point of view.

THE CONTEMPLATIVE VIEW OF EMOTIONS

Unlike some psychological and spiritual approaches that regard emotions as obstacles to awakening, Tibetan Buddhist psychological teachings understand emotions to be part of our wealth and not something to be gotten rid of. From this point of view, emotions are, in essence, energy combined with thoughts, and that energy is simply a manifestation of our natural wisdom (Trungpa, 1976). When the energies in emotions flow freely, without being referenced to a mistaken sense of self, they are expressions of our brilliant sanity as the five wisdoms or, as they are sometimes called, the five wisdom energies (Shambhala, 2013). However, most frequently, these energies become solidified by the stories we attach to them. Anam Thubten (personal communication, May 2012) has described them as becoming "frozen." Then they manifest as painful negative emotions or as misunderstood positive ones.

For example, as we have seen, the direct experience of the energy behind anger is simply clear seeing. We see something and recognize that it is unfair, inappropriate, or harmful in some way. Along with that seeing there is an energetic quality that we feel in our bodies and have learned to call anger. We tend, then, to reference that experience to ourselves and add a story about how it insults us or displeases us personally. In that way, we turn the unconstrained direct experience of anger into a negative emotion. In addition to creating such a self-referenced story, we hang on to our story as reality. The most common negative emotions are desire, anger, ignorance, jealousy, and pride. I sometimes think of the first three, the threes of passion, aggression, and delusion as the three primary colors of emotion (Hanson with Mendius, 2009). They combine to create the multitude of common emotions and feelings.

Positive emotions like happiness or delight can be problematic, too, because we become attached to the good feelings they bring and become unhappy when they inevitably change. Moreover, often while we are still enjoying them, we fear we will lose them, and we begin to grasp them and strategize about how we can keep them around. Once we begin doing that, the good feelings have already begun to turn into something less positive.

Clients, in my experience, tend to regard emotions as somehow more real than other experiences. They are certainly more intense, but from a Buddhist viewpoint, they are essentially empty of any permanence or solidity. Rather, they are part of the ongoing flow of experience. By helping our clients to bring mindfulness and gentleness to the arising and subsiding of emotions, we invite them further into the present moment. In particular, we are interested in supporting our clients in actually feeling their emotions in their bodies and perhaps uncovering the wisdom to be found within them.

METHODS OF WORKING WITH EMOTIONS

Buddhist psychology offers three ways of working with emotions. While our overall intention is to help clients be present with all of their experience, we also need to practice compassion and gentleness by providing them with a path, when necessary, to move gradually toward the intensity of some emotional experiences. By making skillful use of these three methods, we can help clients to moderate their experience and keep it within a zone of workability. Having practiced these methods with us in therapy, clients can begin to apply them in the rest of their lives. First, I note two common ways of dealing with our emotions that are not recommended.

Two Common Mistaken Ways of Approaching Emotions

Two ways in which we commonly approach our emotions are suppressing them or acting out. Both of them are attempts to escape from the discomfort of painful emotions by pushing them away or by expressing them into the environment. Unfortunately, these methods do not work very well. Both suppressing and acting out are ways of not feeling our emotions, either through pushing them out of awareness or by turning them into speech and action before actually experiencing them fully. These emotions that are not fully felt tend to become held in the body as tension, to intrude in thoughts, to show up in dreams, and to pop out of our mouths when we least want them to. They do not just go away.

In the contemplative approach, we would not, therefore, encourage clients to get the feelings out as a way of dissipating their energy. As we have seen, this would probably plant negative seeds in the storehouse consciousness and instead of getting rid of negative experiences would plant the seeds of their repetition. Suppressing them leads to planting seeds of ignoring as well as the seeds of the unacknowledged emotions themselves.

Since the essence of emotions is the energy of wisdom and brilliant sanity, we are more interested in being able to access their positive qualities than in getting rid of them. Instead, Buddhist psychology presents the following three methods for working with emotions, which are ways to include them in our experience rather than trying to eliminate them.

Three Methods of Working With Emotions

Before applying any of the three methods, we need to first accept that our emotions are ours to deal with. The three methods all begin with the idea, expressed in the First Noble Truth, that we are each responsible for how we relate to our experiences, including our emotions.

The three methods are rejecting or boycotting emotions, applying antidotes to emotions, and recognizing the nature of emotions (Wegela, 2009).[1] As always in Contemplative Psychotherapy, the suggestion is to work with these methods oneself before introducing them to clients. While they are presented here as three discrete approaches, we might begin using one method and find that we move naturally into one of the others.

Boycotting Emotions

When I shared some earlier writing on this method with a friend of mine who had been a Buddhist monk for some years, he winced. While he acknowledged that it is found in the Buddhist tradition, he thought of it as very un-Buddhist. In one sense, he is correct. Buddhist psychology, and the contemplative approach based on it, emphasize the importance of direct experience. The boycotting, or rejection, method is based on the opposite. In using this method, instead of feeling what we feel, we back off. We redirect our attention to something else until we feel stronger or more able to be present with what is arising emotionally. This method is especially appropriate for helping clients whose emotions trigger memories of past trauma that they do not yet have the resources to deal with.

To me, this method is an expression of kindness. As a staff member at a meditation retreat once advised me, "The most important thing is to be gentle" (Jonathan Eric, personal communication, January 1980). Instead of encouraging our clients to override their discomfort or their fear of going deeply into some emotion or other, we can teach them how to be gentle with themselves. As noted previously, self-aggression is one of the key sources of suffering in modern culture, and assisting clients in treating themselves kindly is often more important than getting to the bottom of any particular emotion.

Boycotting by Using Mindful Concentration   In applying this method, we advise our clients to pay attention to something other than the emotion with which they are having a hard time. We might suggest that they focus on their breathing or on a particular sense perception. I sometimes suggest to clients, for example, that they close their eyes and notice what they can hear. In this way, they are still practicing being in the present moment, but they are not going more deeply into a difficult emotion. Buddhist psychology teaches that we can pay attention to only one thing at a time, so any kind of concentration practice can be used in this way.

The drawback to this approach is that it works for only as long as we can keep our attention on the chosen object. Still, it is often a useful skill for clients to learn. It may offer them a sense of empowerment, the feeling that they are not at the mercy of uncontrollable emotions. Also, since emotions are impermanent, it is often the case that the original problematic emotion dissipates while the client attends to some other object of attention.

Erin was struggling with feelings of anxiety. She had recently separated from her husband of 5 years, and she was on her own for the first time. Feeling unprotected was bringing up echoes of the defenselessness she had felt growing up with her alcoholic father. When she paid attention to the present feelings of anxiety in her body, she felt even more frightened and panicky. As a child, she would feel terrified when her father would come home drunk at all hours and yell at her mother, her brother, and herself. A few times he had hit her older brother when he tried to intervene between his parents. Once he had slapped Erin. He was unpredictable: sometimes he was warm and loving, and sometimes he was "a monster."

Erin had married right out of high school, and her husband had represented safety and reliability above all. It had been her own choice to separate from him when she realized that these qualities were no longer enough for her. She was surprised to feel scared instead of happy with her newfound independence.

Erin worked with the mindfulness practice of counting her breaths, first in our therapy sessions, and then at home. I taught her a method taught by Thich Nhat Hanh (1988). I told her to take a comfortable seat, preferably sitting up straight, but not necessarily, and then to count breathing out as 1, and breathing in as 1. I suggested that she count 10 outbreaths and 10 inbreaths, and then start again at 1. When she lost track of what number she was up to, she could just start again at 1. Erin found this a useful way to ground herself in the present moment, interrupt her scary thoughts, and remind herself that she was safe now.

Boycotting by Using Mindlessness Practices   Another way to apply the boycotting approach to emotions is described in Chapter 7 as using mindlessness practices to titrate intensity. Instead of using a concentration practice, which makes use of mindfulness, we can also help our clients to boycott emotions by using mindlessness practices. The advantage of mindlessness practices is that they generally require less effort and may work for a longer period of time than concentration.

Applying Antidotes to Emotions

The second method of working with emotions is to apply an antidote to them. Buddhist psychology identifies some specific practices for counteracting the effects of negative emotions with positive ones. As noted in Chapter 6, all experiences plant the seeds of their recurrence. As we saw, something as simple as a smile can plant positive seeds in the storehouse consciousness. When we apply an antidote, we are planting positive seeds in this way even though we are not cutting through the confusion of a mistaken sense of self, and we are probably not uncovering the wisdom aspect of the emotion.

In Chapter 9, we explore practices that cultivate compassion and other related qualities, and they too can serve as antidotes to negative emotional experiences. Here, let us look at some antidotes to ignorance, passion, and jealousy.

The Antidote of Mindfulness   Mindfulness is an all-purpose antidote to being caught up in negative emotions. Specifically, it is the antidote for ignorance, and in Buddhist psychology ignorance about our true nature's lacking any fixed identity underlies all confusion, including negative emotions. Bringing mindfulness to any emotional experience can short-circuit the momentum of spinning the stories that accompany confused emotions. Taking a few moments to bring mindfulness to the body is an especially good antidote for being lost in one's head with any emotional upheaval. I often invite clients to take a moment to come back into the room and ground themselves in their bodies.

Lara was understandably upset when her ex-husband told her three teenage children untrue stories about her in his attempt to gain full custody of them. She was angry and frightened and in telling me had begun to escalate her distress further by imagining all kinds of scenarios in which he would succeed in turning her children against her. She felt helpless in the face of his greater financial resources and his willingness to disregard the rules of common decency.

As she continued her story, I interrupted her at some point and asked if she would like to slow down and connect with me for a moment. With a sigh, she turned toward me. For a few moments, we just looked at each other. I felt sad and angry at her situation, and I worked with bringing mindfulness and maitri to those feelings in my own body and mind. Lara calmed a bit and smiled sadly at me. I invited her to look around and just take a minute or two to be here in the room. As she did that, I noticed that her breathing, which had been rapid and shallow, began to slow down and deepen as she brought her mindfulness to her sense perceptions.

I asked, "How much of what you are talking about has actually happened and how much is what you are afraid might happen?" As long as she was feeling activated, she could not have brought her attention to cutting through her wild thoughts; however, having applied the antidote of mindfulness, she had interrupted their momentum and was able to make use of her own clarity to begin to tease apart what was actually happening from what she feared might happen in the future. Later, we turned to planning together how she could respond to her ex's inappropriate behavior.

A Traditional Antidote to Sexual Craving   The eighth-century Buddhist teacher Shantideva (1979) advised his audience of monks to think about all of the negative qualities of the women they fantasized about. He graphically described the inside of women's bodies, especially their digestive tracts, and also encouraged the monks to think of these women's corpses once they had died. How much would they crave them then? Setting aside the cultural assumption that monks would not have craved male bodies and his limited audience that had no women in it, we can still see a possible antidote even for our own times. That is, we can invite clients to focus not just on the alluring qualities of the men and women they crave as sexual partners, but also on the negative consequences of dwelling on these thoughts or moving into action based on them.

My client Ginny, whose massage therapist she found attractive, continued to think about him even after discovering that he was not available. Nearly every time we met, she would bring up how much she longed to be with him and her daydreams about how that could possibly occur. She imagined being in bed with him and how they could spend their lives together. As she indulged these imaginings, she added more and more detail. She knew that these thoughts only brought her pain, and yet she found it difficult to stop them.

I suggested that she might try balancing them with considering those qualities she did not find so appealing in him. Like many of us, she had ignored those things that did not fit into her fantasy of happily ever after. She began haltingly, but once started, she remembered that there were things about him she had noticed early on and had chosen to dismiss. For example, she did not like how he talked down to her and seemed to assume that he knew more about her than she did about herself. She had liked his attention but had minimized his possible arrogance. Also, she found that she felt some anger at what she now saw as his leading her on by texting and phoning her about things unrelated to their professional relationship. "He knew I was married and couldn't respond, so why did he do that?" Taking him off the pedestal that she had put him on helped her put an obstacle in the way of her runaway thoughts. By bringing awareness to her ignorance and reducing her mindless thinking in this way, she found some relief and also planted some positive seeds.

Rejoicing: The Antidote to Jealousy   The traditional antidote to jealousy is to rejoice in the virtues of others (Gyatso, 1980). It is often described as an antidote to envying the spiritual accomplishments of others, and it is practiced by identifying and then appreciating the good spiritual qualities of those we feel jealous of. For many of us, the spiritual prowess of others is not a source of suffering, but we can still apply the idea of appreciating those we feel jealousy toward as a way of working with that painful experience. Applying this antidote requires a certain amount of counterintuitive effort. Because of that, I usually limit suggesting this approach to those clients who already have a contemplative practice and a commitment to developing not only awareness but also compassion.

Instead of resenting someone who we believe has something we want or even deserve, we try to find things we like or admire in that person. The antidote goes even further: it suggests that we actually feel joy about the good qualities we find. When I applied this antidote myself for the first time, I was surprised by how effective it was. As we will see in Chapter 9, cultivating joy is an important teaching in Mahayana Buddhist teachings.

Marc felt jealous when his girlfriend, Carol, sat talking and laughing with another man, Jeff, at a dinner party. As he described the situation to me, he noticed that he was starting to have feelings similar to those he had at the dinner. He felt scared and angry: scared he would lose Carol and angry that she had made him feel that way. He was jealous of Jeff, and he quickly began to add a number of story lines comparing himself to Jeff: Jeff was better looking; he was smarter and more entertaining; he made more money. Marc went on to find any number of negative qualities in Jeff: he was arrogant, selfish, and mean.

Marc and I had worked together for a while, and I knew that Marc had a contemplative meditation practice. He had no trouble recognizing that he was causing himself to suffer by proliferating and solidifying these thoughts. He had the further insight that being jealous hurt him and not the person he was jealous of. Moreover, he recognized that holding onto his jealousy and blaming Carol for his suffering was more likely to push her away than to help him stay in relationship with her.

I suggested that he might try applying this antidote, and he was willing to give it a try. I invited him to think of what he appreciated in Jeff. First he groaned, and then he begin to think. "Okay, the things I said were true: he is nice looking, intelligent, and makes a good living."

"All right," I said. "Can you find any way to feel happy for him that he has those qualities?"

"That's harder." Marc took some time. Then he said, "You know, I kind of hung out with Jeff a few years ago. We used to play pickup basketball at the gym together. I liked him then. He's an okay guy. I just don't like him stealing my girlfriend."

I encouraged him to go deeper. "Can you imagine being happy for his enjoyment in talking and laughing with Carol?"

"Ouch. Well, all right. I can imagine that, but, you know, I don't want to lose her. That's the scary part."

I shifted gears at that point and invited him to see if he could access happiness for Carol's pleasure in her conversation with Jeff. To Marc's surprise, this turned out to be easier. "Well, sure. I don't want to prevent her enjoying herself. Not really. I want her to be happy. I just hope she feels that with me. I see that I am making up a story about losing her. I would be sad if that happened, but I guess I could survive."

Having touched into his affection and care for Carol, he began to talk about how he could be more supportive of her in their relationship. He had visibly softened at this point.

Replacing Negative Thoughts With Positive Thoughts   Another antidote that may be familiar to readers from cognitive-behavioral psychotherapy can be especially helpful in working with depressed clients: replacing negative thoughts with positive ones. The Buddhist *lojong* teachings present a series of slogans that a practitioner studies and then memorizes (Kongtrul, 1974). The idea is that the slogans will arise in one's mind as appropriate and can interrupt the grasping and fixation in which we may habitually indulge. For example, one slogan is "Be grateful to everyone" (Chödrön, 1994, p. 56). The idea behind it is that everyone, and most especially those with whom we have a difficult time, gives us the opportunity to develop compassion and awareness. Without them, we would remain confused and caught in suffering. Meditation practitioners who have studied it may recall it when they are angry at someone. Instead of acting on their anger, they might consider how they could cultivate gratitude, an experience that is not painful and that might plant positive seeds.

I do not actually teach these slogan to clients, but what we sometimes do together is come up with short sentences or phrases that clients might use in the same way. They are similar to the gathas mentioned in Chapter 7. For example, one client came up with the sentence "I can be ordinary" as an antidote to her painful strivings for perfection. Another used "I don't have to be ready" in order to get herself into her painting studio. It helped her overcome the inertia of resistance. Once in the studio, she usually became engaged, but she needed the boost this slogan gave her to get through the door.

Using Resourcing as an Antidote to Fear   As we have seen above, inviting clients to imagine being in a pleasant or safe place can be an effective way to plant positive seeds in the storehouse consciousness. It is particularly helpful when clients are fearful, and it gives them a way to de-escalate when their fight-flight responses are activated.

When I work with clients who have already been introduced to grounding and resourcing, I check in with them and ask if they want to use those techniques, especially when they are feeling overwhelmed by painful memories.

Seeing the Nature of Emotions

The third method of working with emotions is to experience them directly, free of their story lines. We go toward our physical and energetic experiences and let go of our attachments and preferences about what we might experience in the next moment. When we do this, we automatically drop any mistaken sense of identity and just are fully present with whatever is arising in our body and mind. What remains is the unconfused wisdom energy that is the essence of the emotion.

To repeat what we found in Chapter 3: the wisdom energy contained in ignorance is a sense of spaciousness; in anger, it is clarity; in pride or in feeling inadequate, it is equanimity or generosity; in passion, it is discriminating awareness or compassion; and in jealousy or self-doubt, it is skillful action.

A young woman I know, Amanda, shared the following clinical example with me of her work with a contemplative colleague of mine, Paul Bialek. She had begun by working with an antidote to feeling a poverty mentality and feeling inadequate, and then tapped into recognizing her direct experience, which led, in turn, to a sense of generosity and even equanimity.

Amanda, a single mother who received some support from her ex-husband to take care of their two young children, was always worried about whether she had enough or was enough. As she described it, she felt as though there would never be sufficient resources, especially financially. Would she have enough to pay the bills or to feed the children? She was haunted by these worries all the time.

In addition, she struggled in her intimate relationships with the feeling that she was not good enough. One way she dealt with that was to avoid relationships with men who were actually available. Her most recent relationship had been a classic example of the Padma dance described in Chapter 5.

My colleague suggested to her that she might try working with the antidote of asking herself, "What is not wrong?" Amanda took on this practice and was pleased to note that this let her interrupt her worrisome thoughts. She went further and imagined what it might be like to feel like she did have enough. As she did so, she noticed an unfamiliar feeling of happiness. She felt elated, and reported that she did not often let herself feel good in that way. Usually, it brought up fear, leading to a conviction that she needed to be on guard. By practicing "What is not wrong?" again and again, though, she found that she could stay present both with the good feeling of having enough and also with the anxiety that accompanied it. As Amanda described it, "[When I allow myself] to relax and feel that I have enough and that financial security is possible, I am able to be more present and grounded. I am able to extend the generosity of this state out to others." In addition, she was willing to consider the possibility that just perhaps she herself was enough, too.

Cecilia, a client of mine, was struggling with feelings of jealousy. Unlike Marc, who used the antidote described above, she did not have an ongoing meditation practice or a consciously chosen commitment to cultivating compassion. Nonetheless, she was quite good at being able to track her direct experience. In one session, we practiced the technique of touch and go: bringing mindfulness and awareness to her bodily sensations while also recognizing that the thoughts she was having about her wayward boyfriend were just that, thoughts. She was able to let go of the narrative about him by paying attention to the changing array of sensations in her body: the rising and falling of heat on her face, the tightness in her belly, the changes in her breathing. As she did this, her awareness expanded, and she was able to be present more with me as well as to bring attention to her inner experience.

The next time she had occasion to try this method was at a charity auction where her boyfriend was serving as one of the auctioneers and receiving a good deal of attention. As she sat on the sidelines, she noticed that she felt exhausted and numb. Because we had talked about it, she suspected that what she was really feeling was jealousy. She leaned into her sensations and tracked feelings similar to those that had arisen in our session: waves of hot and cold feelings moved through her body; her breathing became increasingly shallow; her belly and throat tensed up. As she continued to cut the

179

story line, her breathing relaxed and the fatigue began to lift. By attending to her body sensations, she had already moved away from the numbness. As it had in my office, her awareness began to expand, and she noticed what was going on in the room. She noticed a man she knew, and she smiled at him. When he came over and began to chat, she was pleased to note that her tiredness was soon gone. Together they went and looked at the various lots up for bidding, laughing at some of the more absurd offerings. The energy she had constricted by ignoring her jealousy had become available now; it had been transmuted from jealousy and self-doubt into liveliness, connection, and enthusiasm.

By understanding and using the various methods of working with emotions described in this chapter, therapists may help their clients to uncover the natural wisdom contained in their emotions.

Chapter 9

CULTIVATING COMPASSION

The experience of brilliant sanity, or even ordinary mental health, is characterized by concern for others. In this chapter we consider how to connect—or reconnect—with the boundless nature of our own and our clients' innate kindness and wisdom by exploring what are known as the four limitless ones: loving-kindness, compassion, joy, and equanimity. The four limitless ones are drawn from the Buddhist teachings on the ideal of the bodhisattva (Trungpa, 1991). In Mahayana Buddhism, bodhisattvas are people who have committed themselves to benefiting others. A fully realized bodhisattva would manifest the qualities of the four limitless ones. Therapists, too, are committed to the well-being of their clients. While we may not be on the bodhisattva path, we may still aspire to develop these same qualities.

We may feel inspired to cultivate our inherent compassionate qualities for many reasons, and one that pertains to us as therapists might include something like the following: the experience of looking at our appointment calendars, seeing the name of a client with whom we are having difficulty, and thinking, "Oh, no, I don't think I can face that client today!" We may have begun to actively dislike a client or the client's behavior to such a degree that we have lost touch with our tenderness. For whatever reason, we have contracted somehow, and we are not feeling generous or compassionate even though we might think that we should be. The contemplation practices associated with each of the four limitless ones may be especially useful at such times.[1] Going beyond the cultivation of mindfulness and awareness, they are designed to help us open our hearts.

Generally, with all of the four limitless contemplations, it works best if we have first practiced them when we are not faced with an especially challenging situation. If we are already familiar with them, we may find using them can help us more easily shift our attitudes. On the other hand, we can still use these practices when we need them most, regardless of how often we have done them before. We can do them as described in this chapter, or we can do what I think of as a kind of emergency version in which we flash briefly in our minds on the essential idea of each one. The emergency version can be especially helpful in the midst of a session with a challenging client.

Therapists may choose to introduce these practices to their clients, either in the forms in which they are presented here or by adapting them to the needs of particular clients. A practice for cultivating each of the four limitless ones, followed by clinical examples, is presented below.

LOVING-KINDNESS

In Buddhist psychology, loving-kindness is the wish for all beings to be happy. Some readers may be familiar with its Pali name, *metta*, or its Sanskrit name, maitri. In Contemplative Psychotherapy we also use the term "maitri" in a slightly different way, emphasizing nonaggression and friendliness toward oneself, as noted earlier.

When we are having a hard time with relatives, friends, or clients, wishing them happiness may be the furthest thing from our minds. We may be doing our best not to wish that they vanish from our lives or even be harmed. In the Buddhist tradition, though, trying to awaken a genuine experience of loving-kindness—or any of the four limitless ones—toward such people is exactly what is recommended. How do we approach such a task?

Formal Loving-kindness Contemplation: Metta Practice

With the formal practices of the four limitless ones, we can take the same kind of posture we do for meditation practice, or we can do them in any comfortable position. Many people include the metta loving-kindness practice as part of their ongoing meditation routine. They might, for example, do about 10 minutes of metta practice before or after their regular sitting practice. As already mentioned, we may choose to engage in metta practice on an as-needed or emergency basis, too.

In all of the practices of the four limitless ones, we make use of our imagination. Having found a comfortable position, we might begin by sitting in mindfulness meditation for a few minutes. Or we can just notice our bodily experience and track our breathing for a few breaths. Once we feel somewhat grounded and settled, we can begin the contemplations. Many people prefer to do these practices and contemplations with their eyes closed.

Traditionally, one begins metta practice with oneself. The idea is to begin with whatever is easiest (Sharon Salzberg, personal communication, April 3, 2014). Many people find it easier to think of a person or animal whom they love or have positive feelings toward. However you begin, spend a minute or two just thinking about and evoking in your mind a sense of that being. It is not necessary to have a visual image. Tapping into your feelings is completely appropriate in all of the limitless ones contemplations since what we are doing is developing our hearts. Then, begin to say some sentences like the following, silently in your mind, directing them toward yourself or the being you are thinking about: "May I be happy. May I be safe. May I have food, shelter, and comfort. May I be free from suffering. May I be peaceful." If you begin with someone, a person or animal, other than yourself, use "you" instead of "I." It is good to use sentences that feel genuine to you, so feel free to make up your own. Repeat the sentences over and over. You may find that you want to change them as you go along, and that is fine, too. Tap into your affection for the being you have chosen, and let the contemplation be as real for you as you can. Do this for a few minutes. If you did not begin with yourself, be sure to include yourself in the practice at some point.

If you did begin with yourself, next think of someone you love or feel close to. Or, you could pick someone who has been helpful to you and toward whom you feel gratitude. Use the same kind of sentences described just above.

Next, think of someone toward whom you feel neutral. I sometimes think of Mike, who delivers our mail. Or I think of the cashier at the supermarket whom I often see at the checkout. Bring to mind a sense of the being you have thought of. Again, use the same kinds of sentences as before: "May you be happy. May you be safe. May you have food, shelter, and comfort. May you be free from suffering. May you experience peace." As before, tailor the sentences so that they feel genuine and appropriate to you. Spend a few minutes on this part of the contemplation.

Then, move to what most people find the hardest part of the practice: think of someone you actively dislike or feel aversion toward. You might choose to apply the contemplation to a difficult client. Once again, proceed just as you did before. Call up a sense of the person and then repeat the sentences to yourself and wish him or her happiness and well-being as you do so: "May you be happy. May you be safe. May you have food, shelter, and comfort. May you be free from suffering. May you experience peace." Do the best you can while staying true to your genuine feelings. Spend a few minutes on this.

Finally, if you have not already done so, extend the same wishes of goodwill to yourself: "May I be happy. May I be safe. May I have food, shelter, and comfort. May I be free from suffering. May I experience peace." Some therapists and other helpers find this part of the practice the most difficult. It can be fascinating to notice what obstacles arise when we express the same kindness to ourselves that we may readily extend to others.

Complete the contemplation by coming back to your body and your breathing. If you like, you can do some mindfulness meditation at this point.

Loving-kindness: Clinical Examples

I used metta practice in working with my feelings toward a client of mine, Ed, who struggled with depression. Actually, he did not really struggle with it; he sank into it and felt hopeless and stuck. He had a very difficult time getting out of bed or going to work, and dragged himself through his life. In being with him, I often felt heavy and hopeless myself. If I could not even imagine him feeling better, how could I help him to take steps to relieve his suffering? At the same time, I was aware of the need not to impose some agenda of my own on him. Part of what I had a hard time with was his inertia. No matter what he agreed to try, he did not manage to follow up between sessions. Even getting to the psychiatrist to discuss the medications he had been on for many years seemed beyond him. Loosening up my own stuck feelings by practicing metta gave me a way to work with my own issues toward Ed.

In particular, I thought of him in the context of the formal metta practice. The one time I had seen him smile was when he talked about his cat, so I imagined him holding his cat and smiling a little bit as I repeated a series of sentences wishing him well-being and happiness. I included this in my daily practice for a while. Over time, I began to experience sadness instead of the frustration I had been feeling. Did this tenderness affect my work with Ed? It is hard to say for sure, but he made an appointment with a doctor who changed his medications. That helped him some, and he was able to turn his attention to how his negative thinking was adding to his suffering.

I have also had a few clients who did metta practice themselves. One, Jessie, had learned it when she attended a weekend program at a meditation practice center. She had tried a regular mindfulness practice of working with her breath, but she found it was easier not to become lost in worrying thoughts when she did metta. Also, she just liked it better and felt that it was more in line with her own spiritual tradition of Judaism.

COMPASSION

In Buddhist psychology, compassion refers to our wish to relieve suffering. The practice of tonglen, associated with cultivating compassion, is similar to loving-kindness practice, but the emphasis is a little different. In loving-kindness we are wishing for the future happiness of others; in compassion practice we are imagining that the present suffering of others is removed from them right now.

Does compassion practice actually lead to our becoming more compassionate in our actions? Research by Richard Davidson and others suggests that doing this kind of practice actually does affect our brains and our behavior. Davidson and Begley (2012) describe an experiment in which graduate students were taught a compassion practice similar to the metta practice described above. In the same way in which metta practice begins with those close to us and expands outward, the compassion practice used in the research begins with imagining the suffering of others and widening one's circle to gradually include all beings. At the same time, the instructions included saying phrases like, "May you be free from suffering; may you experience joy and ease" (p. 221). The students were also encouraged to feel compassion emotionally, not just intellectually. The conclusion the researchers reached was that "people who are trained in compassion meditation develop a strong disposition to alleviate suffering and wish others to be happy" (p. 223).

Tonglen, the compassion practice introduced here, can be more demanding than metta. Tonglen means "sending and taking," and we practice sending positive feelings to those who are suffering while taking on their suffering ourselves (Chödrön, 2001). My own initial reaction when I was first told about tonglen was that it sounded crazy. Why would I want to experience the suffering of others? Then I realized that as a therapist I was already inviting exactly that: when I was with clients who were in pain, I willingly opened myself to exchange with them. It was not so crazy after all. In fact, it seemed to me that it was simply a description of what we do all the time. Since we are not solid and separate, we pick up on the feelings of others whether we wish to or not. In tonglen we cultivate our ability not to shut down in the presence of that discomfort.

It is important in practicing tonglen that we have some understanding of emptiness. We are not taking others' suffering into a solid self. We are taking that suffering into our spacious brilliant sanity where it can dissolve. Still, we have to be willing to experience discomfort in the same way that we do when we are in the presence of clients who are suffering.

Formal Compassion Contemplation: Tonglen Practice

To begin, do some meditation practice for a few minutes, following the breath and grounding yourself in your body. We always sandwich formal tonglen practice between periods of sitting meditation. It is good to practice tonglen for about 10 minutes in the context of our sitting practice. Not only does mindfulness meditation settle us, it reminds us of our impermanent and empty nature. Having sat a few minutes or longer, follow the four steps of the practice.

Step 1: Flashing on Brilliant Sanity

First, take a moment to flash on brilliant sanity. The idea is abruptly to shift your attention from your usual state of mind to a brief recognition of your basic nature. There are a number of different ways to do this. You can tune in to any one of the three basic qualities of brilliant sanity: openness, clarity, or compassion. If you choose to work with openness, you might simply let go and allow the mind to expand outward. Or you can use your imagination and think of a place with a sense of vastness like the ocean or a spacious meadow. Then you can let yourself feel the peacefulness of being in such a landscape.

You can work with the quality of clarity by reminding yourself of why you are choosing to do tonglen at all. Or you can remember a time when you felt particularly clear and let yourself feel that quality in your mind. Drawing on the third quality of warmth, you can tune in to the quality of compassion or tender heart. Or you can think of someone you know who is suffering now or someone in the past who was. Sometimes I still begin my tonglen practice by thinking of my dog Molly, my companion of 15 years, who died in my arms. Even now, many years later, it brings up sadness, tenderness, and the wish to relieve her suffering and that of others.

However you do the first step, the point is to recognize, and perhaps briefly feel, your desire to become more compassionate and openhearted.

Step 2: Establishing the Texture of the Practice

The focus in the second step is on establishing the rhythm and texture of the practice. As you breathe in, imagine taking in the essence of the feeling of suffering. This is often described as hot and heavy and is more a sensation than a visualization. Breathe in this sense through all the pores of your body. Feel free to use your imagination creatively. I have a colleague, Jeremy, who has taught this practice by suggesting that we take in the awfulness of dirty, stinky water (Jeremy Lowry, personal communication, March 2008). The idea is to have a felt experience, however we can rouse it.

Then, on the outbreath, send out what Buddhist teachings call *bodhichitta*: our soft and open, awakened hearts (Chödrön, 2001). In other words, breathe out the qualities of relief from suffering. These can be imagined as cool, weightless, and bright. At this point, Jeremy described breathing out the sensation of cool, clean, refreshing water. As you breathe out, do your best to have the experience of relief yourself.

As always, use whatever thoughts and images are helpful. Coordinate the alternation of breathing with the qualities of suffering and the qualities of relief, however you can most genuinely feel them. Do this part of the practice for up to a third of the time you have set aside to practice tonglen.

Step 3: Beginning With a Specific Situation

In Step 3, choose a specific situation to work with. It is often best to begin with oneself and with whatever experience is already occurring. It does not need to be a big thing. Perhaps you have a pain someplace in your body, or you have an uncomfortable emotion. You might even start with the feeling of not knowing how to proceed with tonglen practice. Whatever that experience is, breathe it in. "Breathe it in" means feel it. Feel whatever you feel in your body and emotions, and notice any thoughts and images in the mind.

Then, on the outbreath, send yourself some kind of relief. It might be the wish for the pain to dissipate; it might be something concrete like imagining a warm compress on a sore back; or it might be a sense of dropping whatever struggle you might be engaged in. The main point is to treat yourself with kindness and tenderness.

Continue working with whatever situation you began with, breathing in the pain and breathing out relief for a few minutes. If something shifts and changes, that is fine. However the practice naturally develops is all right.

For example, I began my tonglen practice a few days ago with the pain I felt in my thumb where I had cut it badly while slicing onions. Along with physical pain, there were also the self-critical thoughts I had about what a stupid thing it had been to do. On the inbreath, I leaned into the sore feeling in my thumb and recognized the sad and impatient feelings that accompanied my thoughts. I let myself feel the sore thumb and also the heat that rose in my face when I let myself go toward the embarrassing truth of my mindlessness.

On the outbreath I breathed out coolness to my slightly throbbing thumb underneath the big bandage the Urgent Care folks had wrapped it in, and I sent myself kind words like, "It's okay. It is not a big deal." The practice was to let the coolness and kindness actually come in. It took quite a number of breaths to do this.

You might discover a tendency to breathe in suffering and not breathe out relief to yourself. Or you might find that you do the opposite. In tonglen, try to strike a balance with taking in and sending out.

Instead of beginning with something about yourself, you can begin the practice by thinking of the present suffering of someone you know. You might choose to work with a loved one who is ill or dying, or you might begin with a client in this step. Proceed in the same way as you did when you began with yourself, except instead of sending relief to yourself, send it to the person or animal you have brought to mind. Let it be as real for you as you can. As with my thumb situation, you may need to stay with a particular situation for a while. At some point, though, move on to Step 4.

Step 4: Expanding the Practice

In Step 4, we extend the practice to include more beings. Continuing with the example of my thumb and self-criticism, at some point I extended out, breathing in the suffering of the many people who may have mindlessly hurt themselves and who were giving themselves a hard time about it. I pictured sending all of those people some sort of relief, and I imagined them actually receiving it. I could be sure that I was not the only one who experienced that particular kind of suffering.

You can expand first to people you care for, and then to people you feel neutral toward, and finally to people you have a hard time with in the same way as in metta practice. Or you can expand geographically by beginning with others who are nearby and then, including more and more beings, you gradually expand to your town, region, country, hemisphere, and world. You create the practice for yourself as you go along by finding what lets the practice feel real to you. Expand outward in whatever way feels most natural to you.

End the practice by sitting quietly for a few minutes, perhaps practicing mindfulness meditation.

Tonglen on the Spot

Many people find tonglen easier and more accessible if they use it as the occasion arises. Instead of doing it as a formal practice, or in addition to doing it formally, they use it more spontaneously. When we are with someone who is in pain, for example, when we are visiting a friend who just separated from his partner, we might choose to breathe in his suffering and breathe out to him the wish that his suffering lessens. We might imagine his pain becoming dark smoke. We might breathe in that smoke and let it dissipate in the vast spacious sky of our own beings. There is no need to get even that fancy. We could just breathe in, imagining that we are taking away another's suffering, and breathe out, imagining that we are sending peace and goodness in its place. We can do tonglen in this way for just a breath or two even during a session with a client.

As we do this, we could recall the difference between what we have identified as optional suffering as opposed to unavoidable pain. We could imagine removing others' suffering. With my thumb, for example, I could let go of the extra suffering I was putting on top of the simple experience of what was actually quite manageable pain.

As I have written elsewhere (Wegela, 2011b), I did tonglen practice in this way by the bedside of my father as he was dying. A nurse practitioner sitting next to me quietly did it, too, based on the brief description I had given her of what I was doing myself.

Sometimes when there is nothing else we can do, it can be helpful to us to practice tonglen for loved ones, clients, and strangers across the world.

A Clinical Example of Adapting Tonglen to Work With a Client

As I get older, I seem to attract more therapists into my private practice, though most of them would not describe themselves as contemplative. George had recently completed advanced training in Jungian work and had a woman client whom he had seen as part of that training. He had made an open-ended commitment to work with her until she felt done with her work. He felt torn between honoring his commitment and his strong desire to be free of her endless complaints and lack of progress. An additional issue was the extremely small fee she paid him and the time she took up outside of sessions with frequent phone calls.

Having explored George's own feelings toward this client, I wondered if he would benefit from applying the essence of the tonglen practice to his situation. I asked if he wanted to try a compassion exercise and see where it took him. George readily agreed. I invited him to begin by settling himself in the present moment by feeling his body in the chair and then tracking his breathing.

Once he felt centered, I asked him to begin by letting go of how he thought the exercise should go. Then I asked him to call up the feelings he had when he was with his client. George identified feeling frustrated, annoyed, stuck, stupid, and useless. No matter what he did, this woman kept coming back and nothing he suggested seemed to help her. I asked if he thought that his client might feel any of those feelings. "Yes, definitely. I'm sure she feels all of those feelings, but she probably would not admit it. She just always says she doesn't feel anything."

I suggested that he breathe in the feeling of not knowing how he felt and just notice what arose with that for him. I encouraged him to use as many breaths as he needed. After a little while, George said that he did not like that feeling: he felt numb and lost.

"What would give you relief?" I asked him.

He thought for a moment, and then said, "Knowing that I wasn't doing anything wrong. That would be a relief."

I suggested that on his inbreath he let himself feel the numb and lost feeling and on the outbreath let the knowledge that he wasn't doing anything wrong come into himself. I told him to alternate between those two things until he felt he had established that rhythm.

Once he felt he had done that, I suggested that he imagine breathing in his client's numb and lost feelings and breathing out to her the knowledge that she was not doing anything wrong. George nodded and continued his quiet breathing. A few minutes went by, and then he said, "I see how I am holding onto the belief that she is doing it all wrong, and I see how painful that has to be for her." George had reconnected with his empathy and compassion, and now we could turn our attention to exploring how he could let go of this judgmental attitude.

In this example, asking George to let go of how he thought the exercise should go was similar to the first step of flashing on spacious brilliant sanity. Then I began with his experience of himself and what was probably some exchange with his client. The piece that felt to me to be most about the client's experience, however, was her insistence that she did not feel anything, so I chose to follow up with that.

In a later session, George reported that while he still did not exactly enjoy his work with this client and still had some resentment about the low fee, he felt some relief in knowing he was honoring his commitment. He had continued to feel more sympathy for her suffering, and that had loosened things up for him. He felt more open in his work with her.

JOY

The third limitless one is joy, or sometimes empathetic joy (Wallace, 2004). I was initially surprised to find joy designated as one of the ways we can reconnect with our compassionate nature. Joy had always seemed to me to be a particularly self-centered feeling, and it was not apparent to me what it had to do with extending warmth and kindness to others. Encouraged by my teachers to explore it further, I came to realize that when I feel joy, I tend to be more welcoming to others. Joy does not happen when I shut down, but when I open up.

The particular practice associated with joy is rejoicing (Wallace, 2004). Specifically, it refers to rejoicing in our own and others' good fortune. In other words, the practice of joy is to be happy for the happiness of others. As we saw in Chapter 8, one traditional application of rejoicing in this way is as an antidote to jealousy.

Formal Rejoicing Practice

There are different ways to do formal on-the-cushion rejoicing practice. In the two presented here, we begin by connecting with the direct experience of joy in ourselves. Then, as we do in the other limitless ones practices, we imagine extending out toward others.

As always, we begin with a few minutes of settling ourselves in the present moment by taking a good posture, feeling our bodies, and following our breathing.

Method 1

In the first method, suggested by Pema Chödrön (2001), we start by thinking of our own good fortune and rejoice in it. When I do this practice myself, I might think of the good fortune of having been born at a time and place where women have the opportunity to work as I do and to learn as I have. If I had been born only a few decades earlier, I would not have been exposed to the Tibetan teachings, for example. I would have had limited choices in how I could earn a living. I think of more things I am grateful for: I had polio when I was six, only a few years after Sister Kenny's cure became widespread in America (Cohn, 1975). Without it, I might have been disabled for life. I continue to list the things for which I am appreciative and in which I rejoice: good friends, meaningful work, good health, and living in a safe place where I am generally free from danger. I find more and more things to add. Simply shifting my attention in this direction leads me to feeling appreciation and delight.

Having thought of what in our lives we can rejoice about, our next step in this method is to imagine others feeling joy and rejoicing in their happiness. Many people find that once they are in touch with joy themselves, they easily feel joy for others, too. Then, in a still further step, we think of people we know and imagine them rejoicing themselves. Unlike metta practice, where we wish happiness to others, in rejoicing we imagine others rejoicing on behalf of the others in their own lives. So, for example, I might wish happiness to my niece, Debbie, in metta practice. In rejoicing practice I might imagine the delight Debbie feels in watching her daughter, Sarah, growing into a bright young woman.

As with the metta and tonglen practices, we then expand out to people we feel neutral toward and finally people we have a hard time with. I often find that by the time I get to the last category it is easier to wish joy for others I do not especially warm to, or even actively feel repelled by, when I imagine them rejoicing on behalf of someone else.

Method 2

The second method, presented by B. Alan Wallace (2004) is a little different. In particular, it makes use of our ability to empathize and imagine being someone else. We begin by thinking of someone who is already filled with joy and delight. It might be a child or a pet or even a fictional character. Then, using empathy, we imagine what it would be like to be that being and feel what he or she feels. For example, one of our three dogs is a little 8-pound cutie. She is such a happy creature that even her breeder named her Sunny. Sunny likes to lie on her back and wiggle back and forth while making little yippy pleasure noises. I sometimes take Sunny to school with me, and my students often come to my office for what they call, "Sunny therapy." It is hard not to be cheerful around her. I have a few clients who like to have Sunny in their sessions, and one man who is often quite depressed brightens up and laughs when she is with him.

So we begin the practice by identifying with a happy being, perhaps someone like Sunny, and in that way evoke feelings of happiness and delight in ourselves. Then we rejoice for whatever being we have been thinking of.

We expand the practice, as usual, by thinking of those toward whom we feel neutrality, and then antipathy. We imagine those people feeling utterly delighted and, as we did at the beginning of the practice, we identify with them and put ourselves in their shoes. Then we feel joy ourselves about their happiness.

As always, with any exercise or practice, we do what we can do and just let go of any part of the practice that feels unworkable. I often find that I can expand my understanding and view of a person when I include him or her in this practice. It sometimes reveals to me a one-dimensional view I have been holding onto, especially toward someone I find challenging. B. Alan Wallace (2004) warns us not to imagine someone finding joy in harming another being. It is good to remember that we are doing this practice to cultivate our hearts and feel kindness for other beings.

We conclude the practice by practicing mindfulness meditation.

Helping Our Clients Connect With Joy

We have already seen the example of how I worked with Marc, who felt jealous of his partner at a dinner party. Most often the way I include the practice of rejoicing in my clinical work is by asking clients more about potentially joyful situations that they have brought up on their own. When clients talk of those they care about—partners, children, grandchildren, friends, pets, and anyone who is dear to them—I might ask to hear more. For example, when a lonely client mentioned her cat, I asked her to tell me more about him. She told me about how she had first gotten Emperor as a tiny kitten and went on to describe how they play together with his favorite "mousie" string toy. As she told me about Emperor, she seemed happy. In her case it seemed possible to go further, so I asked about what she imagined it was like for Emperor when they played together. "I think he loves it. He's like a kitten when he jumps after the mousie. He seems to seek it out."

What good is it to invite this client to talk about her cat? In itself, it is of value to help her tune in to the expansive feeling of happiness. Beyond that, it can also provide a way for us to connect with each other. We can share a few moments of joy as we think of Emperor and his toy. Having tapped into some openness and mutual connection, we can then explore more difficult topics such as how she might take some steps toward her stated goal of having more people in her life.

EQUANIMITY

Equanimity, in Buddhist psychology, refers to having boundless "affectionate loving-kindness" toward all beings (Wallace, 2004, p. 161). It is also described as having a welcoming attitude toward all emotions and states of mind (Chödrön, 2001). We can cultivate this attitude through the sitting meditation practice of unconditional mindfulness and in the equanimity practices described below. Equanimity points to our common ground and basic similarities. As the Dalai Lama has pointed out, "every human being wants happiness and does not want suffering." A key aspect of equanimity is recognizing that we might very well have responded to life as others have if we had found ourselves in circumstances like theirs.

Thich Nhat Hanh's (1987a, pp. 62–64) powerful poem "Please Call Me by My True Names" highlights this idea. He writes about a young woman, one of the boat people after the Vietnam War, who killed herself after being raped by sea pirates. In the poem he imagines being the child who grew up to be the pirate who raped her. He thinks about how if he had been born into a life of ignorance and poverty with no future prospects, he, too, might have followed the example of all his peers and raped the young woman.

As we did in the B. Alan Wallace approach to joy, we practice equanimity by putting ourselves inside someone else's skin through the use of our imagination and empathy. Equanimity practices are specifically about letting go of attachment to our fixed views about others. Before we go further, let me clarify a bit what Buddhist psychology means by "attachment." In the Buddhist use of the word, attachment refers to objectifying people, or other beings, as separate and solid, and then responding to them with the three poisons of passion, aggression, or ignorance. Attachment is attributing to others the kind of fixed identity that Buddhist psychology regards as the source of suffering. This understanding of attachment is not a denial of the need for healthy attachments to parents or caregivers that we all require growing up.[2] In equanimity practice, we are cultivating our ability to see others not as objects but instead as the subjects of their own experience. It is this subjectivity with which we imagine identifying. There are several ways to do equanimity practice.

"Just Like Me" Practice

A simple and very portable equanimity practice is to remind ourselves, whenever we see or meet someone we want to ignore or reject, "This person is just like me" (Wallace, 2004; Chödrön, 2005). When I receive yet another unwanted phone call from someone selling billing systems for my private practice, I just want to hang up on him. If I can remember that he is just like me, trying to make a living and perhaps supporting a family, I can be more polite as I tell him I am not interested. When I hear the news of how the political party of which I am not a member has once again held on to what I see as a stubborn and wrong view, preventing my preferred political agenda from being moved forward, I can remind myself that all of those people are just like me and have their reasons for their convictions. I can easily imagine that if I had grown up hearing particular opinions espoused by those who loved and cared for me, I might well now sympathize with the views I currently find unacceptable. The practice of "just like me" helps us let go of fixed opinions about others and lets us see that there just might be some goodness even in those we find difficult.

As noted earlier, we need to remember that emphasizing how we are all alike should not be an excuse to dismiss the genuine differences in experience we each have. In fact, equanimity practice may give those who are privileged in various ways the chance to develop a more personal appreciation of what it is like to be on the receiving end of injustice and oppression.

A Formal Equanimity Practice

As we did with the first three limitless ones, we can cultivate equanimity in the context of our sitting practice. To begin, we settle ourselves with a few minutes of mindfulness practice. Then, we begin by thinking of someone we care for like a friend, lover, or family member. As before, we move on to a neutral person and then someone we do not like (Wallace, 2004). For each of these people, we consider how the circumstances of their lives and our own have come together to create the relationships we now have. We might, for example, recognize that the person we now view as a distrusted rival could, in a different set of causes and conditions, have been a close friend. The close friend whose infidelity we have done our best to understand might in another context be someone we would condemn. The point of this practice is to see how our positive and negative attachments are based on temporary and changing conditions. As we do these contemplations for each of those three people, we may find that we can let go of some of our own solidified opinions and perceptions. Take a few minutes to work with each person, and end the practice with a few minutes of mindfulness meditation.

The Empty Mirror

Some years ago I was teaching a class on the eighth-century Mahayana classic, *A Guide to the Bodhisattva's Way of Life* (Bodhicharyvatara) to some third-year students in Naropa's contemplative program. The author, Shantideva (1979), presents a particular teaching known as "exchanging self for other," which my students were having a hard time relating to. The particulars of the practice did not speak to their modern experience, focusing as they did on relationships between superiors and inferiors. Instead, we came up with a variation which we then called he difficult person exercise. Over the years I have tinkered with it more, and the empty mirror exercise, presented here, is my latest reworking of it. I have led this empty mirror exercise with many different groups of people at various

197

workshops and conferences in this country and elsewhere. It is a potentially powerful equanimity practice.

There are four steps to the exercise. As always, if any part of the exercise feels like it is too much or unworkable for you, for any reason at all, do not do it. Stay with as much of it as you like. As you do this exercise for the first time, I do not recommend choosing a person who could be retraumatizing for you. You might choose to do that at some later point, but do not begin there.

Step 1: Choosing a Challenging Relationship

Begin by taking a comfortable posture. It is best, for this exercise, to be sitting on a chair or cushion. As usual, relax into your body and track your breathing for a few minutes. Then think of a person in your current life with whom you are having a difficult relationship. It may be a friend with whom you have unfinished business; it may be a family member with whom you disagree or from whom you have become estranged; it may be a client who drives you crazy; or it may be a colleague or boss whose actions are causing you to worry and lose sleep. It should be someone with whom you have an emotional charge.

Step 2: Imagining the Other Person

Now imagine the other person seated opposite you at eye level. In this step, do your best to come up with a vivid sense of this other person. Imagine what he or she looks like: the clothing, the posture, the hair. Then go further and think about that person's life circumstances. How does this person spend time, and with whom? What are the other relationships in that person's life? What are his or her concerns? What do you know about his or her personal history and how it affects the present? And what is that person's relationship with you? How do you feel when you are with that person, and how do you feel now as you think about him or her? Spend some time on this step until you have a good sense of the person and your own feelings toward him or her.

Step 3: Trading Places

In this step, imagine trading seats with the other person. That is, you become the other person. Take a few minutes, probably with your eyes closed, to feel into this new identity. Notice what you are wearing, and spend time seeing what it is like to have this body and whatever physical challenges and strengths come with it. Consider how you spend your time and who the important people are in your life. As much as you can, tune in to your emotions and thoughts.

Then imagine lifting your gaze and noticing the person seated opposite you. This is the person you began as. As you look at that person, what do you think of him or her? How do you understand your relationship? Spend some time with this, and consider your history together and the state of your present connection. Notice what feelings arise as you do this.

Then, continuing in this seat, consider what it is you want from that person sitting opposite you. Then imagine that you actually receive what you want. Notice what arises for you once you have received whatever that is. Take whatever time you need.

Step 4: Returning to Ourselves

Now imagine returning to your original place. Once you feel seated again in your original identity, notice what you are feeling now. What do you experience in your body and mind? And, as you imagine lifting your gaze to look again at the person opposite you, what do you feel? How is it for you to know that the person has received what he or she wanted from you? Once again, take as much time as you need.

End the exercise with a few minutes of mindfulness meditation. It is usually helpful to have your eyes open at this point.

Some Comments on the Empty Mirror Exercise

This practice can be very powerful for some people. For example, I have known a few conference participants who transformed their relationships with estranged siblings after doing this practice. Others have told me of how their relationships with parents and children have softened after doing it. Still others, of course, have found it to be nothing special. Many people have reported to me that they chose not to give the challenging person what he or she wanted. For them, it felt inappropriate, offensive, or too soon. Many others have said how surprised they were to discover that what the other person wanted was merely to be seen and acknowledged. This they were happy to do. Like sitting practice, the empty mirror is a unique experience for whoever does it, and it is different each time it is done.

An Example of Doing the Empty Mirror Contemplation for a Client

Loretta had always been a difficult client for me. She called me frequently, leaving urgent messages with my answering service that she needed to be called back immediately. When I would call back, she would ramble somewhat incoherently about wanting to kill herself. I realized after a few of these calls that she had been drinking, but she always denied it. When I pressed her further she would say that she did not want to kill herself, but if nothing changed she sure would. I called the police once to do a wellness check to see if she really was suicidal. They were satisfied that she was not.

Loretta was often angry and would raise her voice, accusing me of not helping her and not knowing my job. Mostly she complained about the people in her life who were disappointing or inadequate somehow. Once she very briefly mentioned losing a bet to a staff member when she was in high school and blaming herself for not winning it. She completely refused to discuss it further in the same way that she also refused to discuss her sexual relationship with her husband. We met, sometimes twice a week, for over a year. Our work ended when she moved out of town. My failure to provide her with any useful help, or to find out what was most deeply troubling her, haunted me for quite awhile after she left. Then, about 5 years later, I was surprised to receive a phone call from her. She was visiting friends in town, and she wanted to see me for one session. I agreed to meet her despite my misgivings.

When she came in, she surprised me by thanking me for all I had done for her. I asked if she recalled her dissatisfaction with me, and she said no, I had always been helpful. After she left, I did the empty mirror exercise as a way to relate to my own bewilderment.

As I settled myself and began to think about doing the exercise while focusing on Loretta, the familiar feelings of helplessness and anxiety arose. As I went on to picturing her sitting opposite me, I imagined her brows knitted in a frown as she listed all the things that were terrible in her life. The litany of complaints was familiar, as was her anger at me for not helping. I pictured her overweight body, wearing her usual knit pants and loose top. Her short dark brown hair was tousled.

I imagined changing places and becoming Loretta. As I felt my way into her body and mind, I noticed how sad and alone I felt. No one understood my pain: not my husband, not my children, not my friends. I would keep everything to myself and no one could help me. As I looked up at Karen, I saw that she was trying hard to understand. I needed her to let me be angry, but I could never tell her why. What I wanted was her kindness and her not giving up on me. That was all.

Switching back to myself, I could see how my being kind and persistent might actually be what she had been seeking from me. I now remembered a few incidents in which she had said as much. It seemed to me now that her way of connecting with me had been through her angry complaints. She had found a precise solution to the problem of wanting to connect beyond her loneliness but not wanting to become vulnerable. My willingness to stay there with her, without giving up on her, was what she had valued: that, and simple human kindness. I felt softhearted as I thought about her. I had, for a long time, thought that she had probably been sexually abused by the high school staff person, and her insistence that losing the bet had been her own fault was perhaps a defense against recognizing her own powerlessness. Maybe if we had met for a longer time she might have told me the truth of what had happened to her. Maybe I had that wrong. In any case, doing the empty mirror helped me connect with our shared essential humanity, and I could see how she could think that I had helped her despite my not recognizing it myself.

Chapter 10

CONTEMPLATIVE APPROACHES
TO ANGER

In this chapter, we explore how Buddhist psychology suggests working with anger. Although we have already looked at how to work
with emotions in Chapter 8, anger can be especially challenging for
clients and therapists, so I have chosen to devote a separate chapter
to it. As we have seen in earlier chapters, anger may be confused or
unconfused. Unconfused or clean anger is not a problem. It is an
expression of our natural wisdom, our brilliant sanity.

Confused anger, on the other hand, is permeated with aggression
and may also contain the desire to harm its object. I focus largely on
this confused, or what I sometimes call ordinary, anger in this chapter. As we have seen already, in Contemplative Psychotherapy, we
define aggression differently from some common usages of the term.
It is not the same, for example, as assertiveness or forcefulness.
Those might be quite healthy. Instead, we define it as rejecting our
experience. Aggression, from this point of view, is always a pushing
away of the truth of the moment and is thus never an expression of
brilliant sanity.

First, we look at how we might work with anger when it arises in
ourselves or in our clients. We also note what the Buddhist teachings
suggest we do when we are the objects of the anger of others. Finally,
we explore the four powers as a way of working with what is often
the residue of anger: feelings of guilt and shame (Gyatso, 1994).

The Buddhist approach to working with confused anger is to cultivate its antidote: patience (Gyatso, 1980). I know my own first reaction to this notion was that it sounded pretty passive, even doormat-like. I imagined patience as being a good girl, sitting quietly, hands folded in my lap, while I waited for something I wanted in the future. As a woman who was in her 20s during much of the women's movement of the 1960s, I was especially leery of any suggestion of losing my hard-won voice. However, I discovered that patience, from this point of view, is basically nonaggression. That is, patience is the ability to see things as they are and not reject them. Note that this is not the same as making the judgment that things are just fine. It may be that things are not fine at all, and that action needs to be taken. Skillful action cannot be undertaken, however, without the clarity that is revealed only when we let go of our attachment to how we want things to be as well as our rejection of how they are now. That is to say, our ability to be skillful rests on our willingness to let go of aggression. Having seen many well-intentioned activists fall into the very aggression and inflexibility they were opposing, this approach of cultivating patience made sense to me.

Drawing on Buddhist psychology, we can identify three kinds of patience.[1] The first is the patience that comes from understanding how anger arises; the second is the patience of tolerating discomfort; and the third is the patience of not retaliating.

THE PATIENCE OF UNDERSTANDING HOW ANGER ARISES

When we understand how anger arises, we are better prepared to recognize and track it as it builds and even to interrupt its momentum. This can let us find the seed of clarity that exists underneath all anger.

How Anger Arises

The first stage in the development of any kind of anger, unconfused or confused, is a moment or more of clear perception. Along with this clear perception there may be some degree of discomfort or pain. The next stage is where the development of confused anger parts company with that of unconfused or clean anger. At that point, we either open further to the clear perception, or we reject it and push it away with aggression. In the former, especially when the perception is based on the recognition of injustice, unfairness, or abuse, the arising of anger may simply be an expression of compassion and brilliant sanity. For example, we may have been ignored or harmed because of our race, gender, or sexual orientation. This kind of anger contains energy that we may skillfully direct toward remedying a harmful situation. It need not contain aggression: it can be seeing what is happening in the moment, not pushing it away.

In the development of confused anger, based on aggression, however, we reject the message of the moment of clear perception. We perceive something in our inner or outer world that we do not like or wish not to experience. For example, it could be as small as the market not having the brand of toothpaste we like or being cut off by another driver. Or we may find our plans and desires are not met. Or we feel hurt, fear, embarrassment, or some other kind of pain and want to escape it.

In that pushing away, there is a loss of contact with things as they are. Instead, there is an increasingly solidified and inaccurate interpretation of what has occurred. This is then maintained and enhanced by negative thoughts about the object of one's anger. Often this means beginning to interpret the situation through the lens of our fixed sense of a personal identity. We may identify ourselves with the experience of anger. In addition, if we are angry with other persons or groups, we solidify them even further as "other" and "different from me." Even experiences of clean anger may become confused anger if we try to create and hold onto an identity as the one who is rightfully angry.

Until there is some recognition of one's mistaken viewpoint or an external interruption, the anger and increasing physical signs of the fight response can keep building until some confused action is taken. That action is very likely to be harmful to oneself or others and result in unwanted consequences.

The following example may illustrate how ordinary, confused anger might arise. The other day, Kobe, one of our dogs, slipped on our back deck. He is no longer young, and he began to limp and could not manage to lie down. We took him to the dog version of urgent care where a very pleasant veterinarian diagnosed an injured groin muscle. He prescribed some medications, and since we already had a leftover supply of the painkiller he recommended, we did not buy still more of it. The vet told us to follow the dosage instructions on the label of what we had at home.

Once home, it became apparent that we had two different sets of instructions on two bottles of the same size pills: one bottle said to take two tablets three to four times a day, and the other said to use only one tablet twice a day. It was quite a difference even though both had previously been prescribed for Kobe. When we phoned the urgent care office, the young woman who answered the phone gave us the message to "follow the instructions on the label," because the doctor had said that he could not comment on someone else's prescription. I expressed my belief to her that this was an unacceptable answer and that we needed to know the proper dose. She promised to ask him and call back.

So far, my initial response had been mostly clear: Kobe was in pain; he needed the right amount of medicine; and it was necessary to know the correct dose. I hung up the phone, and as I awaited her return call, I began to feel irritated and to find reasons to criticize the vet for not telling us what we needed to know. I added more thoughts: I questioned the vet's motivation and his skill. I doubted his compassion and suitability for the work he was doing. I soon had a familiar experience, which I call my "Yeah" moment. It is as though at that point I say, "Yeah, I'm right!" The emphasis is on the I who is right. Sometimes I can recognize that moment and interrupt the building anger.

That day, though, I kept it cooking. At some level, I was enjoying the rush of energy that accompanied the rising momentum of my anger. I began to voice my complaints aloud, in an increasingly strong voice. I could feel blood rushing to my face. I began to spin out more and more judgmental thoughts and comments about this terrible man. As is often the case, I mindlessly exaggerated his negative qualities. I was soon completely enraged and utterly convinced of my version of things.

Then the phone rang, and it was the vet himself. He was pleasant and reasonable. I began to realize that there was little correspondence between my rage and what he was saying. I finally managed to let go of my anger and begin to actually hear his words. I had to ask him to repeat the first part of what he had said. He explained exactly what dosage to give Kobe and what signs to look for if he needed more or less medication. With good wishes to Kobe for a speedy recovery, he hung up.

This example illustrates how confused anger arises. It begins with a clear perception and then is followed by becoming attached to an increasingly solid conviction of one's own point of view, bolstered by stories with varying degrees of accuracy. The problem is that we often miss the earliest stages of our growing anger and can become certain of our rightness and the truth of all sorts of inaccuracies that we do not bother to verify. In this example, my anger rose and became solid quite quickly. I have heard this called a sudden wind of anger. However, anger can also build much more slowly over time. Instead of erupting, as mine did, it can smolder and gather without our noticing until we are furious without recognizing where our rage has come from. Whether it builds quickly or slowly, the same process is the essence of how anger at all levels develops and can lead to long-standing animosities and hostilities, including war.

Helping Clients Cultivate the Patience of Understanding How Anger Arises

Cultivating the patience of understanding how anger arises can be very useful to clients who struggle with inappropriate anger and the acting out based on it. Helping them learn to recognize the felt experience of anger, the earlier in the process the better, can provide them with opportunities to make choices. In confused anger, there is a loss of curiosity, and therapists can help their clients to reawaken it. Learning their personal patterns related to anger is also important. Each of us has different landmarks. For me, it is the "Yeah" moment and the tightening of my jaw. I have also learned that when my anger is fueled by fear for the well-being of someone I care about, it is more likely to escalate than at other times. In the process of feeding my anger, I lose touch with the fear and also with the tenderness and care on which the fear is based. This is, of course, not an unusual pattern. What I really need to explore in such situations is what will actually be helpful to the one I care about. Instead, if my energy and attention is caught up in nursing my anger, I am not able to address what needs to be addressed. To take such skillful action, I need mindfulness and awareness. In turn, as noted before, mindfulness and awareness are more accessible if we can calm our fight-flight responses. In order to take the steps that will help us regulate our nervous systems, we have to notice that we need to do so. Again, it is increasing our ability to recognize the early signs and the direct experience of anger that are key.

In Chapter 4, I described how my client Sarah learned how to track her inner experience of fear in order to know when she was in a potentially dangerous situation with her partner, Barbara. Sarah also needed to learn how to track her experience of anger. Both she and Barbara came from sexually and physically abusive families, and when they were in conflict, either one of them might rapidly fall into abusive language. Name calling quickly could become shoving and then hitting. Sometimes alcohol was involved. In the same way that Sarah did not recognize the early signs of fear, she often also failed to track her own mounting dissatisfaction and anger with Barbara until it required only the smallest trigger for her to become very angry.

For example, one day they fell into an argument when they were sitting side by side at a picnic table in a park. The topic almost did not matter, but it happened to be about who was going to do the grocery shopping that week. Barbara said that she had done it the previous week. Sarah heard this as a criticism of herself. There was some accuracy, perhaps, in that perception. Perhaps not. In any case, it felt like the last straw to her. She started to yell at Barbara, listing all the things that she, Sarah, took care of around the house, and who did Barbara think she was? Her slave? Barbara replied in kind. Neither was willing to let go. They began to push each other as they sat on the bench attached to the table. The conflict escalated to hitting. Sarah ended up lying on the ground with a bruise on her face. In telling me the story, Sarah was still enraged at her perception that Barbara had charmed the police into identifying Sarah as the perpetrator even though she was the one with the physical injury. Sarah ended up being court ordered to therapy for domestic violence. When our county could provide only a group with male perpetrators, she was allowed to use our work together to meet this requirement. She continued to live with Barbara even after this.

In our work, we focused on a number of issues, including her anger. We worked on improving her ability to track small signs of fear and anger before they exploded in the rage that felt like it was about protecting her survival. One of the first things we did was to focus on language. Like many clients, Sarah used words that she did not recognize as anger related. We began to identify those feeling words together: for example, "upset," "irritated," and "frustrated."

Like many clients who work with anger, another part of our work was teasing apart what was appropriate, unconfused anger from what was confused and based on distorted perceptions. For Sarah this included not only working with her past sexual abuse as a teenager but also the abuse in her present relationship with Barbara.

Another thing we explored was the role of alcohol in her anger. In particular, we noted how drinking made it even more difficult to recognize the early signs of fear or anger. She did not drink frequently, but it was often the case that when she and Barbara drank wine at dinner, arguments followed. She learned to reduce her drinking, to recognize her negative, angry thoughts, and to leave the house before she erupted in rage. In addition, she began to identify the physical signs in her body indicating that she was becoming frightened and activated. Over time she was able to recognize the tightening in her belly and a feeling of numbness that were the signs she was beginning to be afraid. With them came increasing tension, and she became more likely to react with anger. Given her own and Barbara's histories, it took very little for either of them to become triggered. Sarah learned some basic techniques for calming herself. We worked with her trauma history and also with recognizing her own good qualities to counter her deeply held conviction of herself as not good enough. It took some months after her domestic violence conviction, but she finally moved out of the home they had bought together. Eventually, she ended the relationship with Barbara, found a new career she was drawn to, and went back to school to get the training she needed.

THE PATIENCE OF TOLERATING DISCOMFORT

The second kind of patience is willingly tolerating the painful experience of anger without moving into action. As we noted in working with emotions, acting out or mindlessly expressing our emotions is often an attempt to eliminate them. The suggestion with this kind of patience is to fully experience our anger in our body and mind and not try to get rid of it. Pema Chödrön has described this as "learning to relax with the edginess of our energy" (2005, p. 165).

Why would we choose this option? First, with any experience of anger, we might want to connect with its underlying clarity before taking any action. Confused anger, in particular, has a number of drawbacks to just reacting instead of letting ourselves feel what we feel. The rest of the discussion of this kind of patience focuses on working only with confused anger even though it is referred to simply as "anger."

Traditional Disadvantages of Anger

From the point of view of Buddhist psychology, anger leads only to more anger and not to satisfaction. According to Geshe Kelsang Gyatso (1980), in his commentary on Shantideva, there are a number of problems in giving in to our urge to express our anger instead of willingly experiencing it. First, giving in to anger is said to destroy many of the good seeds we have planted in the storehouse consciousness. Because anger plants so many negative seeds, they more than cancel out the good ones. With unrestrained anger, we are likely to say and do things that we will later regret. We may actually harm others or ourselves, and these actions plant negative seeds that will bring us future suffering.

Anger prevents us from reaching many of the goals we may have, such as having more peace of mind or being more discerning. It tends to be painful, in itself, something we may not recognize if we are caught up in its momentum. Anger makes us less mindful and aware. As with other kinds of mindless states, we lose touch with our compassionate hearts as well as our clarity. We are likely to be swept away by our rage and become less connected with what is actually happening. Geshe Kelsang Gyatso says that when we are ruled by anger, "it robs us of our reason and our good sense" (1980, p. 168).

We also open ourselves to danger when we entertain and express our anger. We are more likely to cause others to be angry with us, and they, too, will be unclear and likely to become aggressive or violent. People who are known to become angry often tend to be avoided by others and may find themselves abandoned by those they care about.

Unlike the popular myth that we sometimes hear, "You're so beautiful when you're angry," the Dalai Lama has pointed out that anger makes people who are "good-looking and normally peaceful" become "ugly" (Gyatso, 1994, pp. 53–54). Moreover, those people find that "anger upsets their physical well-being and disturbs their rest; it destroys their appetites and makes them age prematurely." They become unreliable, and "can no longer be counted on" (p. 54).

Buddhism teaches that confused anger has "no other function than to destroy our positive actions and make us suffer" (Gyatso, 1994, p. 55).

Practicing the Patience of Tolerating Discomfort

Given all of those negative consequences of confused anger, it makes sense to refrain from feeding it or acting upon it. Instead, the suggestion is not to repress it or ignore it, but to go toward it and experience it fully and with mindfulness and awareness. Thich Nhat Hanh (1992b, p. 61) has suggested how we can practice with our anger by doing walking meditation. As we walk, we breathe and say things to ourselves like

> Breathing in, I know that anger is here.
> Breathing out, I know that the anger is in me.
> Breathing in, I know that anger is unpleasant.
> Breathing out, I know this feeling will pass.
> Breathing in, I am calm.
> Breathing out, I am strong enough to take care of this
>   anger.

We keep walking and saying whatever is true in the moment. We can include what is happening in our bodies and also in our minds.

It can take an hour for anger to settle down and dissipate, but it is impermanent and, if we do not feed it, it will eventually dissolve. If we are too angry to do this practice, or one like it, we can use the method introduced in Chapter 8 of using mindlessness practices mindfully or any of the compassion practices found in Chapter 9. The important point is that we are not pushing our anger away or rejecting it. To do so would be treating our already aggressive anger with aggression. Instead we can practice patience, letting be. The

Dalai Lama (Gyatso, 1994) has suggested that cultivating this kind of patience is an expression of strength, not weakness; weakness is giving in to our anger.

Helping Clients Tolerate the Discomfort of Anger

I have suggested the walking practice to some clients. Anger brings a lot of energy with it, and having a physically based mindfulness exercise can be useful. Part of the problem with anger is that we can feel so revved up that we feel we have to do something, anything.

A young man with whom I work, Carl, was feeling hurt and angry when he discovered, soon after they broke up, that his girlfriend had been lying to him about seeing another man during the last several months of their relationship. We explored his feelings, and when he said that he did not want to keep the angry thoughts and feelings "festering," I suggested that he might try walking outside with his anger as a way to befriend it instead of fueling it. I described how he might do that, and he decided to try it. When he returned for his next session, he reported that the walking practice had been helpful, but that he could still get caught up in painful thoughts and lose track of himself. I suggested that he continue doing the walking exercise, when it seemed helpful, and also add some other activities to gain some respite from the anger without rejecting it. We discussed what those might be, and he chose to continue walking and also to sometimes listen to inspiring recordings while he did so. He was fond of Pema Chödrön's recordings, so he chose to listen to those, especially since they reminded him to be in the present moment. Finally, he also decided to listen to other recorded books while he walked, such as the spy novels he liked, when he could not otherwise interrupt his busy mind.

Having practiced willingly experiencing his discomfort in tandem with taking breaks from it, Carl came to a decision. He chose to tell his ex-girlfriend how her behavior had affected him. Having phoned her, because he wanted to have her hear his voice and because he did not want to "hide behind" a text message or e-mail, he told her that he had always treated her with kindness and that he had not deserved to be treated so badly. In telling me about it, he was pleased and proud that he had been able to speak up for himself. He noted that this was something he would not have been able to do during the time they had been together, and he noted how this reflected his increasing feelings of self-confidence and self-worth.

THE PATIENCE OF NOT RETALIATING

The third kind of patience is especially helpful in working with our minds when we are the objects of another's anger. We look here at dealing with clients who are angry at us as well as helping clients who deal with similar situations themselves. As in the second kind of patience, in the patience of not retaliating we choose to experience our feelings without reacting with speech or action. It can be extremely challenging to practice this method, especially when we believe that we are in the right. The suggestion is, as always in working with anger, that we begin by being present with our own experience before we take any steps in communicating further with others.

Practicing the Patience of Not Retaliating

In Contemplative Psychotherapy we sometimes say that it is harder to work with clients who deal with aggression than with clients whose issues are based on passion. Clients working with passion-based issues are often more interested in drawing us in somehow, gaining our approval, or becoming dependent on us. Since they are right there, trying to get what they want from us, we have the opportunity to address our relationships with them. In contrast, by their very nature, aggression and anger push others away, so our clients might be actively pushing us away, too. It can be quite difficult to make use of our relationship with clients as they are backing away from us. This is not to say, of course, that being angry with us is not relating to us.

Being the recipient of our clients' anger can be painful. Clients who are angry with us are often quite perceptive in their accusations, and we may feel hurt by the accuracy of what they might say. There is, after all, always some clarity in anger.

We may have our own personal reactions to anger directed at us. Therapists who have been abused in childhood may feel triggered in addition to any other responses they might have. It probably goes without saying that if we believe we might be putting ourselves in harm's way, we should leave and seek assistance or call the police.

Beyond all of that, it may be painful to exchange with a client who is experiencing anger or rage.

What, then, are the suggestions for practicing the patience of not retaliating? First, we are encouraged to continue developing the mindfulness and awareness that let us know what we are experiencing. As therapists, the ability to hold space, discussed in Chapter 3, is important because it can give us a sense of perspective, allowing us not to be reactive.

Traditionally, we are taught to recognize that when people are angry, they are not in control of themselves. Shantideva (1979) suggests that it does not make sense to become angry at a person who wants to harm us. He points out that the person is controlled by anger and confusion, and if we are going to be angry, it should be at the anger, not at the person. He uses a famous metaphor to describe this: being angry at the person is like being angry at the stick someone might try to use to beat us instead of at the person wielding the stick.

Another understanding that helps us not retaliate is the recognition that a person who is angry is in pain. This can help us connect with our compassion.

Finally, knowing that anger and aggression lead only to more anger and aggression can help us refrain from meeting anger with more anger. Not only does becoming angry not work, it would just make us less clear, and thus less skillful ourselves.

If a client has crossed the line into becoming abusive, threatening harm, or escalating into racial epithets or other inappropriate name calling, we need to set clear boundaries. We need to say what is not allowed without pushing away the client or the client's anger, if we can. This may mean asking clients to describe their experience and say what is making them angry without acting out. If clients can do that, then we can continue to invite them into relationship. If they cannot, then we need to take appropriate steps to protect ourselves. Being compassionate toward our clients means doing what we can to prevent them not only from directly harming themselves but also from indirectly causing themselves future suffering by planting more negative seeds. Where that boundary lies is a personal choice therapists can make based on their own clinical judgment. It may well be different with different clients and in different situations.

If we can continue working with clients, knowing that clients who are presently angry may be quite out of touch with us and with their own brilliant sanity, we will probably choose not to engage in a rational argument at that point. Instead, we need to call on what Buddhist psychology might call pacifying actions (Trungpa, 1991). Generally, they are actions that create a peaceful environment. For therapists, this can mean applying basic listening skills and asking simple questions. Asking closed questions such as those which require simple factual or yes or no answers and setting clear boundaries can help clients to calm down.

If we can hold the space for clients' anger, they may begin to settle down. We can ask if they want help with that, but if we are the bad guy, they may not choose that option. If they do accept our help, we can help them calm their nervous systems with things like grounding, resourcing, breathing exercises, and so on.

The key point is not to model that anger and angry people are bad and need to be rejected.

Clinical Examples of Working With the Patience of Not Retaliating

As I wrote this chapter, I realized I have been fortunate in not having very many clients who directed their anger at me. In Chapter 9, I described my experience with Loretta. I often called on the practices associated with this kind of patience in doing my best to stay present with her. Most often, I reminded myself that her anger was caused by pain.

Dennis, the man who was too strange to be accepted on the intramural softball team (Chapter 7), once became very angry with me.[2] Even though he was no longer fit, he still had the build of a football player, and I was scared when he began yelling at me. We were in the group room of the residential facility where he lived, and other members of his therapy team were present. When he yelled at me, I became scared and noticed he was between me and the door. His face became red, and then he abruptly turned, throwing a notebook in my direction as he did so, and left the room. Later we talked about what had happened, and what he said surprised me. He told me that he had noticed how frightened I was. "I saw in your eyes how terrified you were," he told me. "I didn't want to scare you. I just wanted the team to understand that they had made the wrong decision."

I was very touched by his kindness, knowing also how hard it may have been for him to recognize what was happening with someone else in the environment when he was caught up in anger. It was Dennis's own inherent brilliant sanity, his glimpse of clarity and compassion, that had interrupted his tirade. Perhaps my genuine fear had been helpful to him. Certainly, I had been too frozen to make a conscious choice about how I responded to him.

My client Lara struggled with the anger directed at her by her ex-husband, Martin, with whom she still had to communicate about their three teenage children. He would phone and berate her, listing all the ways he thought she was a bad and incompetent mother. A doctor with a successful practice, he had more money than she did and was, moreover, used to being in charge and having his way. Lara was a high school science teacher and could not match his ability to buy expensive things for the children. When she tried to set boundaries about what the children should have, for example, not being comfortable with his giving a motorcycle to their 17-year-old, she was quickly cast as the bad mother by Martin and by the teenagers. Martin ignored other kinds of boundaries, too. For example, he sometimes showed up at her condo when it was not his day to pick up the kids. Lara knew from their 10 years of marriage that she was likely to lose any actual arguments with Martin. She felt helpless and stuck.

Our work began with acknowledging the experience of anger. Many women have learned not to allow themselves to recognize their anger. Instead, they might feel sad and weep, or they might describe frustration, but deny feeling anger. That was the case with Lara. Attending to her felt experience in her body in the context of our relationship, she came to recognize her anger toward Martin. As she contacted her long-buried anger, her first thought was to take action in ways that would humiliate and harm him as he had done to her. In other words, she wanted to retaliate. As we talked through how she might take such actions and their likely consequences, she realized that she did not want to escalate the situation by just making Martin more angry and giving him more ammunition to use against her in his bid to gain sole custody. She saw that retaliating would harm her and possibly the children without producing any good result.

We talked about how she could set useful boundaries and what kind of legal help she might get. After contacting her attorney, they came up with a plan together. Instead of reading Martin's texts or listening to his voice mail tirades, she simply forwarded his e-mails and texts to her attorney and kept all of his abusive voice mails. She would listen or read only long enough to discover if there were anything she needed to know. Cutting off this source of abuse was helpful. Then with the evidence she had collected she was able to obtain a restraining order: Martin was not to come to her condo or phone her. She was no longer available for his verbal abuse.

During this time, Martin had insisted she let the children decide with whom they wanted to live, and two of them had chosen to stay with him. This was extremely painful for Lara. She reminded herself frequently that she could not change Martin, but she could do her best to take care of herself. With that in mind, she started going to the gym again after not going for some months. She sought out friends and spent time with them. Another thing she found helpful, once the weather permitted it, was working in her small garden. All of these activities helped her ground herself in the present moment.

After living only a few days a month with Lara and the rest of the time with Martin, the teenagers soon came to realize that his version of Lara was quite distorted. Lara was able to return to family court and obtain a new agreement with which she was happy. The teenagers, with the exception of her oldest daughter, who was ready to leave for college, once again given the choice by the court, chose to live full time with her.

THE FOUR POWERS

The four powers are a traditional method of purifying the mind, in this case, of anger. The point is that it is possible to reconnect with the mind's natural purity and goodness, its brilliant sanity, even after one has indulged in harmful thoughts and actions. Although some teachers use different names, or present the four powers in a different order, they agree on the main points. Here I use the names presented by the Dalai Lama (Gyatso, 1994) and in the order used by Geshe Kelsang Gyatso (1980): the power of regret, the power of support, the power of antidotes, and the power of resolve.

The four powers are connected with the traditional activity of acknowledging one's misconduct and are known as the four powers of confession. Many spiritual traditions have practices of confessing one's wrongdoing, and Buddhism does as well. The word "confession" has negative connotations for many clients, and I avoid using it with them, but I often think that an important part of our work as therapists is to listen as clients confess their real and imagined bad qualities and behavior. Sometimes we help clients see that what they imagine to be their terrible qualities are not evidence of their badness and may not even be problematic at all. Other times, when clients' words and actions have actually been harmful, being met by our openness and by our not rejecting them can be extremely powerful. Many clients feel guilt and shame about having given in to anger, especially when it has led to harming themselves or others. Our job is not to condone harmful behavior, but by helping clients work with the four powers we may provide them with a path to recognizing that they are still members of the human community, that they are still basically worthy people, and that they may be able to make amends for the damage they may have caused. The four powers may also be useful in helping clients struggling with addictions or other harmful habitual patterns.

The Power of Regret

The first of the four powers is the power of regret. This power has a couple of aspects in working with clients. The first is helping them to recognize and take responsibility for how their behavior has led to harm and to their current suffering. The second is helping them to release self-aggression, guilt, or shame and to connect with the experience of regret or sadness.

Unless clients can see how their own actions have been the cause of suffering for themselves or others, they cannot take responsibility. Without taking responsibility, there is little chance of moving out of a fixed position of blaming others or ignoring the consequences of what one has done. Often clients are already well aware of their part in causing harm. Sometimes clients take on more responsibility for situations than is properly their own. This is a different issue, but it is one that we should attend to as well. It is common, for example, for children and adults to feel responsible for causing the sexual or physical abuse of which they were the victims.

In working with helping clients to take responsibility, we may need to help them see the part they have played, or are still playing, in causing suffering before we can do much else. In general, unless clients have been court ordered into therapy, they may have some sense of this before they come to us. In court-ordered situations, taking responsibility is frequently a key issue. A former student of mine who did her internship working with perpetrators of domestic violence found that when clients could take responsibility, they could make good use of the four powers. In its simplest form, seeing the action of cause and effect can help clients see where their responsibility may lie.

The second aspect of the power of regret is an especially important one for contemplative therapists. Once clients take responsibility for their actions, they often have feelings of guilt or shame, both of which can contain a good deal of self-aggression. I sometimes tell clients that there is a little bit of good information in guilt and shame: they indicate that we have violated our own sense of what is right. But, I tell them, beyond recognizing that information, keeping those emotions going is not particularly useful. Just as with confused anger, there is some clarity in those feelings, but it quickly can become self-aggression, which only harms oneself to no purpose. I invite clients to notice their inner bodily experience, and more often than not, they are able to touch into a feeling of sadness. When I invite them to further explore the direct experience of sadness, they often say that there is a soft or sore area in their heart region. With my support, they might find that they can experience it without turning it into a belief that they are bad. It has been my experience with clients that if they can find that sense of tenderness, soreness, or sadness, they can move in the direction of regret.

Another avenue to regret is the experience of revulsion. A traditional Buddhist teaching suggests that revulsion "is the foot of meditation" (Nalanda Translation Committee, n.d.). That is, revulsion brings one to the spiritual path. At the heart of revulsion with one's confusion and harmful actions is the desire not to cause further suffering, and it is a reflection of our natural clarity and compassion. As we will see below, recognizing revulsion can be an opportunity to choose a different path forward. Therapists can help their clients recognize such moments and invite them to experience them directly without getting caught up in accompanying, self-critical thoughts.

Regret refers most simply to the feeling of sadness that comes with accepting responsibility for having caused suffering. It is the wish that one did not cause harm but at the same time seeing that one has done so. If clients do not spontaneously express some kind of regret after contacting a sense of responsibility and sadness, I may ask them if that is something they are experiencing.

The Power of Support

In the traditional presentations of the four powers, the second power, reliance or support, is about seeking help from one's teacher or taking refuge in the three jewels of the Buddha (as an example of wakefulness), the dharma (the teachings), and the sangha (the community of practitioners) (Trungpa, 1991). Needless to say, I do not suggest this to my clients. Instead, I invite them to identify what and who in their lives could support them as they work with the suffering they are experiencing: "Who can you rely on? Who do you turn to? What gives you comfort?" Richard Hanson (with Mendius, 2009, p. 93) has suggested that it can be helpful to identify our own refuges, and he gives the examples of "people, places, memories, ideas, and ideals—anyone or anything that provides reliable sanctuary and protection so that you can let down your guard and gather wisdom and strength."

When clients identify their sources of support, they may begin by naming their therapeutic relationship with me. Many clients have support systems that include friends and family members. Many find comfort in their dogs, cats, and other pets. Others have few sources of support. With those clients, I encourage them to make use of the skills we may have reviewed for regulating their nervous systems. I have been known to explore with clients whether it is time to get that little dog they have been talking about wanting.

Some clients turn to their religious traditions for a sense of support. Many feel they can turn to Jesus or to God. Those who work with 12-step groups may rely on their sense of a higher power. Still others may have an sense of inner support from a "wise mind" or inner guide of some kind.

An obstacle to asking for help from others can be the embarrassment and shame clients may feel about what they have done. When those feelings arise, I once again invite them into directly experiencing those feelings and the power of regret. We explore whether they want to express their regret and sadness to some people and perhaps not to others. This may move us into the third power.

The Power of Antidotes

The third power is about what actions one can take to remedy or make amends for what one has done. In psychotherapy, this usually begins with clients telling their therapists what they have done, if they have not already done so. This confession can be quite challenging. Simply saying aloud to another person what one has done can bring up a host of emotions that clients may not already be aware of. Often, before any further actions can be taken, therapists may need to help clients recognize and work with the emotions they are experiencing. This may even need to occur before clients can take responsibility or feel regret. The four powers do not always happen neatly in the order presented here.

Having taken responsibility for one's actions, experienced regret, and identified sources of support for working with one's own suffering, clients may feel inspired to take some kind of reparative action. Therapists can help their clients to sort through what they want to do. They can assist clients in identifying whom they believe they have harmed and what they think might be helpful to those beings. Sometimes therapists can help clients to clarify what they think might happen as a result of some proposed actions. For example, is a proposed action going to benefit a person who was injured or is it a way to assuage the client's own sense of guilt? Whom is the action going to benefit? Would bringing up an injury caused years ago be more painful than not bringing it up? Would writing a letter be better than asking for a face-to-face conversation? Or perhaps doing it the other way around would be better? Every situation is unique, and therapists can be a useful resource in helping clients to negotiate what can be a tricky path. Returning to the direct experiences of guilt and regret can be helpful in this context.

The Power of Resolve

The last of the four powers is about the commitment not to repeat harmful behaviors. It refers to forming the conscious intention to refrain from specific actions of body and speech. Many times what inspires any of us to make such a commitment is the experience of revulsion. Because of our natural compassion, we genuinely do not want to harm ourselves or others, and so we feel revolted when we fully recognize how we have been the cause of pain or injury. Letting ourselves feel such revulsion can be painful. This is why helping our clients tap into regret and sadness can be so important as it provides an antidote to turning revulsion into self-aggression.

Unfortunately, moving from the experience of revulsion into self-aggression is extremely easy. As noted above, we may cultivate feelings of guilt or shame. We might even turn it into aggression expressed outward toward the very ones we originally harmed in a misguided attempt to escape the pain of revulsion. When we move into aggression toward ourselves or others, we lose track of the compassion underlying the revulsion and instead become caught up with ourselves and with negative story lines. We also become disconnected from the clarity that the revulsion also reflects.

In therapy, this is a powerful choice point. With their therapists' assistance, clients can make use of the wisdom within revulsion and use it as the inspiration to make a commitment to refraining from further harm. I often explain this choice directly to clients. I might say something like the following: "This feeling of being disgusted by what you did is actually very good news. It shows that you really do not want to hurt someone else. It is an expression of your compassion. This is a kind of crossroads: you can use it to give yourself a hard time, or you can use it to become even more compassionate."

Then I might invite them to think about what, if any, choices they might want to make about that now. We may talk about how to recognize when they have fallen into self-aggression and how they can connect with the compassion that does not want to harm others. The Buddhist word for such a choice is "renunciation" (Trungpa & Nalanda Translation Committee 1980). Clients might choose to renounce the original harmful behavior as well as the self-aggression it may have brought up.

From the perspective of Buddhist psychology, making such a commitment is understood to plant seeds in the storehouse consciousness. Sometimes people choose to make an ongoing daily practice of stating such intentions as part of their morning routines. In the same way that making a confession to another person carries

221

more intensity than just thinking about it silently on one's own, stating an intention aloud either to another person like one's therapist or saying it aloud as a daily practice can feel quite significant and carry weight. It also plants still more positive seeds.

The Example of Cynthia

In my work with Cynthia we made use of the four powers in working with her guilt and shame about having been a verbally and physically abusive mother to her now adult daughter.[3] In her mid-70s when we worked together, Cynthia still easily tapped into the belief that she was a bad person and often fell into feelings of depression fueled by self-aggressive thoughts.

Cynthia and I had met for a few sessions, and I had learned how she often used negative thinking to support feelings of worthlessness. She had made a fairly solid identity for herself as basically bad. The proof of that, she explained, was her failure as a mother. Her daughter, Marie, rarely contacted Cynthia, and when Cynthia phoned Marie, she answered mostly in words of one syllable and quickly got off the phone. Marie, now in her early 40s, had a 9-year-old son, Ronnie, whom she did her best to keep away from Cynthia. Cynthia felt a lot of pain about being cut off from her grandson.

Our work with the four powers began with exploring how her guilt and shame might both be reflections of her belief that how she had treated Marie was wrong and that she had been unkind in always criticizing and sometimes hitting her daughter. I told her, as described above, that I saw her feelings as evidence of her insight and compassion and suggested that we might be able to strengthen those qualities. She was a bit skeptical about having those qualities, but she was willing to give it a go.

We worked with bringing mindfulness to her direct experience in the present moment of feeling ashamed about what she had done in the past. It took a little time, but Cynthia learned how to track her inner sensations and recognize her judgments as thoughts, not feelings. This was a new experience for her, and once she caught on, she discovered an appetite for exploring her sensory world.

Once when she felt into the tightness in her chest, it shifted into a feeling of soreness and tenderness. With this came a torrent of tears and sobbing. I encouraged her to let that come and reassured her that I would stay with her as she felt this pain. For a few sessions, this was all that arose: tightness, soreness, tears. We also talked about her own childhood, growing up with an angry and often absent mother. She had not known her father. Another emotion that she began to recognize was anger toward her mother. She saw that she had not, in fact, been a bad child undeserving of her mother's attention, and she felt a softening toward herself. Seeing that she had never experienced parental kindness herself, she began to feel some maitri. Tracking her inner experiences and working with her feelings toward her own mother led to sadness and simple regret about having harmed Marie. Over time, she discovered some sympathy for her own mother, who she realized was struggling with little money and no partner. "None of us had the help we needed," she said. "We were all alone."

Cynthia had already been able to take responsibility for her treatment of Marie, and feeling sadness and regret helped her move to the next steps in healing. The sorrow she felt about having been so alone in her life led to our exploring how she might find more supportive people and activities. Cynthia began to exercise, going every day to a nearby gym to swim. She had previously complained about how Boulder's bus system made no sense to her, and she contacted the company for help. They surprised her by putting her in touch with a young woman who came and rode the buses with Cynthia until she knew her way around. Once she knew how to take the bus, she joined a book club at the library and began to make some friends. She felt as shy as a teenager.

For Cynthia, the last two powers came together. First, she made a commitment never to repeat the unkind behavior in which she had indulged with her daughter and also as a bad-tempered employee at a job she held for many years prior to moving to Boulder. How to work with anger became a big part of our work together, and we practiced the skills of tracking its arising and refraining from moving into speech and action. As she became more adept at recognizing anger and interrupting self-judging thoughts, she noticed that she was less depressed.

The last part of our work with the four powers had to do with reconnecting with Marie. Cynthia now felt that she could really take responsibility for how she had abused Marie, and we talked at length about how she might apologize and seek some forgiveness. She decided to write a letter to Marie. Later, when Marie agreed to a phone conversation, Cynthia and I practiced what she might say and how she could listen without reacting to whatever Marie said in response. It was a difficult phone call, but over time it led to Marie allowing Cynthia to visit and spend time with Ronnie.

To her great delight, Cynthia discovered that she could be a very good grandmother even though she had been a very poor mother. This pleased Marie, as well, who gradually recognized that her mother had actually changed. Cynthia and I began to talk about how she could be a good grandmother to herself, too, and this became a metaphor we used for cultivating maitri toward herself. My favorite thing she chose to do was to read children's stories aloud to herself at bedtime. No one had ever done that for her, and she decided to do it for herself.

Working with the four powers in this way helped Cynthia not only to begin to recognize her own goodness, it also helped to repair some of the harm she had caused years before.

Chapter 11

MANDALA APPROACHES TO SUPERVISION AND CONSULTATION

The word "mandala" has a number of different meanings in Buddhism, one of which is a visual representation, often in the form of a circle, of some totality or whole situation (Fremantle, 2001). The mandala techniques presented in this chapter are used by contemplative therapists as ways of deepening their understanding of their relationships with their clients. These mandalas give us a fuller picture of our clients and their worlds, and they also help us understand our own obstacles to being fully present with clients. I originally came up with two of these approaches, the mandala of brilliant sanity and the mandala of the client's world, for use by my students when they were doing their clinical internships, and I chose to call them mandalas because they help us to have more of an overall sense of our clients' lives and their natural wisdom. They are methods that may be used by oneself or with a supervisor or colleague. The third mandala, the mandala of strengths, is a spinoff of the mandala of brilliant sanity and is included here even though it is not a supervision or consultation approach. Instead, it is an interactive technique therapists can use with clients to explore their brilliant sanity and to cultivate maitri.

The fourth mandala approach, the mandala of body-speech-mind, is a group supervision or consulation practice that has been used by contemplative therapists since the late 1970s. No presentation on Contemplative Psychotherapy would be complete without including body-speech-mind (Rabin & Walker, 1987; Walker, 2008; Wegela, 2011b).[1] It, too, is a kind of mandala since it helps us view "the client's world . . . in terms of the whole" (Rabin & Walker, 1987, p. 136).

As contemplative therapists, as much as we can, we try to put ourselves in our clients' shoes and gain a sense of what it is like to be them. These four techniques help us to approach that sense. Since we cannot, of course, ever completely do that, we need to hold lightly anything we come up with in applying these mandala techniques. A discipline we bring to working with all of the mandala techniques is to be as specific and descriptive as we can, rather than interpretative or diagnostic, in whatever we come up with. This helps us see more clearly. For example, instead of saying, "This client is depressed," we might say something like, "This client has trouble getting out of bed in the morning and often thinks about killing himself."

The first three mandala techniques draw in different ways on the five competencies that we have looked at before. The first, the mandala of brilliant sanity, is an assessment tool for identifying the undistorted and distorted signs of brilliant sanity in clients. Next, the mandala of strengths is an interactive tool used by therapists with their clients as a way of highlighting their strengths and offering them an opportunity to experience maitri. And the third one, the mandala of the client's world, is a tool for helping therapists enhance their sense of how clients experience their worlds. Each of these mandalas invites us to think about, and even experience, our clients in different ways. Sometimes they highlight what we do not know, which can be useful as well.

I would encourage readers to adapt these techniques and play with them in any way that seems useful. With the mandalas of brilliant sanity and of the client's world, a straightforward way to use them, either on one's own or with a supervisor or peer consultant, is to contemplate, or think about, how a client may be described by the different aspects mentioned under each one. A further step would be to jot down or talk about what we think of as we do these contemplations with examples as illustrations.

Another method, which a former student of mine came up with when I first introduced the mandala of the client's world, is to actu-

FIGURE 11.1 The Five Competencies

ally create a visual mandala. What she did, and what I and others sometimes do, is to make a representation, including brief written comments, within a large encompassing circle. She used different colors for each of her client's life areas and ended up with a colorful illustration of the client's world.

If we draw a mandala picture in this way, we can make use of the traditional color of each of the competencies (Figure 11.1). In the center of a big circle, we would place the first competency of being present and letting be, which would traditionally be white. I use a black pen since my paper or dry erase board is usually white already. Then, the second competency, seeing clearly, is blue and belongs in the east. Some people like to use the traditional Tibetan directions. Then east would be at the bottom of the page, south on the left side, west at the top, and north on the right side. Here I will use our customary placements and put east to the right of the center and so on. The third competency, appreciating oneself and others, is yellow or gold and goes in the south. I usually use an orange pen because it is easier to see on a white background. The fourth competency, connecting with others and cultivating connection, is red and goes in the west. And finally, the fifth competency, acting skillfully and letting go, is green and belongs in the north.

We certainly do not have to get this elaborate. Even just sitting down and thinking about each item as it relates to a particular client may be enough to expand our sense of a client's possibilities and positive qualities.

While I am not doing it here myself, it can be quite useful to use all three mandalas with the same client, saving the interactive mandala of strengths for last. I have found that doing the mandala of strengths, in particular, reveals to me areas I have overlooked or in which I have held onto inaccurate projections.

THE MANDALA OF BRILLIANT SANITY TECHNIQUE

The purpose of this technique is to help us see our clients' brilliant sanity as it already manifests and where it may have the potential to appear as well. In using this mandala, therapists simply apply each of the categories introduced in Chapter 5 as they contemplate or present a client. Therapists may also choose to add their own categories. With the next two mandala techniques, fuller clinical examples based on single clients are included below. For this mandala, I am not including such an illustration since many examples are already provided in Chapters 5, which can guide the reader in applying this mandala.

To assist readers, a listing of the different aspects of the five competencies as they might appear in unconfused and confused forms is included in Chapter 5, Figure 5.1.

THE MANDALA OF STRENGTHS TECHNIQUE

As mentioned above, the mandala of strengths is an interactive technique done together with a client. It is analogous, perhaps, to the way family therapists create genograms, sometimes alone and sometimes with their clients. The first time I tried this method with one of my clients, I was surprised by how quickly she became engaged with the process. At the end of it, she said that it had made her problems seem smaller. In using it with other clients, I have found it to be a useful tool in helping clients experience maitri toward themselves.

I usually introduce this method by saying that it is a way of helping both of us identify the client's strengths and resources. We use a big white marker board on an easel and erasable pens in five colors. At the end, I sometimes take photos with my smartphone or iPad and send them to the clients who want to keep and think about what we come up with.

Originally I had envisioned using both the basic and the distorted aspects of each competency with clients as we do in the mandala of brilliant sanity. It soon became apparent, however, that it could be useful in helping clients experience maitri. For that reason, I chose to use only the unconfused aspects of each competency (Figure 11.2). I have found that clients quickly tune in to a feeling of encouragement that I do not want to interrupt. Also, my clients have been more than capable of bringing up the ways in which they do not manifest a particular competency without any help from me. One part of my job, when we do this practice, is to bring us back to the task at hand of identifying clients' strengths and positive qualities. At the same time, I try to introduce this technique only when clients feel open to it. For some clients, it is quite challenging to focus on their positive qualities. They may even feel shame about having trouble doing it. Therapists need to be sensitive to this and be willing to be flexible and responsive to clients' present needs and feelings.

Generally, my clients have enjoyed doing it, and it has provided us with another resource to draw on in our work together. It has let me be overt in referring to clients' positive qualities and in asking them to think about how they might apply their strengths to a particular situation with which they are dealing.

As a way of getting to know this approach, my students have found it helpful to try it out with a classmate before using it with clients, and I would suggest that readers might also find it valuable to experiment by taking both roles with a colleague, too. It works best if we do not role-play but instead be ourselves when we take the role of client.

I. Signs of being present and letting be
Inspiration to enter therapy
Moments of letting go
Body awareness
Waking up through sense perceptions
Being present with emotions
Having a sense of sacredness
Feeling spacious
Humor

II. Signs of seeing clearly and not judging
Being curious
Recognizing patterns and thinking logically
Clarifying meaning and values
Skillful use of the imagination
Recognizing thoughts as thoughts

III. Signs of appreciating oneself and others
Appreciating the richness of experience
Recognizing the richness of others
Maitri
Showing generosity

IV. Signs of connecting with others and cultivating relationship
Discriminating awareness
Precise attention to the sense perceptions, especially in the arts
Compassion and empathy
Ongoing relationships
Solitude and aloneness
Experiencing exchange

V. Signs of acting skillfully and letting go
Efficiency
Discipline
Setting and holding boundaries
Creative accomplishment
Cutting and pruning
Forgiveness
Playfulness

FIGURE 11.2 Signs of Brilliant Sanity for the Mandala of Strengths

The Clinical Example of Whitney

Whitney is a young woman with whom I have worked for more than 4 years. We began our work together when she entered a graduate counseling program (not the one in which I teach). Now she works as a counselor at an independent living program for young adults. We did the mandala of strengths toward the end of our third year of work together.

Whitney is in her early 30s. Married about 2 years ago to David, she has no children, although she looks forward to being a mother at some point. Her beloved dog, Sally, died a few months ago, and she has been surprised to find how attached she has already become to Molly, an adolescent Labradoodle. Instead of presenting the problems here that brought her into therapy, let's focus on her positive qualities and strengths as they came out in our two sessions focusing on the mandala of strengths.

At the start of the first session I gave Whitney a copy of the list of the positive signs of each of the five competencies (Figure 11.2). Although I asked about them in order, it was not important to make sure her answers were being listed in the right category. As needed, I clarified what items might include, and occasionally I reminded her of things I knew about from our therapy together that might go under a particular category. Mostly, though, I let her take the lead with what she wanted to include. It is important in using a technique that focuses on clients' strengths not to undermine them by indirectly suggesting that they are not able to do the task correctly. After each of the five main categories, I checked in with Whitney about what she was experiencing.

Being Present and Letting Be: Whitney's First-Competency Strengths

We began with Whitney's ongoing inspiration to be in therapy. She quickly identified the area of relationships as one in which she wished she could be more clear. Her hope was that increased clarity would give her the confidence to speak up more about what she needed in relationships and where she needed to set boundaries. In addition, she longed for more clarity about her relationship with alcohol and with prescription medications, with which she had long struggled.

As she moved on to the idea of letting be, she said that she felt that she is good at dropping an agenda when she works with young adults at her workplace. It is almost always easy to drop negative feelings and the sense of having had a bad day when she spends time with her girlfriends. Lately she has become more skilled in interrupting her ruminations about current situations within her family of origin. Whitney grew up in a very dysfunctional family, and her mother and two older sisters often try to engage her in emotionally charged conflicts. Historically, when she declined to participate in these quarrels or refused to take sides, they criticized, blamed, or shamed her. As we will see below, finding the internal resources to deal with her family has been very important for Whitney.

Whitney described a variety of body awareness practices she uses to bring herself back into the present moment, including grounding and resourcing, touching her lips, skiing, swimming, running, and "even walking from the car to the office or a client's house." In all of these, she makes use of her sense perceptions to notice what is happening in the present.

As for using emotions to wake up, she said that she is able to stay with her emotions except when she drinks alcohol or smokes pot. As I did throughout these sessions, I invited her back to the task of focusing on what she did well rather than on her challenges. In this case I did that by saying, "It sounds like there are a lot of ways you stay present."

Whitney experiences a sense of sacredness when she is in the mountains or in nature generally. Another time she experiences sacredness is when she is in any kind of water: in nature, swimming pools, and even in the bath. She likes to sit by lakes, creeks, and the ocean.

She enjoys humor and easily laughs at her own and others' foibles. Seeing humor in situations "brings up a lot of spaciousness," she said. "I only feel trapped when family stuff comes up."

As we came to the end of the list under the first competency, I asked how doing this was for her so far. She began to tear up and said that she was experiencing a sense of appreciating herself and was especially grateful for her ability to feel spacious. The contrast with her clients who were "trapped in chatter" was especially poignant for her.

Seeing Clearly and Not Judging: Whitney's Second-Competency Strengths

We began the second competency by looking at curiosity. She described how she shows a lot of curiosity about her clients. Sometimes she feels as though she is saying what she is supposed to say, and she would like it to be more "genuine and effortless." She noted that she has a good deal of curiosity about herself. When I mentioned that she seems to bring curiosity about herself into our work together and is rarely overtly judgmental about what she finds, she agreed that this was so.

Turning to the ability to recognize patterns, once again Whitney talked about how she has brought curiosity to her issues with drinking, and that she has noticed the cause-and-effect relationship between her emotions and her craving for alcohol. In a similar vein, she quickly saw how many of her current feelings and behaviors had their roots in her family history. She said, "It's a real no-brainer at this point."

In her relationship with David, Whitney saw how she contributes to distance between them. While she longs for greater intimacy, she also fears it and increasingly recognizes how she does what she calls the "push-pull" of inviting him closer and then backing away.

One area in which she displays clear thinking and good planning is gardening. Before the growing season, she and David plan the garden and gather what they need. Another area of clear thinking is taking care of her health. She researches what kinds of health professionals she wants to work with and then figures out how she can incorporate their advice into her daily life.

It took a few moments to come up with the places in her life where she feels knowledgeable, and then she was able to say that she does know a good deal about how to work with clients.

In clarifying meaning and values, Whitney saw that she does a good job of this with her clients. She particularly likes using the Acceptance and Commitment Therapy approach (ACT) with them. "It helps me, too, to see that what I value are meaningful, supportive relationships."

At that point, Whitney noted that she feels more present when she takes care of her body, mind, and spirit. Another value in this context is feeling more connected to the earth, and she feels this when she hears the birds or plays with her dog, Molly. Along with this, taking care of others and serving as "a good mom" brings her into the present and is an expression of the value she places on being of service.

In using her imagination skillfully, Whitney loves to imagine food and recipes, and she said she is really good at it. She added that cooking and working with recipes bring her into the present and engage her senses. It also expresses her ability to plan and think things through.

Like other clients, once Whitney began to think in terms of what she did well, she found more and more things to add. I jotted them down on the board without being concerned with which subcategory they belonged under.

Returning to her imagination, she said that she loves to imagine occupations in which she could be of service. "What would be my favorite job?"

Next, Whitney mentioned that she is very good at using grounding and resourcing. We often make use of those skills in therapy, and she also practices them at home to evoke a sense of peacefulness and strength when she becomes activated.

When we looked at the ability to recognize thoughts as thoughts, she reported, "I'm sort of skilled at that." This is an ability she feels that she has worked hard to develop and takes some pride in how readily she does it now.

As we came to the end of the second competency, I asked what was going on for her at that point. She said, "This is fun! I like it."

Appreciating Oneself and Others: Whitney's Third-Competency Strengths

As we began looking at the third competency, Whitney began to talk about her father, who died a few years ago. Her dad was appreciative of all kinds of things: "nature, parades, anything!" He was always enthusiastic, and Whitney saw that she is often like this as well. When she began to talk about how sometimes she goes a bit "overboard," I brought her back to limiting our conversation to the positive aspect of this quality. In contrast to the display of enthusiasm, she is also appreciative of stillness, especially in nature.

She appreciates the richness of her clients. "For sure. I think they're all so great." Other people she also appreciates are David and her friends. She noted that she is more appreciative of David when she is not actually with him. "'Isn't he great!' I'll say when he's not around, but when I'm with him, not so much."

I asked her when she experiences a sense of kindness or maitri toward herself. "Now. Doing this exercise. It also reminds me that I can be kinder to myself." Areas in which she feels she has developed more kindness toward herself are in slowing down and not feeling guilty when she needs to say no. "That's a good one," she noted.

The last item on the list of the third competency is showing generosity. Again Whitney compared herself to her father, who was often generous. "You don't see it so much in here [in our sessions], but I'm extremely generous." She reported that giving to others brings her great pleasure, and she does it frequently. For example, just before she came to our session that day, she had sent some food to "a sort of friend" who had just had a baby. "And that's just a tiny example." She has been learning, for the first time, how to track her experience and say no when she needs to. Otherwise, as she knows from experience, she can burn out.

When I checked in with her at this point, she said, "I really like it. I am reminded that I have all these coping skills. Some things came out that I didn't expect. 'Being a good mom' was a really good one."

Connecting With Others and Cultivating Relationships: Whitney's Fourth-Competency Strengths

We had done one session working with the first three competencies in the mandala of strengths, and we did this second session a few weeks later. As we began to look at the fourth competency, I explained that discriminating awareness, the first aspect of this competency, is about being able to tell the difference between things that are beneficial to one's own and others' well-being and things that are harmful. I added that this ability is important in cultivating relationships and connecting with others.

The first thing Whitney identified was her ability to recognize red flags in relationships sooner than she used to. She described examples of this happening in her work with clients, with David, with friends, with her family of origin, and with her dog.

In her relationship with David, she said that they were practicing identifying "What's mine and what's yours" after doing a few sessions of couples therapy. She is working with owning her own reactions when David has done something that annoys her. Instead of trying to get him to change, she does her best to be curious about why his behavior bothers her. "That's pretty huge," she said. "And we've actually gotten a lot more intimate from just that work itself."

She has also been working with telling friends when she needs to leave or when she needs them to leave her home. Learning to identify the boundaries she wants to set has been an ongoing issue in our work together. When we began she could not imagine setting such boundaries. Now, she not only is identifying her own needs but has also been practicing telling friends she invites over when she will need to end the festivities and go to bed herself. She applies discriminating awareness, as well, in recognizing how the scary and sometimes hopeless feelings that arise for her in considering setting boundaries have their roots in her chaotic family of origin.

She described a couple of specific examples with her family members in which she declined to become hooked into triangulating. Another place she exercises good judgment is in training her dog, Molly.

When I asked where she displays creativity, she brightened and described her delight in planning and working in her flower and vegetable gardens. She is also creative in paying attention to color and comfort in decorating her home. She noted that the main room in their open-plan home is not conducive to intimate relationships, and she would like to address that. Other creative activities include dance and "free movement."

As for compassion and empathy, the main arena in which she displays this is with her clients. Seeing the goodness in others—in her clients, in her friends, and in David—is another strength she identified.

Whitney has quite a number of ongoing relationships with friends and colleagues, and reported that she has the ability to make friends and to build rapport easily with clients. When she began to tell me that conflict was more difficult for her to deal with, I invited her back to focusing on strengths for this session.

Enjoying spending time alone is a new thing for Whitney. Now that she is working full time with constant interactions with others, she has discovered the need to set aside more alone time. She has found that having "me time" each evening is important to her.

Since we had previously talked about the phenomenon of exchange in our work together, she knew what it was when I asked about it. Her experience is that she readily exchanges with others and many times this leads to her feeling depleted after work. To address this, she works with grounding and resourcing between clients. In contrast, she noted she might also be experiencing exchange when David's low-key demeanor helps her to calm down when she is feeling agitated.

As we finished this section, I again checked in with how Whitney was feeling. Her response was, "I like doing this because so many times I think I'm really bad at relationships. I must be doing something right. This is encouraging."

Skillful Action and Letting Go: Whitney's Fifth-Competency Strengths

As we turned to the fifth competency, I began by asking about the times when Whitney is efficient. She gave me quite a long list of things, including her efficiency with clients and with taking care of her house and gardens. Getting the gear together and arranging for training classes so that she and David could go on kayaking trips was especially important to her. For her it was getting back in touch with her love of kayaking, an activity she had lost touch with following what she called the trauma of her father's death.

Being steady and dedicated to the work we have been doing together in therapy is another example of skillful action that Whitney identified. Both in our work and in her own work with clients, she said, "I'm persistent. I keep coming, and I keep doing the work. I don't give up."

Moving from knowing what to cultivate and what to refrain from and into action is often a challenge for Whitney, in particular in dealing with her addictive relationships with alcohol and Adderall. She identified stopping smoking 2 years ago as an example of following through on what she knew she needed to do. As she described it, "I know it before I can do it." She noted that she was far more disciplined about alcohol than ever before. It has been many months since she has abused Adderall, though the craving continues to arise.

Similarly, applying what she knows about her need to set boundaries has been challenging. I encouraged her to identify where in her life she is actually doing it. She immediately responded, "With David!" As noted above, she sets a boundary each evening so that she has alone time after work.

Whitney liked the heading "cutting and pruning." She does this literally in her garden, and, increasingly, she lets go of doing things that no longer serve her. Recently, she withdrew from a women's personal and spiritual growth group that had become a burden rather than a support. Unlike previous times in her life, she reported that in doing so she was able to say no without feeling that she was being bad.

Speaking up has been an ongoing challenge as well, and she has been working hard at it. She was very pleased to report how she told her supervisor what tasks she was good at and which ones were not a good fit. This led to her being given the job of providing nutritional support to clients, an area in which she is knowledgeable. As she described it, speaking up took some courage.

When we got to "forgiveness" on the list, she began quietly to weep. "This is it. I'm really touched by that word." She described how she had come far in forgiving herself, especially for drugs, drinking, cutting herself, getting kicked out of boarding school, and "for thinking it was my fault that I was raped [at age 12]."

She noted that she needed to forgive herself before she could forgive others. In particular, she identified her desire to forgive her family members for shaming, mistreating, and dismissing her. "I'm still angry, but I'm really working on it."

We were quiet together for a few minutes as she felt the tenderness of having begun to forgive herself and the longing to forgive others.

The final category, "playfulness," was one Whitney perked up at. "I feel playful most of the time." She loves being playful with clients, making what could be tedious life skills fun. "I make it fun, using humor and being silly."

She also identified a variety of physical activities she enjoys: tennis, biking, hip-hop dance classes, skiing, swimming, and camping. And last, but not least, she said, "I never thought having a new dog would be so much joy!"

At our final check-in, she repeated her enthusiasm and noted the tenderness that had come up at the forgiveness category. It seemed to me that Whitney had not only reported on expressions of her brilliant sanity, but she had also directly experienced it a number of times as we applied the mandala of strengths.

THE MANDALA OF THE CLIENT'S WORLD TECHNIQUE

By using this mandala technique, illustrated in Figure 11.3, we attempt to enter the client's world and see it as the client does. We are looking less at the qualities clients have than at how they are experiencing their lives. We include history only to the extent that it illuminates the importance of any particular area right now. As we try to get inside how clients experience their lives, we increase our sense of empathy with them. In using this technique, and also the body-speech-mind practice introduced below, we can work with our own obstacles to being available to exchange with clients. This technique tends to highlight the places where we have trouble staying present with them. It can be especially helpful in deepening our understanding both of ourselves and of our clients.

Sometimes, we do not know enough about clients to use this technique until we have worked with them for a while. Because we are using our imagination a good deal, it is especially important with this mandala to recognize that what we come up with are projections that may contain varying degrees of accuracy. Still, it can help us have a more compassionate and larger view of our relationships with clients.

When my students are learning how to use this mandala, they often find it helpful to apply it to themselves or to a close relative or friend. My students have come up with quite elaborate projects when I have given them the assignment to create such a mandala. One person made a colorful mobile, and another knitted large portions of hers. Personally, I just write out my thoughts. To help us look at how to use this mandala, I have included two occasions when I applied it to my long-term client Pamela. For the purposes of this chapter, I have shortened some of what I originally wrote, but I could have included a good deal more, and readers may choose to do so as well when they try it out. The first time I used it was early in my work with Pamela, after about 2 months, and the second time included here was after we been seeing each other for about 3 years.

FIGURE 11.3 Mandala of the Client's World

We eventually worked together for nearly 6 years. We can use this method at any time to get a sense of a client's path in therapy, especially when we feel like we are becoming confused ourselves or unusually challenged in our work with a particular client. As is the case with the mandala of brilliant sanity, we can work with this approach alone or with another person. Here I have applied it on my own.

Pamela's Mandala After 2 Months

When I met Pamela she was in her mid-40s. A very pretty woman, she rarely used makeup and wore her hair in a short easy-to-care-for style. During our first 2 months Pamela and I mostly spent our time in building our relationship and establishing a safe enough container in which she could begin to explore some frightening events from her past and how they were still affecting her life. She is the client referred to in Chapter 5 whose goal was no longer to miss her life.

The Center of the Pamela's Mandala After 2 Months

Each of the five competencies is traditionally associated with one of the five elements identified in the Tibetan Buddhist approach: space, water, earth, fire, and wind. The center of the mandala is the space within which everything else happens. By extension, it refers to what we most take for granted, what we simply assume is important. That is, around what is everything else organized? Identifying what is in the center of a client's mandala is a key element in using this technique. Often, when we use this technique, we cannot begin with the center. What belongs in the center may become clear only as we work our way through some or all of the four directions outside of the center.

Some examples of what might be in the center of a particular client's mandala are things like being admired by others, staying sober or staying intoxicated, being a decent person, avoiding pain or death, benefiting others, seeking revenge, providing for one's family, or feeling safe. Note that the center of the mandala can be something we might think of as healthy or not. Notice also that whatever is in the center of the mandala is impermanent and may very well change. As we use this technique, we keep in mind that we are creating a portrait of a client's present situation only.

In Pamela's case, it was clear quite early in our work that in the center of her mandala was her concern about the members of her family: her husband, Jack, and her two children, Mark who was 20 and Rachael who was 17. It was only after completing the whole mandala that I reconsidered and saw that another aspect of the center of Pamela's mandala was maintaining a sense of safety and predictability, as well as the fear that lay underneath that desire.

Almost everything Pamela talked about concerned her family members. A distant second was her interest in writing. Soon after we began our work together, she told me that an important goal in her life was to be able to write again, and she wondered if therapy might help her reconnect with that long-neglected passion. Although she had written poetry and fiction as a young woman, she had stopped writing when her first child, Mark, was born and somehow had never gotten back to it.

The immediate incident that had brought Pamela into therapy was a terrifying experience of disorientation, after which her son Mark had insisted that she seek therapy. Without a family member urging her, I doubt that Pamela would have come to therapy on her own.

Pamela suspected that her father had sexually abused her, but she had no clear memories of it. It seemed likely to her since he had abused other children in the extended family who did very clearly remember it. It became apparent that her experience of disorientation was a more extreme version of what she described as experiencing a sense of numbness most of the time. I guessed that this habit of not being fully present probably began as a way to protect herself from the suspected abuse.

As I worked with this mandala, I used my imagination to try to get a sense of what it would be like for me to move through the world, as Pamela did, being only halfway present. There was a sense of things having fuzzy edges and of never being sure of what I knew. The thought of going deeply into my own experience was alarming, and I did not want even to consider doing it.

Instead of having a sense of being present and letting be, the wisdom aspect that resides in the center of the mandala of the five wisdom energies, Pamela's most familiar state of mind was mindlessness about her own experience and, at the same time, concern for the well-being of her husband and children. As I imagined experiencing this myself, I could see how having my attention outside myself could feel safer and more tender at the same time.

The East Side of Pamela's Mandala After 2 Months

The east corresponds to the second competency: seeing clearly and not judging. This competency is associated with the element of water: both clear, calm water through which we can easily see and turbulent and cloudy water that obscures our vision.

In the east, we look particularly at the client's thinking and cognition. What does she think about; what is meaningful? What intellectual pursuits does she have? In Pamela's case, her thoughts in our first months of working together centered on Jack and the children. Was Jack's business going well? Would his newest project be a success? She talked about how the outcome of this project could affect the family's finances and whether they could move to a larger house.

She talked often about her disapproval of Rachael's current boyfriend. She worried that Rachael might marry him and end up divorced. It was important to her that Mark's activities make him appear well rounded when he entered the workforce in another couple of years.

As I considered what it would be like to have my thoughts focus on my family members in this way, I realized how this kind of thinking about the future, and not about the past, was a kind of island of clarity. I could think about Jack, Mark, and Rachael as much as I wanted without fear of tapping into the hidden places inside myself.

The South Side of Pamela's Mandala After 2 Months

The south part of the mandala, corresponding to the element of earth and its solidity, has to do with dealing with money and possessions, including one's talents and skills. It has to do with giving and providing resources to others. It includes the things a client desires or craves, so it also includes addictions. Pamela's financial situation was comfortable but not luxurious. Jack made a good living, and Pamela took care of the home and the children. She liked to cook for guests and host dinner parties, and often spoke of those occasions either as plans or as reports on how they went. She enjoyed shopping and was proud when she found the exactly right thing to decorate their home.

Pamela and Jack drank wine every evening, usually finishing a bottle of wine at dinner. Pamela told me that she needed it "to take the edge off things."

As I thought about what it might be like to be in Pamela's situation in this area, I liked not having to think about where the money came from, as it freed me up to do the things I liked. I felt a bit like a well-cared-for child, and I wondered if Pamela felt that way, too.

The West Side of Pamela's Mandala After 2 Months

The west side of this mandala is about relationships, communication, and emotions, and is associated with the element of fire: fire that warms but can also burn. While Pamela focused on her family and on the friends she invited to her home, she rarely mentioned how she felt toward any of them. When I asked about her emotions, most of the time she did not know how she felt. Other times, she would say something like, "I think I feel sad about that," or "I might be angry, but I'm not sure." Sometimes she would express love for Jack or for the children, but if I inquired about her experience of feeling love, she would draw a blank.

A troubling aspect of her life was how to deal with the children, who acted out by arguing with each other and defying the rules laid down by their parents. Mark refused to participate in family gatherings, preferring to stay away even over holiday breaks from school, and was very critical of both Jack and Pamela. He accused them of not caring about him. Pamela thought that Rachael might be experimenting with drugs, but she was not sure about it. Sometimes she worried about what she should do about Rachael, and other times she reached for a glass of wine. When she and Jack discussed how to deal with what was going on with the children, they usually disagreed about how to proceed, and then would take no action.

Despite her lack of connection with her inner experience, Pamela had a few long-term good friends whom she had known for many years.

One relationship that had no conflicts or unnamable emotions was her connection with her dog. The family had a Great Pyrenees dog, Max, and he was clearly most attached to Pamela. When Pamela talked about him, her face would soften, and she readily contacted a sense of warmth and tenderness for him.

An aspect of this part of this mandala is tracking the therapist's experiences of exchange. When I considered this, I noted that I often felt quite flat when I was with Pamela. I might even space out a bit and begin thinking about what I was going to do that evening. Knowing that this is not one of my own habitual patterns, I attributed it tentatively to exchange with Pamela. Other times I felt waves of anger toward Jack, Mark, and Rachael. I noticed intense anger arising toward Pamela's father. In all those instances, the anger lasted barely a moment before dissolving back into flatness. I suspected that these, too, were exchanges since they were mere glimpses. A pervasive feeling for me, when I was with Pamela, was sadness. This sadness may or may not have been exchange. Since I liked Pamela very much and felt touched by her, I might very well have felt sad anyway. It could also have been both.

The other aspect of this part of the mandala of the client's world is sexuality. Pamela reported that she felt no sexual feelings at all, and she regarded Jack's sexual desires as a burden. If she felt anything, it was a sense of revulsion. When she could, she avoided having sex altogether, and when she did have sex with Jack, she was hardly present. This caused conflict with Jack, who felt abandoned by her. She reported that on the one hand she would welcome Jack's finding someone else to satisfy his sexual needs and that on the other hand she did not want him to leave her for someone else. When Pamela talked about these two options, I felt a flash of fear.

The North Side of Pamela's Mandala After 2 Months

The northern part of the mandala has to do with action and is connected with the moving element of wind. Here we consider all the ways clients spend their time, including work and other activities. Unlike her close friends who were always very busy and often speedy, Pamela tended to move somewhat slowly and did not fill up her time. She put much of her attention on taking care of her home and was quite particular about the details of how beds were made, what meals she prepared and offered to her family and to guests, and how her gardens were tended. She did much of this work herself and also was deeply engaged when outside workers were hired to take care of some of the heavier labor.

Aside from walking Max and gardening, she did not report any other kind of physical exercise. Her writing remained an unfulfilled wish. She read novels and rarely watched television.

It was Pamela's job to make arrangements for the social activities she and Jack engaged in. Often this involved coordinating with her friends and their husbands for evenings out. Other times, she arranged for social occasions, usually dinner parties at their home, with some of Jack's business associates.

When I tried to feel my way into what this part of Pamela's world might be like for her, I was intrigued by how slowed down I felt. I had a sense of great space, which I attributed not only to her habitual lack of being fully present but also, at least potentially, to a genuine sense of spaciousness. In addition, I tapped into feelings of pride and satisfaction when I thought about what it might be like to feel my home environment was so well taken care of. Beyond that, I noticed that as I thought about being in her home with Jack, I felt safety and relief. In contrast, imagining Jack's business colleagues coming over for dinner brought up a sense of invasion, obligation, and strain. Still, I felt confident that I knew how to put together a good dinner and an entertaining evening for them.

General Comments on Pamela's Mandala After 2 Months of Therapy

The most outstanding thing for me as I put together this mandala was how little attention Pamela paid to herself. She seemed absent from much of her life. Nearly all of her overt concerns were about other people. She spent little time on things intended for her own pleasure or well-being. Her ways of not being fully present appeared in every aspect of the mandala.

It was only after trying to enter her world through completing this mandala that I saw how, at least in my own imagination, how narrow it was. It seemed to me that she had arranged her life to be as predictable and safe as she possibly could. In protecting herself from anything unexpected, especially danger (like what she may have experienced with her father), I saw her brilliant sanity at work. At the same time, her world seemed quite constricted, and both her husband and her children wanted her to be more present.

Pamela's Mandala After 3 Years of Therapy

Pamela and I worked together for a long time, and I was often impressed by her determination and persistence.

The Center of Pamela's Mandala After 3 Years

After 3 years, curiosity had replaced fear to a great extent in the center of Pamela's mandala, and her concern for the well-being of her family members had expanded to include herself as well. She and I had spent a great many sessions on cultivating mindfulness, and she had extended that into many areas of her life, including her evening wine drinking. Moreover, she had internalized some of the questions I had often asked her. She would catch herself when she said, "I think I feel . . . " and say, "You want to know about feelings, not thoughts, right?" Although she was still often out of touch with what she was experiencing physically, she knew to scan her body and see if she could identify where in her body she felt tightness or discomfort.

Pamela had begun to write again and felt excited about it. She did not feel ready to show her writing to anyone, but she was keeping a journal and reported that she had written a few poems and had some ideas for some short fiction pieces.

Having a sense of predictability and safety was still important to Pamela, and she continued to put energy into making her home a safe haven. Although we had done a fair amount of work with the suspected sexual abuse, she had not recovered clear memories and still struggled with situations that triggered fear.

As I imagined being Pamela, I no longer had a sense of fuzziness. Instead, I noted a sense of feeling strong and clear minded. I felt more grounded as I thought about exploring the remaining unknown areas and, at the same time, I guessed that Pamela felt a sense of anxiety about going into them. In thinking about family members, especially Rachael, based on our interactions, I suspected she felt worry and also a sense of determination.

The East Side of Pamela's Mandala at 3 Years

Pamela's thinking had also expanded to include more than her family members. As noted, she now thought more about her own needs and her writing.

She continued to express a good deal of concern about Jack, Rachael, and Mark. In particular, she was quite worried about Rachael, who was 20 now and no longer living at home. Her experimentation with drugs had become a full-blown problem with addiction to alcohol and abuse of marijuana. Pamela reported that her worries about what might happen dominated her days and kept her awake at night.

In addition to the work we did together, Pamela sought out professional advice on how best to help Rachael without enabling her. Attending some Al-Anon meetings was also helpful.

As I considered how this part of Pamela's life would feel to me, I touched into a good deal of fear. Rachael was my baby. I noticed that the sense of fogginess I had seen earlier in our work was no longer there. Instead, my thinking was quite focused. I also recognized that I felt a painful quality in not being able to take a break from worrying about Rachael.

The South Side of Pamela's Mandala at 3 Years

In the intervening years, Jack and Pamela had moved to a new home. Pamela had been very involved in the building design and in decorating it. These were talents she had previously exercised only in her imagination. As she saw her ideas incorporated into the plans and actual building, she had become increasingly confident in her abilities. Both Jack and the architect had learned to value her judgment, and she had been buoyed by the respect with which they had treated her.

At one point she invited me to come see the new house, and I accepted her invitation. I was deeply impressed by the beauty and comfort of her home. Her design skills were also reflected in the flower gardens and landscaping. Her pride in her accomplishments was visible and well deserved.

As I imagined this part of the mandala would feel to me and how it would affect my sense of myself at this point, I noted that the little-girl feeling of being taken care of was no longer there for me. Instead, there was a sense of being engaged and interested. At the same time, I also had the sense that my home, while being less of a hideout from the outside world, was still a much-valued refuge.

The West Side of Pamela's Mandala at 3 Years

Pamela's relationships with her family continued to be very important, and she spoke often about Jack, Rachael, and Mark. Mark had married his college sweetheart and had a baby daughter, Susan. Pamela loved being a grandmother and doted on her granddaughter. Mark still kept his distance, living out of state, and Pamela longed to see more of both her son and grandchild. In talking about Mark, Pamela now readily accessed sadness. She believed that her emotional absence while Mark was growing up was a big cause of his maintaining so much distance between them now. Sometimes Pamela reported feeling guilty about that. Her emotional repertoire had definitely expanded.

She also felt guilty about Rachael's problems with alcohol and marijuana. Her daily wine drinking was something we had explored, and she believed that she and Jack had modeled drinking as a way to avoid dealing with thorny issues.

There had been some changes in her feelings toward her parents. Pamela had previously cut off all communication with both of her parents some years earlier when they had refused to discuss her father's sexual abuse of children in the family and the possibility of his having abused her as well. Both her parents had denied that anything had occurred. While she did not recall sexual contact, she did remember being hit and always being afraid. She connected now with anger toward both of her parents.

This newly found experience of anger led to an unexpected result one night.[2] Pamela told me that Jack had just gone out of town, and she was frightened of staying home alone that night. She was glad to have Max with her for protection, but she said that she would be scared and probably would want to dull out with wine. As we talked about the source of her fear, she realized that it went back to feelings about her father. She had always been scared of being alone with him. As she felt into this fear, it was replaced with intense anger. She was not only mad about his behavior in the past, she was angry that he was the cause of her present fear. I asked if she felt afraid now as she talked about her past fear. She said, "No, I feel angry!"

When we met next, she told me that when she began to feel anxious that evening, she called up her anger at her father and felt empowered by it. She was proud of conquering her fear of being home alone.

As I imagined what it would be like for me to have as many emotionally challenging things going on as Pamela did, I felt intensely alive and, at the same time, exhausted and overwhelmed. Fear, anger, sadness, and worry were all in a big soup of feelings. I noticed that I also felt proud and pleased that I was more in touch with my inner world. It did not feel easy, but I was grateful to be coming out of the thick fog in which I had been cocooned. When I thought about going more deeply into my feelings about my father, I felt some hope. Maybe I could do it, after all. Still, I was in no hurry.

The North Side of Pamela's Mandala After 3 Years

As I have already indicated, Pamela was much more engaged in her life and taking a more active role in a number of areas, including the building of her new home, attending Al-Anon meetings, and taking more responsibility for her drinking as well as how her past actions (or lack of them) may have affected her children. She continued to enjoy planning and working in her gardens and designing landscaping for her home. In finding ways to visit with her son and granddaughter, she was proactive in arranging to travel by herself to visit them out of state. Finally, she was actually writing.

As I imagined this aspect of Pamela's life, I again felt the sense of aliveness and active engagement that had been missing earlier. Looming large was worry about Rachael, but there was also more confidence that I could actually take care of some things. I did not have to wait for Jack or someone else to tell me what to do. There was a glimpse of joy as I noticed that growing confidence.

General Comments on Pamela's Mandala After 3 Years

Overall, I noticed how far Pamela had come in becoming engaged in her life. In therapy, she was more active and taking more risks in going toward her emotions and bringing mindfulness to all aspects of her current life. I felt encouraged myself, and I knew that she did as well. In doing this mandala, I recognized that Pamela had made the kind of progress she had been seeking in many areas. A big area that was still difficult was her sexual relationship with Jack and the emotions it triggered related to the still mostly unremembered abuse. Enough small memories had emerged, though, that she no longer doubted that it had occurred. With Jack, she was able to stay more present during sex even though she did not especially enjoy it.

As I write this now, I would like to let the reader know that Pamela never fully remembered the details of what happened with her father. She was able to track her emotions, though, in the present and uncovered both anger and also tenderness. Unlike her distant and absent mother, her father had shown her affection apart from the inappropriate sexual contact. While this was very confusing and unsettling, bringing up a host of other issues, Pamela had been able to stay present and explore many of them.

She was able to set appropriate boundaries and find ways to connect with Rachael while her daughter continued to battle her own demons. Mark softened a bit, and he and his mother had somewhat warmer interactions when Pamela visited him and his family.

At this point, Pamela comes in for a tune-up session every year or so, and we check in on how things are going. She is happy with Jack and sometimes enjoys sex. She definitely enjoys their other kinds of intimacy. I think she is no longer missing her life.

THE MANDALA OF BODY-SPEECH-MIND

As we have seen, as contemplative therapists we make use of a variety of ways to help us be more present and compassionate, including mindfulness-awareness meditation, metta, tonglen, empathetic joy, and equanimity practices (introduced in Chapters 2 and 10). As mentioned, two of the mandala techniques introduced in this chapter, the mandala of brilliant sanity and the mandala of the client's world, are useful either as self-supervision techniques or with one other person.

In addition to these, contemplative psychotherapists often make use of the body-speech-mind small-group practice. It may be used by as few as two colleagues together, but it is most powerful when it is done in a group of four or more. I have used it in a workshop with a group as large as 18 people. Ongoing body-speech-mind groups that meet weekly, biweekly, or monthly usually have three to seven members.

The purpose of the body-speech-mind group practice is to experientially identify our obstacles to being present and to experiencing exchange with our clients. Those obstacles may include our difficulties in experiencing certain emotions through exchange or being triggered by events in our own histories. We may have expectations and projections that get in the way of our seeing a client clearly, or we may find it difficult to like a client. Whatever these obstacles might be, we may be able to clarify them, and perhaps go beyond them, through participating in a body-speech-mind group.

Basic Guidelines for Body-Speech-Mind Practice

Body-speech-mind is, in itself, a contemplative practice, requiring us to track our inner experience with mindfulness while we also bring awareness to the dynamics of the group. Even though the clients who we are presenting are not literally there, we like to say that we are bringing clients into the room by presenting them using the body-speech-mind practice. Or as Rabin and Walker put it, "the body-speech-mind discipline allows the client who is being described to emerge as a living presence in the supervision group environment" (1987, p. 138). Actually, when we present clients, we are inevitably presenting our relationships with them since the dynamics between presenters and their clients tend to manifest themselves in the room during the presentation. A working guideline that has shown its usefulness over the years is to assume that everything that happens during a presentation has something to do with the relationship between the presenter and the client being presented. Most groups meet for an hour and a half, but a good presentation could happen in an hour's meeting if everyone is familiar with the form.

Body-speech-mind groups can be used for supervision and have a leader, or they can be used as consultation by a group of peers. The role of the leader of a body-speech-mind group is to remind the group's members of the form and to invite the group to stay on topic. Moreover, a group leader may help the members notice the tone and content of the interactions between its members. Groups of peers may choose to rotate leadership of the group, while some other groups manage just fine without any leader at all.

The presenter's job is to describe in great detail the body, speech, and mind of the client being presented. What belongs in each of those three categories is explained below and summarized in Figure 11.4. By describing and letting go of all interpretive words, we have a chance to experience the uniqueness of a client. Instead of trying to see what a particular client has in common with others, as we do when we identify clients' diagnoses, in body-speech-mind we are most interested in the unique humanity of one specific person. For many traditionally trained therapists, the discipline of describing and not interpreting takes some getting used to.

The group helps by inviting the presenter to use descriptive words. For example, instead of beginning with something like, "The client is a 28-year-old African American woman with a history of social anxiety," we might say, "Sylvia is about 5 feet 7, and her face is very smooth and the color of strong coffee with just a little bit of cream."

The role of the group members is to track their own experiences and to describe what they notice. They also ask questions of the presenter. Some groups prefer to wait until there is a break between the

---

Body
Physical appearance, including posture and movement
Ethnicity, gender, and group memberships
Environments
Work and how time is spent
Health and addictions

Speech
Communication and expression
Relationships and significant others
Emotions
Sexuality
Relationship between presenter and person being presented
Presenter's experience when with the person being presented

Mind
Quality of awareness
Thoughts and assumptions
Practices of mindfulness and mindlessness
Spirituality

FIGURE 11.4 Body-Speech-Mind Presentations: Main Categories

various parts of the presentation. Personally, I like group members to listen at the start of the presentation, but then to chime in as they feel so moved. Part of what is interesting is to notice how different presentations evoke quite different styles of response from group members.

I remember one presentation when the presenter kept being interrupted by the group members. He grew increasingly frustrated and irritated. What became clear, as the group went on, was that his own way of relating with the client whom he was presenting was similar to how the group was treating him. He worked with court-ordered clients, and he often asked them questions they were not interested in answering. Now he experienced firsthand what it was like to have questions lobbed at him that were not the things he wanted to talk about. It shifted his attitude toward the particular client he was presenting and perhaps affected his work with his other clients as well.

It is most useful to present a client with whom the presenter is experiencing some difficulty. As group members exchange with or just pick up on different aspects of a client, the presenter may gain a deeper and more thorough understanding of the client.

Body

The category of body includes a detailed description of clients' physical bodies as well as the environments in which they live, work, and spend time. We usually begin by offering the person's first name unless it is so unusual that it could identify the person in our relatively small town. People's names tend to evoke their presence for the presenter. I usually begin at the top of a person's head and describe hair, face, eyes, skin, nose, mouth, brows, and so on. Then I move on to what the rest of the body looks like. How much do we guess the person weighs? What about height? Age? How does the person move? Can the presenter show us? Does the person appear to be embodied?

I am always curious when presenters leave out parts of the body. For example, I have heard a number of presentations in which the presenter described a woman's hairdo, makeup, and clothing: all the things that were not the woman herself. As the presentation continued, it became apparent that these clients were not in touch with their bodies and there were particular reasons in each instance why that was so.

We note clients' ethnicity and any membership in marginalized or privileged groups. We include health in this section, but not medications that might suggest a psychological diagnosis. Does the person have any addictions? If the person smokes, what brand? How do people spend their time? What work, if any, do they do? What other ways do they spend time? Do they cook for themselves? What is in their refrigerator? How do they get around? Do they drive? What kind of car? Do they bike? Walk? Stay home? Do they play? If so, at what?

An important part of the body section of the presentation is the environments in which the presented clients spend time: What are their living situations? Are they homeless? With whom do they live? Do they have ex-partners? Children? Parents? We do not describe these relationships yet; that will happen in the next category. Here we just name the people in their world.

As you can see, nothing is too trivial to be included.

Speech

Speech includes all kinds of communication and expression, not just verbal. I like to include clothing here since it is a way people express themselves. Speech includes all of the ways a person communicates: with words, gestures, or silence. What is the person's first language? If it is not the language of the dominant culture, does this cause any problems?

An important part of speech is relationships of all kinds. Here is the place where we talk about the qualities of relationships with family members, with partners, and with people at work or school. Any significant relationship can be mentioned. For example, as we have seen before, sometimes those relationships are with animals. In speech, we include sexuality and sexual orientation. Are people comfortable with sexuality? Or do they have a conflicted relationship with it? If so, what is the nature of the conflict?

Emotions are another important aspect of speech since they often arise in the context of relationship. What emotions are people able to express or describe?

The relationship between the presenter and the person being presented is another part of the speech section. What does the presenter experience in the presence of the person being presented? What emotions does the presenter notice? Or does the presenter feel flat? Is there a sense of connection between the presenter and the person or does the presenter feel disconnection? If the client weeps, what does the presenter feel? Does the presenter feel safe with the client?

The speech section of the presentation is often quite juicy, and it is especially tempting to fall into interpreting and not describing. The group leader and the group members can be very helpful in reminding each other to come back to the descriptive discipline.

Mind

In presenting body and speech we can rely on what we experience with clients and on what they tell us. In the mind section, we have to depart somewhat from description and make use of inference since we cannot directly access clients' minds. Still, we do our best to stick to what we know and identify when we are guessing about the characteristics of the client that belong in this section. In the mind portion, we attend to the qualities of clients' awareness, their thoughts and assumptions, their mindfulness and mindlessness practices, and their experience of their own minds.

We might describe a client's awareness as scattered or focused, narrow or panoramic, detailed or general. Sometimes we use a gimmick here: we use a metaphor or image to describe our best guess about clients' experiences of their minds. One presenter described a client's mind as a flat plain with no trees, a gray sky, and no wind blowing. Another described a different client's mind as a carnival midway with barkers soliciting people to come into their sideshows and the client feeling attracted to first one and then another amusement.

In the mind portion we talk about the person's relationship, if any, with spirituality or religion. Does the person attend a particular church or other spiritual center? Do clients practice prayer? Meditation? Yoga? Recite mantras? Sing in the choir? If so, what experiences do they have that they would identify as religious or spiritual?

What are the contents of the person's thoughts? What assumptions about the nature of their worlds do clients make? Do they see the world, for example, as dangerous? Welcoming? Hostile? Do they assume they will be liked? Judged? Rejected? Do they have strong political views? Do they ignore the news?

At the End of the Presentation

At the end of a presentation, the group may choose to spend some time talking about how the presenter might go forward in his or her work with the client who has been presented. Other groups may choose not to have any follow-up discussion. When groups take this second approach, it parallels other contemplative practices, like mindfulness awareness meditation. The assumption is that simply being present with whatever has arisen during the practice is already valuable and needs no further explanation. Each group can decide for itself how to proceed. In my own experience, I have found that sometimes discussion is helpful after I make a presentation, and that at other times I prefer to sit with what I have experienced and then just see what I notice when I next meet with the client.

All of these mandala approaches can help us let go of the obstacles that may make it difficult to be fully present with our clients. These mandala techniques provide us with opportunities to explore our work with our clients with gentleness and curiosity.

The more we are able to bring those qualities of maitri, mindful awareness, and courage to our own experience, by making use of the various Buddhist and contemplative practices presented in this book, the more we bring our own brilliant sanity into our therapeutic relationships. When our aspiration is to let our brilliant sanity invite and support our clients' discovery of their own brilliant sanity, we are practicing Contemplative Psychotherapy.

NOTES

INTRODUCTION

1. For more information on EMDR, see EMDR Institute, www.emdr .com. On TRM, see Trauma Resource Institute, http://traumaresource institute.com/trauma-resiliency-model-trm/.

CHAPTER 1

1. Brilliant sanity was part of the logo designed by Chögyam Trungpa for the cover of the first volume of the *Naropa Institute Journal of Psychology*. The logo featured "Brilliant Sanity" arching over a Bodhi leaf, which, in turn, contained the Buddhist symbol of the wheel of life, or dharmachakra. The board of editors explains that the wheel "stands for the principle of discipline," while the Bodhi leaf "represents the possibility of extending . . . gentleness to others" (1980, p. 1).

2. This incident is described for a different purpose in Wegela (2011a).

3. In ancient India, medical knowledge was presented in the form of disease, diagnosis, cure, treatment. "The Four Noble Truths seem to be modeled on this, but apply to our spiritual wellbeing" (Eshin, n.d.).

4. See Hanh (2013) for a dharma talk on interbeing. Thich Nhat Hanh (1987b) also uses the term when he describes his approach to engaged Buddhism called the Tiep Hien Order.

5. For more on neuroscience and our interconnectedness, see D. J. Siegel (2010), Watson (2008), Dow (2008), or Loizzo (2012).

6. For more on the notion of emptiness, see Thrangu (2012) or Gyamtso (1994).

7. For more on the dzogchen teachings, see Gyatso (2000) or Tsoknyi (1998).

8. Different sources list variations of the eightfold path. C. Taylor, for example, lists "right understanding, right thought, right speech, right action, right livelihood, right effort, right mindfulness, and right meditation" (2010, p. 172). Khenpo Karthar lists "perfect view, thought,

speech, action, livelihood, effort, memory, and meditation" (1992, p. 276).

CHAPTER 2

1. Readers who are interested in pursuing further the particular meditation practice introduced in this chapter may locate a qualified meditation instructor through www.shambhala.org. Many other organizations provide meditation instruction and practice opportunities as well, including the Insight Meditation Society (www.dharma.org), various Zen groups, and other Tibetan-based groups. Most Buddhist meditation teachers have Web sites providing both meditation instruction and directions for finding an individual to speak with about one's practice. Many of the books listed in the references also provide leads to locating a meditation instructor.

CHAPTER 3

1. Another example of applying the four powers in therapeutic work may be found in Wegela (2009, pp. 124–126).

CHAPTER 4

1. Using my hair as an example of interdependence and emptiness appears also in Wegela (2009, pp. 36–37).

2. A traditional presentation of the five skandhas may be found in Sangharakshita (1977). A different version, more developmental in nature, may be found in Trungpa (1987).

CHAPTER 5

1. For more on positive psychology, see Epstein (2001) or Fredrickson (2009).

2. This incident is referred to also in Wegela (2009, p. 193).

CHAPTER 7

1. An earlier description of Dennis's softball try-out appears in Wegela (2003, p. 17).

2. An earlier description of my professor's chalk-rolling practice appears in Wegela (1996, p. 98).

3. Previous descriptions of this mindlessness practice appear in Wegela (1996, p. 183) and in Wegela (2009, p. 173).

CHAPTER 8

1. I was introduced to these three methods of working with emotions by Drubwang Tsoknyi Rinpoche at a meditation retreat held in Crestone,

Colorado, in the summer of 2002. I have changed the wording somewhat to make them more readily applicable to psychotherapy.

CHAPTER 9

1. The contemplations presented here are based on my own work with the four limitless ones (also called the four immeasurables). Readers who prefer a more traditional version may want to refer to Wallace (2004). Pema Chödrön (2001) presents yet another version of them.

2. For a more thorough discussion of the differences between a Buddhist understanding and a contemporary Western psychological understanding of attachment, see Aronson (2004).

CHAPTER 10

1. I have adapted the three categories of patience somewhat in order to highlight their application for therapists. Readers interested in digging more deeply into more traditional presentations might like to refer to Gyatso (1980), Chödrön (2005), or Gyatso (1997).

2. A brief description of this incident appears in Wegela (1996, p. 123).

3. Another example of applying the four powers in therapeutic work may be found in Wegela (2009).

CHAPTER 11

1. Two excellent presentations on body-speech-mind groups may be found in Rabin and Walker (1987) and Walker (2008).

2. An earlier description of this incident appears in Wegela (2009, pp. 141–142).

REFERENCES

American Psychiatric Association. (2013). *Diagnostic and statistical manual of mental disorders* (5th ed.). Arlington, VA: American Psychiatric Publishing.

Aronson, H. (2004). *Buddhist practice on Western ground: Reconciling Eastern ideals and Western psychology*. Boston, MA: Shambhala.

Asrael, D. (2012, spring). The question is the answer. *Naropa Magazine*. Retrieved from http://magazine.naropa.edu/2012-spring/features/the-question-is-the-answer.php

Badenoch, B. (2008). *Being a brain-wise therapist: A practical guide to interpersonal neurobiology*. New York, NY: Norton.

Bayda, E. (2005). Three breaths at a time. *Shambhala Sun, 13*(6), 19–20.

Beck, C. J. (1989). *Everyday Zen: Love and work* (S. Smith, Ed.). San Francisco, CA: HarperSanFrancisco.

Bettelheim, B. (1972). *The empty fortress: Infantile autism and the birth of the self*. New York, NY: Free Press.

Chödrön, P. (1994). *Start where you are: A guide to compassionate living*. Boston, MA: Shambhala.

Chödrön, P. (1998). To know yourself is to forget yourself. *Shambhala Sun, 7*(1), 13–14.

Chödrön, P. (2001). *The places that scare you: A guide to fearlessness in difficult times*. Boston, MA: Shambhala.

Chödrön, P. (2005). *No time to lose: A timely guide to the way of the bodhisattva*. Boston, MA: Shambhala.

Cohn, V. (1975). *Sister Kenny: The woman who challenged the doctors*. Minneapolis, MN: University of Minnesota Press.

Davidson, R. J., & Begley, S. (2012). *The emotional life of your brain: How its unique patterns affect the way you think, feel, and live—and how you can change them*. New York, NY: Plume.

Dow, M. (2008). Buddhism, psychology, and neuroscience: The promises and pitfalls of a neurobiologically informed contemplative psychotherapy. In F. J. Kaklauskas, S. Nimanheminda, L. Hoffman, &

M. S. Jack (Eds.), *Brilliant sanity: Buddhist approaches to psychotherapy* (pp. 99–129). Colorado Springs, CO: University of the Rockies Press.

Dowman, K. (Trans.) (1980). *The divine madman: The sublime life and songs of Drukpa Kunley.* Clearlake, CA: Dawn Horse Press.

Epstein, M. (1998). *Going to pieces without falling apart: A Buddhist perspective on wholeness: Lessons from meditation and psychotherapy.* New York, NY: Broadway.

Epstein, M. (2001). *Going on being: Buddhism and the way of change: A positive psychology for the West.* New York, NY: Broadway.

Eshin, J. (n.d.). Four Noble Truths. Retrieved from http://www.budd histdoor.com/OldWeb/bdoor/0009e/sources/truths.htm

Fortuna, J. (1987). Therapeutic households. *Journal of Contemplative Psychotherapy, 4,* 49–73.

Fredrickson, B. L. (2009). *Positivity: Groundbreaking research reveals how to embrace the hidden strength of positive emotions, overcome negativity, and thrive.* New York, NY: Crown.

Fremantle, F. (2001). *Luminous emptiness: Understanding "The Tibetan Book of the Dead."* Boston, MA: Shambhala.

Gunaratana, B. H. (2002). *Mindfulness in plain English.* Boston, MA: Wisdom.

Gyamtso, T. (1994). *Progressive stages of meditation on emptiness* (S. Hookham, Ed.). Oxford, UK: Longchen Foundation.

Gyatso, K. (1980). *Meaningful to behold: A commentary to Shantideva's guide to the bodhisattva's way of life* (T. P. Phunrabpa, Trans., & J. Landaw with J. Marshall, Eds.). London, UK: Tharpa.

Gyatso, T. (n.d.). Compassion and the individual. Retrieved from http:// www.dalailama.com/messages/compassion

Gyatso, T. (1994). *A flash of lightning in the dark of night: A guide to the bodhisattva's way of life* (Padmakara Translation Group, Trans.). Boston, MA: Shambhala.

Gyatso, T. (1996). *The good heart: A Buddhist perspective on the teachings of Jesus* (T. Jinpa, Trans., & R. Kiely, Ed.). Boston, MA: Wisdom.

Gyatso, T. (1997). *Healing anger: The power of patience from a Buddhist perspective* (T. Jinpa, Trans.). Ithaca, NY: Snow Lion.

Gyatso, T. (2000). *Dzogchen: The heart essence of the great perfection* (T. Jinpa & R. Barron, Trans., & P. Gaffney, Ed.). Ithaca, NY: Snow Lion.

Hanh, T. N. (1987a). *Being peace.* Berkeley, CA: Parallax Press.

Hanh, T. N. (1987b). *Interbeing: Commentaries on the Tiep Hien precepts.* Berkeley, CA: Parallax Press.

Hanh, T. N. (1988). *The sutra on the full awareness of breathing* (A. Laity, Trans.). Berkeley, CA: Parallax Press.

Hanh, T. N. (1990). *Transformation and healing: Sutra on the four establishments of mindfulness.* Berkeley, CA: Parallax Press.

Hanh, T. N. (1992a). Buddhism and psychotherapy: Planting good seeds. *Journal of Contemplative Psychotherapy, 7,* 97–107.

Hanh, T. N. (1992b). *Peace in every step: The path of mindfulness in everyday life* (A. Kotler, Ed.). New York, NY: Bantam.

Hanh, T. N. (2006). This is the Buddha's love [An interview with M. McLeod]. *Shambhala Sun, 14*(4), 50–57.

Hanh, T. N. (2013). Dharma talk: Protecting the environment. Retrieved from http://www.mindfulnessbell.org/wp/tag/interbeing/

Hanson, R., with Mendius, R. (2009). *Buddha's brain: The practical neuroscience of happiness, love, and wisdom.* Oakland, CA: New Harbinger.

Kabat-Zinn, J. (1990). *Full catastrophe living: Using the wisdom of your body and mind to face stress, pain, and illness.* New York, NY: Delta.

Karthar, K. (1992). *Dharma paths* (N. Burshar & C. Radha, Trans., & L. M. Roth, Ed.). Ithaca, NY: Snow Lion.

Kongtrul, J. (1974). *A direct path to enlightenment* (K. McLeod, Trans.). Vancouver, BC: Dharmadata.

Leitch, L., & Miller-Karas, E. (2010). It takes a community. *Psychotherapy Networker, 34*(6), 34–39, 62.

Linehan, M. M. (1993). *Cognitive-behavioral treatment of borderline personality disorder.* New York, NY: Guilford.

Loizzo, J. (2012). *Sustainable happiness: The mind science of well-being, altruism, and inspiration.* New York, NY: Routledge.

Maté, G. (2010). *In the realm of the hungry ghosts.* Berkeley, CA: North Atlantic Books.

Maitri five wisdom energies practice. (n.d.). Retrieved from http://shambhala.org/maitri.php

May, R. (1989). The empathic relationship: A foundation of healing. In R. Carlson & B. Shield (Eds.), *Healers on healing.* Los Angeles, CA: Jeremy P. Tarcher.

Melville, H. (2010). *Billy Budd.* New York, NY: Digireads.

Midal, F. (2004). *Chögyam Trungpa: His life and vision.* Boston, MA: Shambhala.

Mingyur, Y. (2007). *The joy of living: Unlocking the secret and science of happiness.* New York, NY: Harmony.

Murakami, H. (2008). *What I talk about when I talk about running.* New York, NY: Knopf.

Nalanda Translation Committee. (n.d.). Kagyu lineage prayer: The mahamudra lineage supplicaton. Retrieved from http://www.khandro.net/prayer_Kagyu_lineage.htm

Narada. (1992). *A manual of Buddhism.* Kuala Lumpur, Malaysia: Buddha Missionary Society Malaysia.

Nichtern, D. (2010, March 25). Stay on your cushion: The importance of "hot" and "cool" boredom during meditation. Retrieved from http://www.huffingtonpost.com/david-nichtern/boredom-as-medicine_b_509917.html

Olson, E., Unger, H., Kaklauskas, F. J., & Swann, L. E. (2008). Mothering the moment: Explorations of mindfulness in mothering and therapeutic experiences. In F. J. Kaklauskas, S. Nimanheminda, L. Hoffman, & M. S. Jack (Eds.), *Brilliant sanity: Buddhist approaches to psychotherapy* (pp. 309–334). Colorado Springs, CO: University of the Rockies Press.

Perls, F. (1969). *Gestalt therapy verbatim* (J. O. Stevens, Ed.). Lafayette, CA: Real People Press.

Podvoll, E. M. (1983). The history of sanity in contemplative psychotherapy. *Naropa Institute Journal of Psychology, 2*, 11–32.

Ponlop, D. (2006). *Mind beyond death*. Boulder, CO: Snow Lion.

Rabin, B., & Walker, R. (1987). A contemplative approach to clinical supervision. *Journal of Contemplative Psychotherapy, 4*, 135–149.

Rogers, C. R. (1961). *On becoming a person: A therapist's view of psychotherapy*. Boston, MA: Houghton-Mifflin.

Roth, G. (1982). *Feeding the hungry heart: The experience of compulsive eating*. New York, NY: Macmillan.

Sangharakshita, M. S. (1977). *The three jewels: An introduction to Buddhism*. Cambridge, UK: Windhorse.

Shahani-Denning, C. (2003). Physical attractiveness bias in hiring: What is beautiful is good. Retrieved from http://www.hofstra.edu/pdf/orsp _shahani-denning_spring03.pdf

Shantideva. (1979). *A guide to the bodhisattva's way of life* (S. Batchelor, Trans.). Dharamsala, India: Library of Tibetan Works and Archives.

Siegel, D. J. (2010). *The mindful therapist: A clinician's guide to mindsight and neural integration*. New York, NY: Norton.

Siegel, R. D. (2010). *The mindfulness solution: Everyday practices for everyday problems*. New York, NY: Guilford.

Silverberg, F. (2008). Resonance and exchange in contemplative psychotherapy. In F. J. Kaklauskas, S. Nimanheminda, L. Hoffman, & M. S. Jack (Eds.), *Brilliant sanity: Buddhist approaches to psychotherapy* (pp. 239–257). Colorado Springs, CO: University of the Rockies Press.

Simmer-Brown, J. (2002). The crisis of consumerism? Retrieved from http://www.mro.org/mr/archive/21-3/articles/crisisofcon.html

Sogyal. (1992). *The Tibetan book of living and dying* (P. Gaffney & A. Harvey, Eds.). San Francisco, CA: HarperSanFrancisco.

Taylor, C. (2010). *A Buddhist approach to finding release from addictive patterns*. Ithaca, NY: Snow Lion.

Thrangu, K. (2012). *Open door to emptiness: An introduction to Madhyamaka logic* (3rd ed., S. Dorje, Trans., & M. L. Lewis, Ed.). Glastonbury, CT: Namo Buddha.

Trungpa, C. (1969). *Meditation in action*. Boston, MA: Shambhala.

Trungpa, C. (1976). *The myth of freedom and the way of meditation*. Boston, MA: Shambhala.

Trungpa, C. (1987). *Cutting through spiritual materialism* (J. Baker & M. Casper, Eds.). Boston, MA: Shambhala.

Trungpa, C. (1991). *The heart of the Buddha* (J. Lief, Ed.). Boston, MA: Shambhala.

Trungpa, C. (1995). *The path is the goal: A basic handbook of Buddhist meditation* (S. Chödzin, Ed.). Boston, MA: Shambhala.

Trungpa, C. (2005). *The sanity we are born with: A Buddhist approach to psychology* (C. R. Gimian, Ed.). Boston, MA: Shambhala.

Trungpa, C., & Nalanda Translation Committee. (1980). *The rain of wisdom: The essence of the ocean of true meaning: The vajra songs of the Kagyü gurus*. Boston, MA: Shambhala.

Tsoknyi, D. (1998). Carefree dignity: Discourses on training in the nature of mind (E. P. Kunsang & M. B. Schmidt, Trans., & K. Moran, Ed.). Boudhanath, Nepal: Rangjung Yeshe.

Walker, R. (2008). A discipline of inquisitiveness: The "body-speech-mind" approach to contemplative supervision. In F. J. Kaklauskas, S. Nimanheminda, L. Hoffman, & M. S. Jack (Eds.), *Brilliant sanity: Buddhist approaches to psychotherapy* (pp. 175–194). Colorado Springs, CO: University of the Rockies Press.

Wallace, B. A. (2004). *The four immeasurables: Cultivating a boundless heart* (2nd ed., Z. Houshmand, Ed.). Ithaca, NY: Snow Lion.

Watson, G. (2008). *Beyond happiness: Deepening the dialogue between Buddhism, psychotherapy, and the mind sciences*. London, UK: Karnac Books.

Watson, M. (2013). Case study: The black shadow: Facing the taboo issue of race in the consulting room. *Psychotherapy Networker, 37*(6), 63–66.

Wegela, K. K. (1988). "Touch and go" in clinical practice: Some implications of the view of intrinsic health for psychotherapy. *Journal of Contemplative Psychotherapy, 5*, 3–23.

Wegela, K. K. (2009). *The courage to be present: Buddhism, psychotherapy, and the awakening of natural wisdom*. Boston, MA: Shambhala.

Wegela, K. K. (2011a). I think we should stop seeing each other. In A. Miller et al. (Eds.), *Right here with you: Bringing mindful awareness into our relationships* (pp. 150–153). Boston, MA: Shambhala.

Wegela, K. K. (2011b). *What really helps: Using mindfulness and compassionate presence to help, support, and encourage others*. Boston, MA: Shambhala.

Welwood, J. (1992). The healing power of unconditional presence. In J. Welwood (Ed.), *Ordinary magic: Everyday life as spiritual path* (pp. 159–170). Boston, MA: Shambhala.

Welwood, J. (2002). *Toward a psychology of awakening: Buddhism, psycho-*

therapy, and the path of personal and spiritual awakening. Boston, MA: Shambhala.

Winnicott, D. W. (1992). *The child, the family, and the outside world* (2nd ed.). Reading, PA: Perseus.

Yeats, W. B. (1990). *Collected Poems*. Picador: London, U.K.

Yontef, G. (1993). Gestalt therapy: An introduction. Retrieved from http://www.gestalt.org/yontef.htm

INDEX

Index

Thich Nhat Hanh, 13, 70, 125, 126,
127, 153, 172, 195, 210
thinking, labeling, 32, 33, 35, 40,
139
thoughts
east side of client's mandala and,
240, 242–43, 247–48
recognizing as thoughts, 95, 230,
234
Tibetan Buddhism, 15
"crazy wisdom" lineage of, 44
emotions and, 168
five Buddha family wisdoms or
energies in, 37
mandala of the client's world and
five elements in, 240, 241
Vajrayana tradition of, 4
visualization in, 95
timing meditation, 27
tobacco, 160
tonglen practice, 80, 185, 186, 193,
251
adapting to work with a client,
190–92
beginning with a specific situation, 188–89
establishing texture of, 187–88
expanding, 189
flashing on brilliant sanity, 187
on the spot, 189–90
touch and go technique, 55–57,
135, 136, 150, 179
exchange and, 76
sports and, 147
touch and grab technique, 56, 57
transitions
mindlessness practices and, 166–
67
spacious feelings and, 89
trauma, 95
boycotting emotions and, 171
mindful application of mindfulness and working with, 166
mindfulness practices guidelines
for clients with history of, 157–
58

planting negative seeds and, 126–
27
Trauma Resiliency Model (TRM),
xiv, 52, 127, 128, 259n
treatment plan, four noble truths
and, 16
triggers, 125
TRM. see Trauma Resiliency Model
(TRM)
Trungpa, C., xv, 130, 139, 259n

unconditional mindfulness, 17
Unger, R., 48
uniqueness of each moment, recognizing, 140–41
upaya (skillful action), 51

Vajrayana Buddhism, 4, 44
values, clarifying, 94, 230, 233
Vietnam War, 195
visualization, 95
volleyball, mindfulness and, 147

Walker, R., 252
walking meditation practice, 156,
210, 211
Wallace, B. A., 193, 194, 195
wandering, mindful, 156
wanting, paying attention to, 134–
35
war, 206
warmth, 68
water, east side of client's mandala
and, 240, 242
Whitaker, C., 38
wind, north side of client's mandala
and, 240, 245–46
wisdom, 69, 83, 84
of all-encompassing space, 39
of discriminating awareness, 130
emotions and, 168
inherent, discovering, 68
mirror-like, 42
natural, 81, 84, 92, 97, 105, 124,
180
skillful action and, 51

284

witnessing, 139
working out, mindfulness and, 146–
    47
worrying, as distortion of acting
    skillfully and letting go, 83,
    121–22
writing, mindfulness and, 150

Yeats, W. B., 6
yoga, 142, 143, 254

zabuton, 28
zafus, Japanese-style, 28
Zen masters, 44